Music and the Crises of the Modern Subject

MUSICAL MEANING AND INTERPRETATION
Robert S. Hatten, editor

MICHAEL L. KLEIN

Music and the Crises of the Modern Subject

INDIANA UNIVERSITY PRESS

Bloomington & Indianapolis

This book is a publication of

Indiana University Press
Office of Scholarly Publishing
Herman B Wells Library 350
1320 East 10th Street
Bloomington, Indiana 47405 USA

iupress.indiana.edu

Manufactured in the United States of America

Library of Congress Cataloging-in-Publication Data

Klein, Michael Leslie, author.
    Music and the crises of the modern subject / Michael L. Klein.
    pages cm — (Musical meaning and interpretation)
    Includes bibliographical references and index.
    ISBN 978-0-253-01720-8 (cloth : alkaline paper) — ISBN 978-0-253-
01722-2 (ebook) 1. Music—Psychological aspects. 2. Music—Philosophy
and aesthetics. 3. Lacan, Jacques, 1901–1981—Philosophy. 4. Musical
analysis. I. Title. II. Series: Musical meaning and interpretation.
    ML3845.K598 2015
    781.1'7—dc23

                                                          2014047870

1 2 3 4 5   20 19 18 17 16 15

For Michelle,
who can read it
to Tamae,
who could use the sleep

These are really the thoughts of all men in all ages and lands,
they are not original with me.

—Walt Whitman

Contents

Acknowledgments

As always, I am indebted foremost to Robert Hatten, who has supported my research since I started giving lectures on musical meaning. He has guided me through a previous book and a collection of essays, and his guidance was invaluable in completing this book, as well. After I discussed the ideas in this book with him, his usual enthusiasm spurred me to complete it with renewed vigor. His suggestions, ideas, and insights about the manuscript led to a much stronger book than I could have written without his help. I cannot thank him enough for the support he has given me both with this book and throughout my career.

Once the manuscript came back from the outside readers, Patrick McCreless kindly revealed to me that he was one of them. He did this so that I could send him a final draft of the manuscript before I sent it to Indiana University Press. His care in pointing out errors, suggesting additional avenues for research, and encouraging me to clarify many passages went beyond the call of any colleague. He is one of the best-read scholars I know, which made his contribution to the completion of this book immeasurably important.

Raina Polivka, music, film, and humanities editor at Indiana University Press, has now guided two of my projects through the publication process. I would like to thank her for her continuing support of my work at IU Press. In addition, Jenna Whittaker, assistant sponsoring editor at IU Press, has been a valuable resource, managing this project in its later stages, for which she has my thanks. I would also like to thank David Miller, lead project manager and editor at IU Press, and Eric Schramm, who copyedited the text. I am certain that any problems or errors in this book are mine and mine alone.

I would like to thank Robert Stroker, Vice Provost for the Arts, and Dean of the Center for the Arts at Temple University, for supporting my research with a number of grants and reductions in my teaching load. Anne Harlow, Temple University's librarian for music, dance, and theater, made sure I had every score and book I needed to complete my work, for which she has my gratitude. Dr. Julia Alford-Fowler, a tremendous composer and graduate of Temple University, set all the musical examples with great care, for which I thank her. While I was writing this book, I taught several graduate seminars on topics related to subjectivity. After struggling through readings by Freud, Lacan, Deleuze, and others, my students posed questions that prompted me to reexamine my thoughts. They have my thanks.

Material from this book formed the topics of dozens of lectures at conferences and universities that I have given in the last several years. At every turn, questions from my colleagues forced me to reframe my work. In particular, I recall questions about postmodern irony from Matthew Shaftel at Florida State University. Michael Cherlin at the University of Minnesota challenged me to explain the difference between Freudian and Lacanian models of the unconscious. Sumanth Gopinath at the same university pointed out to me that Lacan's formulation of the Symbolic order owes a debt to Hegel's master-slave dialectic. At a conference at Cornell University, Zbigniew Skowron from the University of Warsaw asked me how I could claim that Deleuze's concepts of the molar and molecular failed to function dialectically. Michael Lee at the University of Oklahoma asked me to consider that John Zorn's collage music is also a form of simulacrum. Marianne Kielian-Gilbert at Indiana University reminded me not to ignore Carolyn Abbate's article on Ravel when considering Lacan and the uncanny. Martha Hyde at the University at Buffalo wondered if I should tone down the mapping between Proust and Debussy when considering the time problem in early modernism. So many people asked probing questions. I am only sorry that I cannot thank all of them.

If I follow convention and thank my family last, it does not mean that their support has been of the conventional kind. I don't know what people talk about at their dinner tables, but my poor family has to suffer through talk about Freud, and Lacan, and Marx, and on and on. I am astonished at my daughter, Michelle, and her ability to engage in this conversation and use what she learns from it. I discovered, for example, that during a discussion of the scene in *The Catcher in the Rye* (yes, they still teach that book in high school) involving Holden and his purchase of a record for his younger sister, Michelle's teacher asked each student to jot down an idea or two for discussion. My daughter scribbled on her notepad *objet petit a*. Discussion ensued. I'm glad I won't have to teach Michelle in college. I doubt I could keep up. As for my wife, Tamae, her typical response to any attempt I make to explain my thoughts about music is "That's all? You mean it took you all day to write that?" Tamae is a practicing musician, a violinist who performs all the time. She has a wry sense of the silliness that musical scholarship can often be. I cherish my wife's responses, as I cherish my wife and my daughter. I do what I can to show them my love, though I realize that I often fall short of saying what I mean in its fullest way: a symptom of the Symbolic order, I suppose, but not a good excuse.

* * *

An earlier version of chapter 4 appeared in the journal *19th-Century Music* as "Chopin Dreams: The Mazurka in C♯ Minor, Op. 30, no. 4," 35/3 (2012): 238–60.

The poem "Parfum de l'instant" by Amin Maalouf is reprinted in chapter 2 with the kind permission of the poet.

Music and the Crises of the Modern Subject

Introduction

This is my letter to the world
That never wrote to me . . .
Her message is committed
To hands I cannot see. . . .

—Emily Dickinson

A letter always arrives at its destination . . . There is no speech without a response . . . Thou art that . . . The unconscious is the chapter of my history that is marked by a blank or occupied by a lie . . . The unconscious is the Other's discourse . . . A symptom is language from which speech must be delivered . . . I identify myself in language, but only by losing myself in it as an object . . . Not only can man's being not be understood without madness, but it would not be man's being if it did not bear madness within itself as the limit of his freedom . . . Man is, prior to his birth and beyond his death, caught up in the symbolic chain, a chain that founded his lineage before his history was embroidered upon it . . . What did not come to light in the symbolic appears in the real. . . .

Lacan is a challenge. His more famous statements can puzzle us or spur us to reconsider what constitutes us. His writing thwarts conventional thought (which is the point), expressing an exquisite strangeness in the form of aphorisms tied one to another. We can even shatter Lacan's texts and rearrange their sentences into an aleatoric chain, as appears in the paragraph above, which nonetheless startles us for making just about as much sense as the original configuration of his ideas. But if we are to take Lacan seriously, as I think we should, then we must not be content to treat his famous statements as gobbets to be tossed into our writing, marking us as well read. For Lacan, we are never well read; we always need re-reading. Lacan is a challenge worthy of our best efforts, because once we have some understanding of his project, which was nothing less than a total reconfiguration of what we are as subjects, then we will never see ourselves or the world in the same way. This reconfiguration of our thought about thought has enormous implications for virtually every human endeavor, including music.

This book is about Lacan and music. The association may seem a strange one, since the French psychoanalyst had virtually nothing to say about music.

But music is the product of subjectivity, and since Lacan reconfigured the nineteenth-century model of the subject, we find that he necessarily prompts us to reconsider music. In this book, I try to clarify what Lacan's model of subjectivity means for our approaches to music, and what music means for our approaches to Lacan. Although the analyses herein are often hermeneutic, they promise no new method of hermeneutics. Sometimes the analyses are meant to explain a concept in subjectivity, and other times a concept in subjectivity is meant to illustrate a different way to think about music.

I begin here by unpacking the words in this book's title in reverse order. By *modern subject*, I mean a model of consciousness that begins with Freud and undergoes a structuralist revision with Lacan. I think of the modern subject as what Foucault calls "only a recent invention," resulting from a revolution in thought (episteme) that began in the early nineteenth century (1994: xxiii). If Foucault is correct, then we cannot speak of Faulkner's "old verities and truths of the heart" without acknowledging that they are neither old nor true, except for a particular kind of subjectivity. Neither can we read the subtitle of Harold Bloom's book about Shakespeare, *The Invention of the Human*, without wondering what kind of human the literary critic has in mind. When we read Shakespeare and find universal truths of the heart, we are not reading Shakespeare; we are reading ourselves. As it turns out, though, reading ourselves is not the problem we might imagine. The problem is to believe that subjectivity (more colloquially *the human*) is somehow divorced from history.

In addition to Freud and Lacan, the book turns to Kristeva, and, in the last two chapters, to Deleuze and Guattari, all of whom owed a debt to Lacanian thought. The primary focus, however, is on Lacan, whose notoriously impenetrable writing received a revival in the 1990s thanks largely to Slavoj Žižek. In particular, Žižek's *Enjoy Your Symptom!* popularized Lacan (if such a thing is possible) with its playful use of movies to explain the decentered subject, and with its provocative questions like "Why is *reality* always multiple?" Readers familiar with Žižek will note a similar impulse in this book, which often frames each section with a question, and which uses movies, novels, poetry, and (yes) music to explain Lacan's thorny concepts.

By *crises*, I mean the consequences of Lacan's model of subjectivity, which involves a series of critical disjunctions that both create and challenge personhood. These crises begin at birth and move through the young child's epiphany of separateness, to the acquisition of language, and on to the recognition of symptoms. No one escapes this series of crises, which, according to Lacan, involve a catalog of symptoms that can never be cured, only understood. Turning to music, whenever composers practice their craft, the crises that made them find their way into their music. Resorting to a chiasmus, a favorite rhetorical trope in continental philosophy, we can claim that we interpret music, and music interprets us.

These crises of the modern subject are structural, historical, and cultural. They are structural in the sense mentioned above: that the subject (and here I should be exact in writing *the person born into western society during the period from industrial capitalism to late capitalism*) is formed through a family drama that begins with separation from the mother's body (birth), moves through a second separation in the primordial formation of an ego, and culminates in a final separation in the acquisition of language. This drama is one in which every fully formed subject must participate, and, with its completion, the unconscious is structured by that very drama. These crises are cultural and historical in the sense that any problem a culture addresses will find its expression both in the unconscious of the subject and in every form of speech (words, art, music, etc.) that the subject delivers. For Lacan, this is because when we begin to think in signs, we take on the culture that surrounds us, including its problems, aporias, and contradictions.

By *music,* I refer narrowly to a repertoire that ranges from the early nineteenth century (Beethoven, Schubert, Chopin), to the early twentieth century (Debussy, Stravinsky), to the late twentieth- and the early twenty-first centuries (Lutosławski, Rochberg, Zorn, Higdon, Saariaho). Another chiasmus of the Lacanian variety: I chose this music because it worked in illustrating Lacanian concepts, and the music worked in illustrating these concepts because I chose it.

This is not the first book to tackle Lacan vis-à-vis music. In addition, musicologists (especially) and theorists have been referring to Lacan in their articles and essays for almost two decades. After spending enormous time and energy trying to understand Lacan, though, I confess that the Lacan I read about in musicology and theory is not always the Lacan I recognize from my own poor attempts to interpret his work. Nonetheless, several books have been formative in my approach to Lacan and music. Of these, I should mention first Sarah Reichardt Ellis's admirable monograph on Shostakovich's quartets, *Composing the Modern Subject: Four String Quartets by Dmitri Shostakovich* (2008). Reichardt Ellis's book revealed to me that Lacan was not someone I could afford to ignore. The words *modern subject* in the title of her book find resonance and acknowledgment in the title of this one. In addition, David Schwarz has written two books whose musical-cultural analyses rely on Lacanian concepts: *Listening Subjects: Music, Psychoanalysis, Culture* (1997) and *Listening Awry: Music and Alterity in German Culture* (2006). Schwarz's essays have prompted me to think carefully about Lacan before I make any claims about music. Finally, much of Lawrence Kramer's astonishing work is about subjectivity. But two of Kramer's books, *After the Lovedeath: Sexual Violence and the Making of Culture* (1997) and *Franz Schubert: Sexuality, Subjectivity, Song* (1998), have had a strong impact on my thinking about subjectivity, particularly in the tradition of Freud and Lacan. (I hope that he will not be too embarrassed for me to write that his *After the Lovedeath* is one of my favorite books.)

Despite the work on Lacan that already appears in musicology and theory, I have felt it important to lay the groundwork in explaining Lacan's model of the subject. Chapter 1, therefore, introduces that model, which includes three orders (or registers): the Imaginary, the Symbolic, and the Real. In addition, the chapter discusses Lacan's changing conceptions of the symptom. To illustrate these ideas, the chapter reimagines Edward T. Cone's famous article "Schubert's Promissory Note" (1982) before embarking on Lacanian readings of music by Beethoven and Brahms.

Chapters 2 and 3 turn to the Imaginary and its musical correlate, the *acoustic mirror*. Chapter 2 configures our attraction to music as an extension of the Imaginary, involving a fantasy of return to the mother. Music of Chopin, Brahms, and Saariaho illustrates the impossibility for the subject to fulfill such a fantasy. In addition, the chapter reconsiders Vladimir Jankélévitch's conception of music as ineffable. I argue that Jankélévitch tries to stand at a midpoint between music as a fantasy-object beyond the reach of language and music as a form of cultural communication, which demands the very hermeneutic endeavors that he warns us against. Chapter 3 wonders whether it is possible for the Imaginary to return to us in the form of what Proust called *lost time*. The chapter works through a Lacanian reading of Proust before turning to a correlate in the music of Debussy. The argument also involves the so-called *time/space problem* familiar in the work of Proust's cousin, Henri Bergson. That problem pondered whether industrial conceptions of time-as-space were crowding out the phenomenology of time-as-quality that allowed consciousness to unfold freely. Reconfigured in Lacanian terms, the problem involves the Imaginary as the engine of desire and nostalgia.

Chapter 4 turns to a late notion of the symptom in Lacan's work: the *sinthome*. When a subject experiences a symptom that fails to be cured, he or she turns to an unending search for the meaning of that symptom. In so doing, the subject becomes his or her symptom, which is another way of saying that we define ourselves by the very symptoms we try to understand. Thus, a symptom is a demand for interpretation. But since no language exists to capture the particularity of the subject, no interpretation of the symptom can be fully satisfactory. The chapter illustrates this idea by uncovering layer after layer of meaning in some strange and unsettling passages (symptoms) in a mazurka by Chopin.

Between chapters 4 and 5 a brief interchapter, called "Intermezzo: On Agency," considers the implications of Lacan's thought on the problem of agency in music. Since musical agents are often taken to be correlates to human ones, our understanding of what constitutes a subject (human) necessarily influences our understanding of what constitutes a musical agent. The unspoken ideology behind musical agency is that it follows a model of the subject as closed, independent, and self-determining. But that is not the model that Lacan proposes for subjectivity. The Lacanian subject is shot through with the agencies of the Imaginary (in the form of others who populate our consciousness), the Symbolic (language and culture), and the Real (everything that the Symbolic cannot express). Thus, the human agent is not singular but plural, and we should not be surprised if musical agency reveals similar characteristics.

Chapters 5 and 6 deal with postmodernism and its effects on subjectivity and music. Chapter 5 discusses postmodern music from a Lacanian perspective that understands the constant jostling of quotations and styles as a break in what he called "the signifying chain." As such, both music and the subject suffer a form of cultural psychosis that moves from the alienation of modernity to the fragmentation of postmodernity. The chapter includes discussion of music by Rochberg, Zorn, and Higdon. Chapter 6 moves to Deleuze and Guattari's *A Thousand Plateaus* to offer a less fraught version of the postmodern subject, in which the broken signifying chain is replaced with the notion of the *molar* and the *molecular:* two sides of subjectivity that both create new structures and tear them down in order to acknowledge desire and prevent the fascism implicit in hegemony. The music of this chapter all comes from the oeuvre of Lutosławski.

Patrick McCreless, who kindly read two late drafts of this book, pointed out to me that one of its themes is akin to that of Emily Dickinson's "This Is My Letter to the World," whose opening lines form the epigraph of this introduction. It is a curious coincidence that Dickinson uses the word *letter* instead of *poem,* because the choice anticipates one of Lacan's famous aphorisms: *the letter always arrives at its destination.* We may choose to read the opening lines of Dickinson's poem with an empathy for what it might be like to write without knowing if the world "that never wrote to me" will even care to accept our letter, our poem. From a Lacanian point of view, though, the letter that we write *is* addressed, as Dickinson suggests, to an anonymous world, a culture, the Symbolic, whose only meaningful reply is silence. In that silence of the letter sent without the hope of a reply is the nagging thought that we must make our own answer in the form of another letter, another poem, and another appeal. But also from the Lacanian point of view, we the readers of Dickinson's poem are precisely the ones to whom it is addressed, simply because we have read the poem in the first place. A final Lacanian chiasmus: whoever we are, we are the destination of Dickinson's poem because we have read it, and we have read the poem because we are its destination. As I hope to show in the coming chapters, music is another letter that always arrives at its destination. We are meant to open music's letter to us and make sense of it.

* * *

A few words are in order about how the book approaches Lacan's concepts typographically, and about citations. It has become common practice to distinguish the everyday notion of the word *real* from Lacan's concept of *the Real,* with a capital *R* for the latter. I extend that practice by using capital letters to distinguish Lacan's concepts of *the Symbolic* and *the Imaginary* from the everyday notions of the words *symbolic* and *imaginary.* Finally, there is a distinction between *the Other* (capital *O*) and *the other* (lowercase *o*) in Lacanian thought. *The Other* (also called *the big Other*) is language and the culture that it signifies. *The other,* however, can be the mother, against whom the subject first defines itself, or a person who substitutes for the mother, or even an object that substitutes for the mother. In the last case, *the other* is also called the *objet petit a* (object with a lowercase *a* for *autre:* other).

Concerning citations, the reader will find no footnotes or endnotes as part of the text. I have decided to forgo extended side arguments in tiny print and pro forma lists of other works that deal with a topic at hand. When I have borrowed or quoted a source, an in-text citation is present; and, on occasion, I have pointed to a few other sources that the reader might find useful. Sometimes the text refers to a performance that was available on YouTube at the time that I wrote this book. URLs for these performances are listed in the bibliography.

Regarding Lacan's publications, most of the citations come from his collection of essays, *Écrits*. There are two English editions of this collection (one with more essays than the other), and both English editions include a set of page numbers at the top of each page and a second set of numbers in the outer margins of each page. That second set of numbers is cued to the original French edition, and it is that second set that I use in this book.

1 Music and the Symptom

The subject's personality is structured like a symptom.

—Jacques Lacan, "Variations on the Standard Treatment"

How Did Edward T. Cone Invent the Symptom?

Early in *The Sublime Object of Ideology*, Slavoj Žižek writes that according to Lacan it was Karl Marx who invented the symptom (1989: 3). Žižek's claim is a willful one, given that Lacan never professed an allegiance to Marxist thought, and that references to Marx appear only sporadically in Lacan's writings (see Valente 2003). But the point is that if Marx *did* invent the symptom, it was qualitatively different from the ancient Greek *sēmeiōtikos* (observation of signs), which formed part of the reading of symptoms in medical practice (see Sebeok 1994: 10–14). For Marx, in Žižek's formulation, the symptom begins with the discovery of a hidden content beneath the form of socioeconomic relations: Marx invented the *social* symptom. And if knowledge of the content behind the form is a necessary prerequisite for such an invention, then we might claim that Edward T. Cone (1982) invented the *musical* symptom with his famous study of the promissory note in Schubert's *Moment musical* no. 6. Although the word *symptom* never appears in this celebrated article, when Cone whispers the words *syphilis, desolation,* and *dread* at the end of his study, it becomes evident that his analysis of Schubert's piece has uncovered a social pathology (240).

As we now know, thanks to Cone, the promissory note in Schubert's *Moment musical* is an E♮ that first appears in m. 12 and stands out for a failure to discharge its conventional voice-leading (Example 1.1). Cone tells us promissory notes appear early in a movement and that their reappearances bring the sections of a piece "into more intimate and more interesting connection" (236). A promissory note (symptom) is a "troubling element" that arouses an expectation that a later section will "legitimize" its disturbing features (237). Cone looks briefly at a foil to the *Moment musical,* the first movement of Beethoven's Piano Sonata in F major, op. 10, no. 2, where a promissory chord is left hanging in the exposition only to find its proper resolution in the development (236). By implication, Beethoven's sonata happily overcomes its symptom (though there was probably no doubt that the hijinks of the opening would lead to a felicitous end). By con-

Example 1.1. Schubert, *Moment musical* in A♭

V²/A stands in for E

Emptiness of Death

trast, Schubert's *Moment musical* never finds a cure for its symptom. Instead, a late phrase in the music "is terrifying in its intensity," lending the final section a "devastating effect" (239).

Cone focuses primarily on the Allegretto of this composite form (Allegretto-Trio-Allegretto), beginning with a structural analysis filtered through the problematic E♮ and its consequences. As such, this part of Cone's study plays within a long and still important tradition of tracing the generative impact of early musical features on later ones (see Réti 1961; Rosen 1972: 115–16, 120–29; Kerman 1982; Agawu 1987; McCreless 1991; Spitzer 1996). Cone's notion of the *promissory note,* a pitch or chord that withholds its voice-leading obligations until a later passage, has a place in analyses focused primarily on harmonic, contrapuntal, or formal structures (see, for example, Burstein 1997: 53). More particularly, since Cone focuses on a chromatic pitch, his study involves what many theorists, starting with Steven Laitz (1992), have called a *pitch-class motive.* Reviewing the history of the pitch-class motive, Patrick McCreless writes that because the technique of tracing a chromatic pitch through a piece is so well known, a colleague of his calls it "an easy game to play" (2011: 65–66). As we will see, though, from a Lacanian perspective the game is easy because theorists have played it by the wrong rules.

Despite his strategy of beginning with a review of structural details, Cone really had a hermeneutic impulse from the start, which powerfully directed the kinds of features he was looking for and the ways he would account for them. Cone lets us in on the game later in the article: "An astute reader will have noticed that my analysis has not been wholly objective. I have insinuated a few leading phrases to suggest to him the kind of expression I find in the work, and to encourage him to hear it the same way" (239). Because of his focus on an expressive interpretation, Cone's promissory note is what we would now call a *hermeneutic window* (Kramer 1990: 12). But in 1982, before the hermeneutic impulse had entered the mainstream of American musicology, Cone needed to proceed cautiously, lending an aura of authority to the expressive meaning he would draw from Schubert's music. He began, then, with the accepted scholarly discourse of the period: a structural analysis. Only after reminding us that he is adept at this discourse does Cone edge more openly toward a hermeneutic analysis.

But hermeneutics does not work this way; one does not begin with a structure and move out to a meaning. The meaning is already evident even to a listener who has no knowledge of keys, or phrases, or chromatic pitches breaking their promises. Cone's tentative move from structure to meaning reveals what Lawrence Kramer calls *ekphrastic fear:* the sense that "verbal paraphrase works too well, that it threatens to engross and supplant the representation that it describes" (2002: 18). Ekphrastic fear is still common in music studies, partly because musicologists, theorists, and performers tend to view the otherness of music as sacrosanct. Ironically, from Lacan's point of view, it is language itself that is Other. Music's otherness is a symptom of the very language that the fearful curtail in their approaches to music. We have no choice but to speak. Once we do, much of human experience becomes strange as language falters in signifying the particularity of being. But our only other choice is to remain silent about what compels us to speak in the first place. Our impulses serve us better if we err on the side of *ekphrastic hope,* which aims to overcome the putative otherness of music and rise to a form of eloquence in verbal representations of it (Kramer 2002). One does not need to know about the E♮ to understand the two most striking passages of the *Moment musical:* the utopian vision that materializes unexpectedly in the middle section, and the ominous passage near the conclusion of the Allegretto, where we hear an intimation of a lonely death. Cone surely understood the meanings of these passages long before he looked for their connections via the pitch-class E. Structural analysis as the first step toward hermeneutics is a hopeless methodology because it only reinforces the idea that meaning works like an equation in which a structural detail here is equivalent to an extra-musical meaning there.

But the larger point is that the promissory note is more than a voice-leading oddity; the voice leading is only secondary. The promissory note is a symptom with a pathology. Cone helps us understand this way of thinking in the second part of the article, where he invokes a metaphor at least as old as the nineteenth century: music is analogous to a "human activity or state of mind" (239). Like Schenker and others before him, Cone views music as a model of human agency, whether construed as a series of bodily actions or psychological ones. Music as psychology, or what Daniel Chua calls the "*I*-pod" of the modern self, "closed off from the outside like a sonic monad" (2011: 345), is the metaphor that Cone develops into a narrative for Schubert's piece. Likening the disquieting E♮ to an "injection of a strange, unsettling moment in an otherwise peaceful situation," Cone argues that the promissory note is "at first ignored or suppressed," but it persistently returns until "it bursts out with even greater force, revealing itself as basically inimical to its surroundings, which it proceeds to demolish" (239–40). The narrative takes on an overtly human potency in the final pages of the article, where Cone imagines a person (Schubert) facing something "repressed [that] eventually returns and rises in the end to overwhelm him" (239–40). The promissory note, then, is a symptom of a psychological problem—an unsettling thought that the music-as-agent fails to repress.

More precisely, Cone's narrative for the symptom bears uncanny resemblance to Freud's famous definition of the *unheimlich* as that "class of the terrifying which leads back to something long known to us," whose pathology is linked to "something repressed which recurs" (Freud 1958: 369–70, 394). Freud's essay also features references to strange and unsettling thoughts—notions that find resonance in Cone's analysis. As such, it is tempting to read Schubert's piece in terms of the musical uncanny as theorized separately by Richard Cohn (2004), this writer (Klein 2005: 78–95), and others (Cherlin 1993; Kerman 2001–02; and Kramer 2002: 258–87). Cohn's discussion of the musical uncanny focuses primarily on the unsettling psychology arising from harmonic motion through *hexatonic poles* (chords of opposite mode whose roots are a major third apart, like C major/A♭ minor). The Allegretto would seem to qualify in this regard, because the middle section features a melodic idea presented first in A♭ minor (mm. 21ff.)

and then in E-major (mm. 29), the key of the promissory note. A small problem, though, is that the move between the two keys is so smooth that it mitigates any unsettling effect that would come from their direct juxtaposition. In contrast to Cohn's work, my view of the musical uncanny focuses on the implicit narrative of Freud's conception of the *unheimlich:* a once familiar thought is transformed into an uncanny one through cycles of repression. From this point of view, we could hear the late passage notated in E (m. 65ff.) as a transformation through repression of the more gracious E-major passage in the middle section. The *unheimlich* moment arrives when the A-major chord of m. 68 (enharmonic to the Neapolitan) moves to an A♭ minor $^6_4$ chord in m. 69. A small problem here is finding a plausible argument for repression (pace Cone): is it that E is repressed, or is it that E just goes away for a while? In addition, musical narratives of the uncanny (like Chopin's Sonata in B♭ Minor, or the last movement of Schubert's Sonata in C Minor) tend to have strong musical signs of obsessive compulsion (Klein 2005: 91–95). Although the Allegretto is compulsive, worrying over the suspension figures throughout, the repetitions give the music what Kramer calls a "beset" quality (2002: 22). It is not that the musical agent is trying to escape an unpleasant thought through compulsive behavior but that the music is mulling over a bad situation. The listener must decide if the suspensions are blocking out an unwelcome thought, or if they are a species of *jouissance* that perversely enjoys replaying the scene of some past pain.

Even if we hear the suspensions as beset instead of *unheimlich*, the possibility of a Freudian reading does nudge a corrective swerve on Cone's interpretation, which takes the symptomatic E as a sign for *vice*. In this narrative, Cone argues that vice is like an enticing suggestion that the agent (Schubert) indulges first with fascination (the utopian E-major section) until it dominates him in a "fearful form" (the final passage, beginning in m. 65) (240). Thus Schubert's psychological symptom (vice) brings on a physical symptom (syphilis), accounting for the terrifying collapse of mind and body. The reading has a high moral tone, despite Cone's assertion to the contrary (240). The upshot is that Schubert writes his moral failing into the fabric of the music as a disquieting and unlikely E, making the *Moment musical* a morality tale.

But there is something wrong here. Syphilis is a medical condition, not a moral one; and this confusion has a historical dimension to which I will return. For now, Cone helps us develop an outline of how to deal with the symptom in music. Despite Cone's appeal to musical structure, the symptom is a demand for interpretation of the hermeneutic variety. The musical symptom involves hearing a piece's progress as analogous to a human agency along a psychological or bodily path. Finally, the musical symptom appears more than once, suggesting cycles of repression, during which the musical agent attempts to work out a problem. This outline is a good start, but before we can take the implications of Cone's work further, we need to know more about symptoms outside of their musical manifestations. And before we can understand symptoms, we must turn to a model of subjectivity. That model comes from Lacan.

What Are the Three Orders of Subjectivity?

Lacan's three orders—the Imaginary (the other), the Symbolic (the Other), and the Real—are famously thorny and often misunderstood. It doesn't help that Lacan rarely gives his readers simple definitions: an easy concept is prey to the emptiness of convention. The reader should take what follows, then, as a first sketch of the three orders. Before understanding them, we must realize that for Lacan the development of the subject involves a series of crises, the first of which is birth, since the young infant cannot care for itself in any way. From birth, the subject moves through the Imaginary, which involves thinking in images, to the Symbolic, which involves thinking in language. With the entry into these two orders of subjectivity, though, the subject discovers that they are radically decentered, which may compel a lifelong search to recover a lost oneness and power that they never really had in the first place.

About one year after the crisis of birth, the subject enters the Imaginary, often associated with *the other* or the *(m)other,* which involves the so-called *mirror stage,* when the young child first recognizes itself in the mother's gaze or a mirror's reflection. As such, the subject discovers that he is separate from the mother. Further, while the young subject's image in the mirror is whole, he realizes that he is uncoordinated, powerless, and alone. At this stage, the subject begins to think in images, which parents might recognize as the child's rapid eye-movement during sleep, indicating dreams. The subject also begins to search for acceptable substitutes for the loss of oneness with the mother. Lacan called any such substitute the *objet petit a,* or *the other.* Desire fuels the search for the *objet petit a,* which can never deliver the fulfillment it promises. Like the ring in Wagner's tetralogy, the search for the *objet petit a* drives the subject, though it cannot fulfill the promise of power, satisfaction, and wholeness. Closing the circuit of desire for the *objet petit a,* on the contrary, leads to death or madness.

In the movie *Inception,* for example, Dominick Cobb commits acts of espionage by entering his victim's dreams to extract information. He takes a particularly difficult assignment, involving multiple levels of his victim's dream world, under the promise that if he is successful, his powerful client will reunite him with his children. Because of various flashbacks and images in the dreams that Cobb enters, the viewer realizes that the children are substitutes for a reunion with his wife, who has committed suicide. His children are the *objet petit a,* standing in for his wife who, in turn, stands in for a lost sense of satisfied contentment. Cobb catches various glimpses of his children in his dreams, but he can never quite see their faces and recapture lost time. At the end of the movie, he is reunited with his children, but a small spinning top that helps him keep his grip on reality suggests that he may still be in a dream. The movie leaves the question open: the final scene ends before we can see if the top continues to spin (indicating a dream world) or if it comes to a stop (indicating the real world). But from a Lacanian point of view, there can be only one answer. Cobb's reunion with his children must be a false one, and he has lost his grip on reality, because we can never close the circuit of desire around the *objet petit a*. Like those dreams in which you wake up just before opening a long anticipated gift, the *objet petit a* disappears as we get too close. The Imaginary, then, is where dreams are born and desire is unleashed.

The Symbolic order consists of the many signifying systems with which a culture attempts to represent the world, or more properly, being-in-the-world. Among these systems, Lacan privileges language, which he calls the *big Other*, or *the Other* (with a capital O). Because language is thrust upon us as we enter the Symbolic, we experience the Other as a radical alterity with a power like the law. We do not choose the language we are forced to speak; the language chooses us. And we cannot think, even in the unconscious, without the language of the Other. It is in this way that we can understand one of Lacan's favorite aphorisms: *the unconscious is the Other's discourse* (2006h: 16). Returning to the movie *Inception*, we see that it enacts the idea that even our dreams belong to others. In order for Cobb and his associates to pull off their plan, they use an "architect" to create a dreamscape that acts as the backdrop for all those who will share a dream. In Lacan's vision of the subject, though, the architect of our dreams is the Other, the culture and its others (lowercase *o*) who populate our unconscious.

In the novel *Cities of the Plain*, Cormac McCarthy plays with this idea that the discourse of our unconscious comes from the Other. In the epilogue, the character Billy Parham meets an unnamed traveler with whom he feels compelled to share an old dream. The dream itself involves a traveler, and as Billy recounts the dream, his new friend interrupts with questions. The following dialogue begins with such a question (note that McCarthy never uses quotation marks for dialogue):

Who was the traveler?

I dont know.

Was it you?

I dont think so. But then if we do not know ourselves in the waking world what chance in dreams?

I'd think I'd know if it was me.

Yes. But have you not met people in dreams you never saw before? In dreams or out?

Sure.

And who were they?

I dont know. Dream people.

You think you made them up. In your dream.

I guess. Yeah.

Could you do it waking?

Billy sat with his arms over his knees. No, he said. I guess I couldnt. (271)

Who *are* the people in our dreams who act and think with their own volition? Those others in our dreams who speak to us as if they are not part of us come from the Other. They are the others who make up the Other. And since the first other for us all is the mother, the Imaginary and the Symbolic work together to create dream people who represent the culture around us. The nineteenth-century view of the subject as a self-enclosed monad is a conceit that fails to capture the porous nature of subjectivity.

Steven Spielberg's movie *A.I.* gets the dream problem wrong. David, a mechanical boy with artificial intelligence whom a young couple purchases as a surrogate child, spends much of the movie trying to win the love of his mother, Monica, who tosses him aside after she bears a real child. Two thousand years later, a robotic society revives David from a long sleep and reunites the mechanical boy with a clone of Monica. David spends a perfect day with his now loving mother. In the last scene of the movie, David falls asleep as a voiceover tells us that he has gone "to that place where dreams are born." The ending is sentimental; dreams do not come because we are united with the mother but because we are separated from her. David was really dreaming from the moment Monica turned away from him.

A final example: in the documentary *Jiro Dreams of Sushi,* a master sushi-chef (Jiro) says that he literally has dreams of perfecting his art. He believes that he can only achieve perfection through constant application of the same methods day after day. Although he is eighty-five years old, he thinks that he still has much to learn about sushi, and he hopes to live long enough to reach the perfection he seeks. The documentary reveals the interaction of the Imaginary and the Symbolic. Jiro is driven; making the perfect piece of sushi is his *objet petit a*. But when he speaks of how to reach perfection, he isn't really telling us anything that comes from him. He is repeating ideas common to Japanese culture, especially in Zen Buddhism. Even outside Japan, there is a current of thought that countless hours of repetition lead to mastery, or what Malcolm Gladwell has dubbed the "10,000-Hour Rule" in his popular book *Outliers* (2008). Jiro's idea of mastery through repetition, then, is the Other's discourse speaking through him. Finally, although it is the Imaginary that fuels desire, it is the Symbolic that tells him what he *can* desire. What better way to enter the endless cycle toward the *objet petit a* than by attempting to make the perfect piece of sushi, the *objet petit a* for others who also speak in the discourse of the Other?

If we could erase all signifying systems and experience the world outside the Symbolic, we would be in what Lacan calls *the Real*. The Real must not be confused with the concept of reality, which is already a notion within the Symbolic. Whatever reality might be outside the Symbolic, the search for its truth is a hopeless one. The symptoms that appear to be blocking us from reality are not "some irruption of truth. . . . they *are* truth . . ." (Lacan 2006d: 235). The Real is what lies outside language; and because the Symbolic cannot capture it, our confrontations with the Real are often traumatic. The Real is a stain on the Symbolic: it is what the Symbolic cannot know directly. Since we think within the Symbolic, we cannot think the Real. We can only know the Real through symptoms, which are an attempt by the Real to reach us through the inadequate signs of the Symbolic.

In *The Matrix,* a movie that Žižek also discusses (2008: 242–64), Neo suspects that there is something wrong with the world that he inhabits, though he cannot articulate the nature of the problem. He is in the computer-generated world of the matrix; he is in the Symbolic, where he feels the Real through the symptom of his own anxious search for the truth of his situation. In one scene, the character Morpheus tries to explain to Neo this truth of his existence by showing him a virtual representation of the scorched earth that lies outside the matrix. As Neo looks on the catastrophic landscape, Morpheus says, "Welcome to the desert of the Real." In the movie, the matrix and its virtual reality are analogous to the Symbolic: a set of semiotic structures within which people experience a world. Outside the matrix lies the Real, a traumatic landscape that a subject in the matrix can only intuit but never experience directly. The analogy breaks down in the movie, since the lead characters have the ability to move in and out of their virtual reality—to exit the Symbolic. In the Lacanian model, though, once we enter the Symbolic by taking on language and all the other signifying systems, we exit the Real never to return. The Real does speak to us, but it does so in signs that we never understand fully. Since we cannot exit the Symbolic, there is no escape from our matrix.

These examples illustrating Lacan's three orders are ways of showing. Just as Wittgenstein claims that logic can be shown but not told (1999: 26; point 4.1212), so the Imaginary, the Symbolic, and the Real can only be shown in examples. Whenever we try to pin down the three orders, they collapse into the Symbolic, which ever seeks to deny the Imaginary and the Real. There is no secret code to making associations between the three orders and their manifestations in artworks. Such a methodology would be unsatisfactory even if it were possible, because, as we will see, it is not a matter of classifying sections of pieces into subjective orders, or making things fit. The three orders are an assemblage, delineating crises in history and their manifestations in the subject through everything she does or creates. Thus for music, it is a mistake to imagine a system for translating the hieroglyphs of sound into Lacanian thought. Each piece is an example that requires its own interpretation.

In the Allegretto of Schubert's *Moment musical,* I understand the opening measures as expressions of desire, fueled by the Imaginary. As the music reaches the section in E major (mm. 29–39), with its barcarolle rhythm (mm. 35–38) and its more extended melodic lines, we see a vision of the *objet petit a,* a backward look to a sensuous fulfillment that the rest of the music lacks. Approaching the end of the Allegretto, the music makes a terrible turn toward A♭ minor (mm. 68–69), which brings a tremor from the Real into the field of our experience. The final phrases are a stain that mars the previous sentiments of the piece. As for the Symbolic: the piece must work within the discourse of its culture, its law-like set of conventions. The music often denies that order, moving to the Imaginary or accepting messages from the Real. In these denials, the music fuels a hermeneutic impulse; it tells of its own telling. But the music is also an appeal to the Symbolic. As we see in the following section, the music seeks in the Symbolic the answers to the questions it poses. And when it cannot find those answers, it demands that we return to our hermeneutic stance.

What Is a Symptom?

Having set up Lacan's three orders of subjectivity, we can turn to the symptom. To begin, we must distinguish a medical symptom from a psychiatric one. While a medical symptom is a sign of a specific bodily illness, a psychiatric symptom requires individual interpretation for each patient (Lander 2006: 77–78). Following Freud, then, Lacan finds any simple analogy between a symptom and its meaning to be "repugnant to the spirit of our discipline." A psychiatric symptom is like a rebus, but it presents itself to us in displacements, such as "metaphor, catachresis, antonomasia, allegory, metonymy, and synecdoche" (Lacan 2006a: 262; 268). Just as hermeneutic analysis is unworthy of our efforts when devoted to simple decoding procedures, so analysis of a symptom requires us to distrust an easy interpretation.

A patient's first motivation for disclosing his symptoms to an analyst is to rid himself of them: to seek a cure. Although Lacan admits that certain techniques can ameliorate a patient's symptoms, he also finds that when one symptom disappears, another comes to take its place. Since one symptom always replaces another, Lacan sees interpretation of the symptom as the real task of psychoanalysis. And since the symptom comes from the unconscious, which is structured by the Symbolic, the task of analysis involves making the symptom speak, rendering it in language. "It is already quite clear that symptoms can be entirely resolved in an analysis of language, because a symptom is itself structured like a language: a symptom is language from which speech must be delivered" (2006a: 269). A symptom is a sign addressed to the Symbolic order in the hope that a cure will come once we have discovered its range of signifiers and signifieds. The relationship between the symptom and Cone's promissory note becomes clear: the strange and unsettling passages in Schubert's *Moment musical* are symptoms demanding interpretation.

Although Lacan's notion of the symptom changed through his career, in its final form the symptom is a message from the Real addressed through the unconscious to the Symbolic order (Lander 2006: 82–83). When the patient first speaks about her symptom to the psychoanalyst, her implicit notion is that the analyst represents the Other: the analyst is the one who knows, the one who represents the Symbolic order and possesses the secret code to unlocking the problem of the Real. The stumbling block is that there is no such code or language of the Real. When the patient discovers that the analyst cannot cure symptoms through facile interpretation, she begins the process of interpretation herself, so that the search for a cure becomes the search to understand the message from the Real. Because the Real is beyond our ability to signify, and because what the Real wants to express is literally unsayable, the Real must clothe itself in a symptom, a sign, which only partially discloses what it wants to say (Lander 2006: 83).

When God revealed himself to Moses, he clothed himself as a burning bush. Thus Moses learns that God burns without consuming, is bright, terrible, and traumatic, since God is outside the norms of daily existence (outside the Symbolic). But these descriptions are insufficient to understand a confrontation with God. Thus, the sign of the burning bush discloses something about God while it keeps something hidden. As with the God of Moses, so with the Real. The difference is that God and Moses could speak to one another in a shared language, but the Real has no such means of direct communication. The signs that it uses to confront us require tireless interpretation. From a Lacanian perspective, though, we could say that God was a symptom for Moses.

Once the symptom is out, a first interpretation often comes so easily that the subject can do it without the aid of the psychoanalyst. Whatever problem the Real is trying to point out, "the subject is usually aware of it, even excessively so; it harasses him all the time" (Žižek 1989: 4). A pianist suffers from an obsessive fear that he will forget the keys to his house. Without much effort, he interprets his obsession as a displacement of his real fear, which is that he will have a memory slip in recital. "Key" is the magic word that transforms the fear of forgetting the music (key on the piano) to the fear of being locked out (key to the house). As correct as this first interpretation may be, though, it is a bit of a disappointment. The imagined situation is certainly unpleasant, but it hardly counts for some deep trauma of the unconscious indicating a confrontation with the Real (see Žižek 1989: 5). The Real has clothed itself in a fear that the subject already knows in order to hide a deeper fear that the subject cannot face. The chain of signifiers (loss of memory, loss of keys, outside the house) begins to point to other interpretations: failure of mastery, loss of the mind. And at first, these interpretations do seem more satisfactory, because they are more traumatic. But soon even they will be inadequate for the truer nature of the Real. The analysis must continue and cannot reach a point of satisfactory completion.

Two of the issues surrounding interpretation of the symptom are *master signifiers* and *jouissance*. A master signifier is a key word or concept that a subject uses to organize the otherwise free-floating signifiers in a text. Master signifiers tend to be terms around which a subject defines herself (a Republican, a musician, an American). Like Wittgenstein's family resemblances, master signifiers are difficult to pin down, despite the fact that subjects apprehend them as if they have a stable meaning. Although there are traits shared by many Americans, for example, there is no single trait shared by every American. I catch a statement on television: "We must reform health care." If I discover that the speaker is a Democrat, I may decide the speech means "Tax people more to take care of this problem." If I discover that the speaker is a Republican, I may decide the speech means "Allow the market to take care of itself, leave things as they are, and don't hamper big business." The master signifiers, *Democrat* and *Republican,* have organized my interpretation of the politician's statement. But when I examine more carefully what it means to be a Democrat or a Republican, I find that I cannot separate the chain of signifiers for both terms so easily.

Each new interpretation of a symptom is like a master signifier that reorganizes all the past occurrences of that symptom. "The Lacanian answer to the question, 'From where does the repressed return?' is therefore, paradoxically, 'From the future'" (Žižek 1989: 58). It is the symptom in the future with its new interpretation that bestows meaning on the symptom in the past. Strangely, then, repression, which is always transforming the symptom into something different and more powerful, comes not from the past but from the future. At first, the pianist's compulsion is just a fear of being stranded outside. In the future, though, a new master-signifier, "memory," transforms the symptom into a fear of forgetting the music. And still later, another master-signifier, "sanity," reorganizes the symptoms of the past into a fear of losing the mind. Oddly, the symptom in its fullest consequences is not some discovery of the past but some new master signifier from the future.

As for *jouissance,* taken by itself it means enjoyment, and in Lacan's earlier work this term is associated with the pleasure in pain that comes from the patient's confrontation with the symptom (Hoens and Pluth 2002: 10). But in Lacan's later work, a play on words extends the meaning of *jouissance.* For example, as *jouis-sense* (enjoyment in making sense), *jouissance* is the pleasure that the patient experiences from making sense of the symptom—a making sense, by the way, that is never satisfied (Hoens and Pluth 2002: 10). The symptom becomes part of a process of interpretation that is pleasurable despite the pain associated with the symptom itself. This sense of *jouissance* is one way to understand the title of Žižek's famous book *Enjoy Your Symptom!*

An analogy. You decide to take up golf, and you quickly gain some skill at the game. But after a few weeks, you notice a pain in your wrist. You decide that the pain is the result of a poor grip, which you endeavor to alter. Soon the pain in your wrist disappears, only to be replaced by a pain in your hip. Apparently, the changed grip has influenced your stance. You decide to alter your stance to fix the pain, and although your tactic works, the pain now moves to your shoulder. Thinking about your shoulders as you tee off makes the pain go away, only to have it move to your elbow. And so on. At one level, the pain is literally what it is: a form of suffering that you wish would stop harassing you. At another level, though, the pain has forced you to think hard about the mechanics of your playing. And there is a certain enjoyment in figuring out what the pain means for your grip, your stance, your swing, your posture. In an odd way, then, you enjoy your symptom.

What Does the Symptom Mean for Music?

Using psychoanalytic theory to interpret artistic texts is no news. Within that tradition, Lacan's conception of the symptom can reorganize our thinking when trying to make sense of music. For Lacan, an artistic text is more than a set of signifiers that a psychoanalytic theory helps to organize. In his famous seminar on Poe's "The Purloined Letter," Lacan claims that a story illustrates "that it is the symbolic order which is constitutive for the subject" (12). Implicit is the notion that the story itself stands in for a human subjectivity. Lacan also argues that a story has "the advantage of manifesting symbolic necessity all more purely in that we might be inclined to believe it is governed by the arbitrary" (12). Since subjectivity is formed within the Symbolic, and since even the unconscious is structured like a language, any story, whether the product of conscious or unconscious thought, is bound to the same symbolic necessity that governs the human subject. When we approach a story from a Lacanian position, then, we are doing something more than seeking a meaning. We are taking a story as a demand to be read *as if* it were a human subject. A piece of music is like a subject who announces his symptoms to the Symbolic in the hope of receiving an answer to the puzzle of existence. And like the living subject who speaks to a psychoanalyst in the Lacanian (and Freudian) tradition, the music's appeal is met with silence. But since the music cannot take up the act of interpretation itself, we the listeners must play the part of the music as if it makes an appeal on our behalf. We try to understand the music's symptoms as if they were our own. From this (Lacanian) subjective point of view, the agency of music is quite real. When we say that the music "makes an appeal to the Symbolic," or that the music "demands interpretation," we could think of these statements as metaphors. It is really the composer who makes these appeals. But since Lacan views artistic works as organized by the same symbolic necessities that organize the subject, those artistic works act *as* agents. They may even make an appeal about which the composer has no conscious knowledge.

Returning to Cone's analysis of Schubert's *Moment musical,* we see how closely he navigates toward psychology without falling in. He refuses to psychologize the music fully, perhaps because the time in which he wrote the article (1982) was one more concerned with musical structures than extra-musical meanings. Cone's interpretations come only late in the article, as if they are musings that could be set aside as extraneous. The path of the music for Cone warns us of the dire consequences that come from surrendering to vice. The promissory note "begins as a novel and fascinating suggestion," which "becomes dangerous, however, as its increasing attractiveness encourages investigation and experimentation, leading to possible obsession and eventual addiction" (Cone 1982: 240). And Schubert offers us this quaint *Biedermeier* tale, one imagines, because he had syphilis and knew too well the path from innocence through vice to decay and loss. The debt of vice must be paid. Although a detail of Schubert's biography (syphilis) provides Cone with an extra-musical idea to form this tale, the result has an oddly objective, impersonal quality. In fairness, the school of New Criticism, which formed part of Cone's intellectual heritage, tended to downplay biography as a distraction. In addition, Cone never claimed to be rendering a psychological reading of the music. Still, something is not quite right. One imagines the music-as-subject entering a psychiatrist's office: "Doctor, I have this strange presentiment that my life has fallen into decay." To which the psychiatrist replies: "Of course you have this presentiment. You have syphilis. You brought this problem on yourself through your own moral depravity." In this scenario, the musical subject addresses itself to an analyst (Cone) as representative of the big Other with the power to interpret the symptom and make it disappear. Rather than make clear that there is no secret key to unlocking the symptom, though, Cone closes off the cycle of interpretation with an answer straight from the Symbolic, which in Schubert's time, as in our own, confused medical problems with moral ones.

If we rework Cone's analysis in Lacanian terms, we might begin with the last manifestation of the symptom instead of the first one, since the meaning of the symptom comes not from the past but from the future. Like Cone, I respond to the final in-breaking of pitch-class E in mm. 65–68 and 71–73 as a terrible foreboding, which is confirmed by an uncanny move toward A♭ minor with a half-cadence in mm. 69–70 and a full cadence at the end of the work. Cone construes the empty octave completing the piece as a "neat tactical device," allowing the music to move smoothly into the key of the Trio, D♭ major (239). But if you play the final cadence with a minor third, C♭, you'll find that the effect is a good one: the Trio gains a glow of warmth after an A♭ minor chord. Rather than look at syntax, I think we find a solution to the empty octave by considering its semantic level. Coming after the A♭ minor chord as part of the cadential dominant in m. 74, the empty octave with its deep (as in profound) register is a premonition of death, the ultimate emptiness. The final passage, which Schubert notates in E, confirms this reading, because it isn't really in E at all. The inverted dominant leading into mm. 66 and m. 71 points to A major: the Neapolitan with its strong indication of *ombra*, the supernatural, death, while simultaneously attempting to escape the inevitable turn to A♭ minor. The key signature does help make a connection between this manifestation of the symptom and the earlier passage in E major (mm. 29–39), but it also uses its implication of mortality (pleasure leads to decay) to hide the Neapolitan, A, and its own signification around death. Like the Real, this passage exposes as much as it hides. It forms the master signifier for a series of past symptoms, while it hides the very implications it wishes to make.

Symptoms show us one sign, which, however uncomfortable, hides another that is even more terrible to imagine. Cone's story for the *Moment musical* plays within this clever game of revealing one sign to hide another, preventing us from seeing the deeper ugliness of the Real behind the symptom. With "moral decay" as a master signifier in Cone's reading of the closing passage (a sign already hiding the more ugly syphilis), the earlier passage involving E (mm. 29–39) does make sense as a period of pleasurable experimentation. This reading also protects the healthy from the unpleasant truth that death is the letter that always finds its addressee (see Žižek 2008: 24–25). The clichéd problem of syphilis is its reminder to the sufferer that the postman soon will be knocking. For the healthy, though, the sign of syphilis read as a moral warning is a sign of protection: "Naughty Schubert, if not for that nasty moral lapse, he'd be healthy. Death comes for him because he has disobeyed the Symbolic, while I, who am ready to obey, will be left alone."

Lawrence Kramer interprets the E major section differently, hearing it as "off-kilter, futile" and as an "illusory denial" of a deterioration that has already begun early in the Allegretto (2002: 25–26). The illusory quality of the passage connects it with the Imaginary, as I have indicated. Thus the passage is no area of sexual experimentation, as Cone would have it, but of a desire for some image of wholeness from the past: in this case, literally a desire for the health that the Allegretto-cum-subject has already lost. Kramer's interpretation also focuses on a pitch-class that Cone spends little time discussing: the B♭ that forms a pedal in mm. 29–32. The B's enharmonic cousin, C♭, plays a role as early as m. 17, cluing us to the troubled nature of the piece. If we are satisfied merely with tracing the E♮/F♭ as the symptom of the Allegretto, we will miss the B♮/C♭ as another symptom hiding behind the first. Miraculously, both F♭ and C♭ appear in the chord at m. 17, which opens the development of the Allegretto while questioning whether the music will find a happy end.

Kramer also discusses another symptom in the Allegretto: the opening figure, which expresses a "suffocating paralysis" from its first appearance to its last (2002: 21). This symptom and others in the *Moment musical* are signs of a "diseased" or "Romantic body," plagued by "self-division and self-alienation" (22). Kramer's reading brings into play a historical dimension that both Cone's analysis and the preceding Lacanian one lacked. But it is time to engage that dimension here, since it is the crucial element of Lacan's theory of the subject. "What we teach the subject to recognize as his unconscious is his history—in other words, we help him complete the current historicization of the facts that have already determined a certain number of the historical 'turning points' in his existence" (2006a: 261). We may object that when Lacan speaks of the historical "turning points" (crises) in the subject's history, he refers to the subject's *particular* history. But since that history is enmeshed in the Symbolic, any determination of a particular history must include the larger cultural practices in play. Schubert's crises were his culture's crises. It is to the historical nature of syphilis, what Kramer calls the "inspired guess" in Cone's interpretation of the *Moment musical*, that we must now turn (2002: 20).

How Does Syphilis Form a Power Relation?

Cone's interpretation of the *Moment musical* as a narrative of syphilitic decay may be an inspired guess, but it confuses a medical problem with a moral one, which is evident in the term *vice*. This confusion, especially with regard to sex, performs a great deal of cultural work. In Foucault's terms, sexuality appears "as an especially dense transfer point for relations of power" (1990: 103). Although Foucault never mentions syphilis outright, the disease plays within what he calls the *psychiatrization of perverse pleasure*, which is the impulse of power relations to categorize the sexual anomalies of the "perverse adult" and find a "corrective technology" for them (105). The sexual power-relation has two sides for Foucault, a *deployment of alliance*, involving a system of laws and constraints confining sex to marriage in order to regulate kinship and property, and a *deployment of sexuality*, involving control of the body as the site of sensations, pleasures, and impressions (106). In short, and bluntly, sex must be confined to marriage as a deployment of alliance, and its pleasures must be controlled to the point of denial as a deployment of sexuality. From the standpoint of nineteenth-century Europe, then, Schubert was guilty of two transgressions, which he and his friends understood all too well: not only did he seek extra-marital sex, but also he did so in the pursuit of pleasure. He explored a form of *jouissance* denied by the Symbolic order of his time. Decades after his death, his friend Josef Kenner wrote that "anyone who knew Schubert knows . . . how powerfully the craving for pleasure dragged his soul down to the slough of moral degradation . . . which only too probably caused his premature death and certainly hastened it" (quoted in Hayden 2003: 91). Kenner's description of Schubert's psyche could stand in for Cone's narrative of the *Moments musical*. The first E-major section is the site of a forbidden pleasure, or more properly of pleasure itself. The final reference to E major is the necessary consequence, an intimation of death. Pleasure *is* death in this equation.

But the entanglement of sex, syphilis, prohibition, pleasure, and morality took on a different arrangement once the medical community turned its attention toward curing the disease. In the early decades of the twentieth century, medical professionals began to disarticulate syphilis from any assemblage involving morality. In 1918, for example, Dr. John Stokes argued that syphilis was "a problem of public health rather than of morals" (Stokes 1918: 18). Moral outcry works well for control of the subject, but it fails miserably when we try to understand and cure a disease. From this point of view, it is a bit disappointing to see Cone laying forth an unreflective moral narrative for the *Moment musical*, especially and ironically in 1982, when the first responses to the AIDS crisis were forms of moral clamor.

To be clear, it is perfectly possible that Schubert, who by all accounts felt the shame that his culture (the Symbolic) attached to syphilis, might compose a piano piece whose narrative reflected the very moral censure to which he was vulnerable. But a purely moral narrative can hardly stand as a full picture of the subject. Freud made this point clear in *The Interpretation of Dreams*: "The dictates of morality have no place in dreams" (Freud 1965: 98). Although morality plays a role in the psyche, in the dream itself the dreamer is free to act on every impulse. From a Lacanian point of view, if we interpret the psyche as nothing more than a morality tale, we are playing the part of the Symbolic order and disguising the deeper truth of the Real. Interpretation cannot rest on the first reading.

The first reading of the *Moment musical*, the moral one, thus plays within what Foucault theorizes as the *right of death and power over life* in modernity (Foucault 1990: 135–59). With the effort to control the body, pleasure, and sex, the Symbolic (Lacan's term, not Foucault's) sets up a narrative paradigm that accounts for life and death itself. Simply, life belongs to those who deny the body, pleasure, and sex, while death falls on the side of those who fail to contain themselves. This comforting thought allows the moralist to push Schubert and his intimations of death away, protecting us from the unhappy truth that death might still come for us sooner than expected.

If we stand on the side of the moralist, we are likely to miss the irony that Schubert's music draws us into the side of pleasure from the beginning. Cone's reading, as we have seen, confines the pleasurable moment to the E-major portion of the middle section with its "more sensuous delights of a berceuse" (237). But one way of playing the opening of the Allegretto at the piano engages the body at the outset. All of those seductive suspensions, sighs controlling our desire, or signs that we are beset, solicit an attraction between the body and the keyboard: you lean in to hold the suspended chords, pushing away at the moment of resolution. You feel the pleasure of the suspensions either as forms of desire or forms of pain that solicit the *jouissance* of suffering. Alexandra Pierce describes a similar embodied experience in playing this piece. Asking us to notice the *junctures*, the rests between each sub-phrase of Schubert's piece, Pierce describes how "a simple dance of arm arcing and sideways stepping emerges" (2010: 139). Addressing us directly as the pianist experimenting with junctures at various levels of structure, Pierce notes that "you are swaying forward toward the performance phrase climax" (147). By the end of the first phrase, the body *is* swaying as if it both creates and responds to a berceuse, a barcarolle with the keyboard. Along the way, the body has one place to sit still, just at the point where the suspensions and the iambic patterns stop: we have come to the beginning of the E-major section (m. 29). Here the suspensions fall away, allowing the torso to calm itself so that the mind can gaze on the long-ago scene. I can imagine a pianist like Arthur Rubinstein, who often gazed upward during music's transcendent moments, playing this passage with his body still and his eyes looking to the distance in search of lost time. Now the moment of pleasure is all in our head as a memory of some past indulgence, though the body begins its swaying again once the triplets lead the torso back into the keyboard for the accented chords in mm. 34 and 37. Because Schubert's music draws the body toward the keyboard, we experience the music's pleasure from the start. And this narrative of the music's embrace ends in the Allegretto with the body following the hands into the low register of the keyboard to play the final empty octaves with their intimations of death. We fall into the abyss with Schubert. We fall in headlong.

By contrast, the Trio is almost too conventional a sign of some heavenly recompense. The chaste hymn topic, with its implications of communal simplicity, disciplines the body. There are no suspensions to draw the torso toward the keyboard. No wonder Cone has nothing to say about the Trio: its pleasures are few. Set in the subdominant key, Db, the Trio's song of innocence has a religious unreality that even ventures toward an ironic commonplace with the echoed upper register in the last phrase. Even within the Symbolic, the Trio offers a vision of what cannot be. Departing the Trio, we return to the more intimate satisfaction of the suspended chords. Schubert's music has infected us, and we enjoy his symptom. This piece is intended for mature audiences only: the young girls of the *Biedermeier* household had best leave it alone.

And so we have a series of transferences: the symptom is a sign for moral decay, hiding the fact that the moral decay is a sign for syphilis, hiding the fact that death will come sooner than expected, hiding the fact that death comes for everyone. If we stand on the side of morality in reading the *Moment musical*, we must close down the series of interpretations and deny the function of the body in drawing the pianist into Schubert's symptomatic pleasure. The moral reading lies on the side of the Symbolic, denying the more terrible vision of the Real. But even this series of interpretations from morality to the emptiness of death fails to reach whatever the Real is trying to tell us. In the most general sense, though, the Real indicates a problem in the Symbolic that we hope to recover when we take Schubert's music as our own and understand the history of our consciousness.

If a Symptom Is Cured, Why Does the Patient Die? (I)

It is time to repay a debt concerning the treatment of pitch-class motives in analysis. The well-known game of the pitch-class motive entails viewing a chromatic note as a troubling intrusion into an otherwise smoothly functioning tonal machinery. The rules of the game involve tracing the chromatic pitch-class through a piece until the music is cured, often by a series of enharmonic games in which the chromatic note takes on different implications until it disappears. When staged as a scavenger hunt, this game is an easy one to play, and the analyst always claims victory. But the rules of the game become more difficult if we realize that the troubling pitch-class is open to a number of hermeneutic possibilities. One of the most recent strategies involves disability studies, where the pitch-class motive and its cure are signs of the abnormal becoming normal. Introducing disability as a master signifier in three well-known works that feature pitch-class motives, Joseph Straus explains: "These works, all major-key movements in sonata form, follow a three-part dramatic plan of a balanced, diatonic beginning, the intrusion of a tonal problem leading to extensive harmonic disruptions and formal 'deformations,' and a restorative denouement in which the wound is healed, the disability cured, the balance reestablished, the abnormal normalized" (2006: 154). Straus's methodology follows the rules of the analytical game while forming a correlation between the chromatic note and a disability that requires normalization. The *locus classicus* for this approach is Beethoven's *Eroica* Symphony, where, as we know too well, a troubling C♯ in m. 7 of the first movement throws the music from its heroic path, returns a number of times, transforms into a D♭ while leading into the coda, and disappears as the movement reaches a triumphant end. Straus's twist on this story is to show how we might take the heroism of the music as a form of personal triumph over the adversity of a disabling ailment. Adding a welcome historical dimension to this story, Straus tells us how the early nineteenth century witnessed a new ideology that viewed disability as something that could be "ameliorated—the abnormal body could be normalized" (118).

But does the *Eroica* really normalize its disability? Does it cure its symptom? All the analyses of this symphony—and there have been ever so many—take a cure, or heroic triumph, or normalization as a given. "The power of this conjunction of Beethoven's music with the ethical and mythical implications of the hero and his journey holds the entire reception history of this symphony in its sway, for there has never been a reaction against the basic heroic type, no deconstructive readings of the *Eroica* as antihero or antiwar or antiself" (Burnham 1995:

27). The first movement does end in diatonic triumph, where the only chromatic pitch in earshot is a D♭ that normalizes the troubling C♯ and forms a secondary dominant leading to a subdominant over a tonic pedal (see mm. 677–78).

If the music has triumphed, though, why does the hero die in the second movement, a funeral march? The opening sections of the march adhere to the conventions that followed the French Revolution: we begin with the march itself, move to a Trio whose major mode celebrates the glorious victories of the hero's past, and return to the funeral march. The Trio blasts away in sunny C major before a Neapolitan on D♭ turns the music back to the serious matter of the march. D♭, the normalized pitch-class motive, thus becomes a sender that reawakens the dark reality of the hero's passing. We can get around the difficulty of the hero's death by viewing it as a metaphor for a particularly painful ordeal. As Northrop Frye explains, the hero of a story often goes through a "point of ritual death" that may involve imprisonment or a mortal illness (1990: 179). The larger point, though, is that the cure of the first movement was only temporary. The symptom returns as a troubling D♭ that leads the Trio back to the funeral march.

When the *Eroica* turns to the Scherzo, the symptom appears to be banished; the boisterous energy of the music revives the hero with renewed vigor and purpose. As the Scherzo enters the digression, though, the music moves from E♭ up to F major (m. 41) before reaching the dominant of G minor (m. 57), where progress halts as the strings alternate between D and C♯: the symptomatic pitch-class has returned to darken our path. The reference to G minor also reminds us of a second symptom hidden behind the C♯ in the first movement. When the C♯ in m. 7 resolves, it does so on what I have called elsewhere an *unheimlich* G-minor chord in second inversion (Klein 2005: 82–83; see also Byros 2012: 284–326). By focusing on the C♯, we only disclose the symptom partially: the Real (or what Straus would call the disability) hides behind one symptom (C♯) so that we might miss the other (G minor). The horns of the Trio reestablish the hero's posture, scattering any shadow from the Scherzo. But the Trio never manages to reach a final cadence that could confirm a cure. D♭ returns in a more normative harmonic progression in the coda, while the diatonic (cured) final measures shake their fists, as if to block out any remnant of the symptomatic note.

By now we should expect the symptom to return no matter how the hero confronts it. We are not disappointed. The Finale begins with a G-minor chord in second inversion: the symptom is back. The series of variations in the Finale suggests that a cure has come at last, leaving the hero to revel in a series of harmless adventures. Although a G-minor chord returns to introduce the coda, the symphony reaffirms a diatonic triumph. The theme for the variations, as we all know, was taken from Beethoven's ballet *The Creatures of Prometheus,* whose title character brings to light another symptom. As portrayed in the ballet, Prometheus is "not a suffering victim but . . . the molder of civilization" (Lockwood 2005: 150). The first act features a scene in which Prometheus brings to life two statues, a man and a woman; and the second act focuses on a parade of mythological figures. The only nod to the reality of Prometheus' suffering in the Greek myth is a scene in which the muse of tragedy kills him. But the tragic moment is not upheld, since the muse of comedy brings Prometheus back to life (the parallels to the *Eroica* are obvious in the development of the first movement and in the entire second movement). As Lockwood explains, Prometheus in the ballet is not the rebel whom Zeus punishes by binding him to a rock while his liver is devoured each day. Rather, he is "an Enlightenment philosopher and teacher who brings reason and knowledge" (150). In order to uphold Enlightenment values, the ballet must hide the gruesome truth of the Prometheus myth: his suffering will find no cure.

Variations can be a form of mastery through compulsive repetition. In order to keep at bay the truth of the symptom, the Finale of the *Eroica* must return again and again to the theme and its implications. But the G-minor chords that introduce the Finale and its coda serve to remind us that the whole thing was a trick of forgetting. As with Helen's interpretation of the Fifth Symphony in *Howard's End*, "Beethoven chose to make all right in the end. . . . But the goblins were there. They could return" (Forster 2002: 23). We are never rid of the symptom. Thus in a reading of the *Eroica* as a narrative of disability, we find that the music only manages to adhere to a nineteenth-century vision of normalizing the abnormal by announcing a victory that never occurred. The *Eroica* does not adhere to the ideology of normalization; it denies it. The game of the pitch-class motive is poorly played when it seeks to cure the symptom. The real trick is to use the symptom to provoke understanding. To the question of why the hero dies once his symptom is cured, the first answer is that there was no cure at all. If the C♯ in the *Eroica* is the first note of modernity, as Wagner claimed (1978: 378), then it rides the paradox of the heroic deed that nonetheless fails to mend the rift at the formation of the modern subject.

If a Symptom Is Cured, Why Does the Patient Die? (II)

But what if we convince ourselves of a cure? What if the symptom goes away but the hero still dies? Brahms's Clarinet Sonata in F minor, op. 120, no. 1, another favorite among the pitch-class hunters, will lead to some answers. In this case, the symptom is a G♭ that manifests itself in m. 4 as the final pitch in the piano's brief introduction (Example 1.2 lists appearances of G♭ in this movement). The opening motto proceeds in sturdy monophonic octaves, like the voices of a Greek chorus declaring the tragedy to come. Just before the entrance of the clarinet, a diminuendo casts an uncanny hue on the G♭, which adds a Phrygian tone to the introduction while directing our attention toward the coming scene. G♭ gently infects the first theme of the sonata, usually forming a Neapolitan harmony, a chord whose significations include *ombra* in the eighteenth century, and the uncanny, terror, or death in the nineteenth (Ratner 1980: 24; Klein 2005: 85–87). Rather than repress the G♭, though, the music takes pains to address the symptom during a second key area (in what Hepokoski and Darcy would call a "trimodular block" [2006: 170–77]), where G♭ plays a prominent role both in establishing D♭ major and in forming the outer-voice counterpoint in the piano. With the piano's hushed chorale topic answered by the clarinet's sweet ascents,

Opening Motto and Part of Theme I

End of Transition and Theme 2

Example 1.2. Brahms, Clarinet Sonata in F minor, I (instances of G♭)

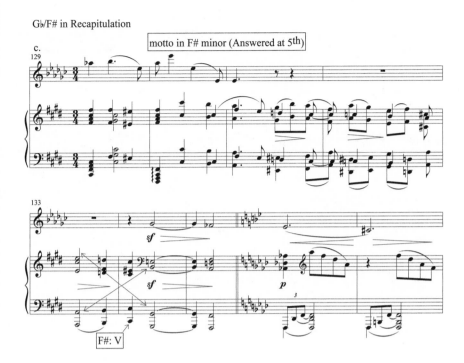

the second key has a faraway *if only* ethos that embraces the symptomatic Gb as a token from a long-ago perfection: a sign from the Imaginary. But the second key fails to find satisfactory closure as a third key enters the scene with stern determination. Despite a dark conclusion in C minor, something must have gone right, because after the second theme the Gb makes virtually no impact on the rest of the exposition.

Nothing in the narrative progress of the sonata, though, suggests a happy end. We already suspect that the symptom will return, and it does so with a vengeance, as the development steers a course to F# minor, the enharmonic twin to Gb, securing a stentorian cadence at the moment when the piano returns to the introductory material (m. 130). Famously, tragically, expectedly, the way to the recapitulation begins in the wrong key, falling into the symptom with a force. This time the Greek chorus has lost its univocal composure, singing the introductory motto with a stretto-like intensification and off-beat slurs.

The off-tonic move to the recapitulation in the enharmonic key (F# minor) of the symptomatic Gb is the music's tragic moment writ large. Here the symptom takes its most threatening posture. Oddly, though, when the clarinet reenters a few measures later to play the first theme, the music finds the home key, F minor, with little difficulty. And with the exception of an anxious diminished-seventh chord on F# (mm. 145–46), which appears near the end of the first theme as an aftershock from the tragic moment, the symptom plays no role in the remainder of the recapitulation. More curiously, for the rest of the movement the music makes

Example 1.3. Brahms, Clarinet Sonata in F minor, I (coda)

no concession to the obvious menace of G♭/F♯, instead running through a pro forma transposition of the second and third themes in the home key with not one note out of place. The formal obligations are fulfilled to the letter, as if no symptom could steer the music from its course. After the recapitulation, another rotation of the first theme ushers in a coda, in whose early measures G♭ makes a final, brief appearance before a long, slower section completes the movement. The remainder of the coda reeks of death, from the mournful melody in the clarinet, to the heavy dominant pedal that eventually releases onto a lament bass-line (mm. 219–21), to the empty (dead) fifths (mm. 229–30) that usher in a last utterance by the clarinet of the introductory motto (see Example 1.3). The Picardy third that completes the movement is more like a nod of acceptance than a turn of the tragedy to a happy end.

No doubt the symptom was a premonition of death. But after the symptom seems to have run its course early in the recapitulation, the overdetermined signifiers for death in the coda make for a puzzling narrative. If we take the first theme to be the present order of things, then the symptom plays a prominent role in the psyche of the sonata from the start, while the introductory motto is an uncanny premonition or a narrator's announcement of the tragedy to come. With the second key, the symptom plays a less ominous role, conjuring the Imaginary as a wish to return to the fulfillment of the past. After the failure of this key, though, the sonata largely represses the symptom until it bursts forth with an anxious, magisterial authority. But this failure of repression finds no traces in the recapitulation, where it appears that the symptom has been cured. Still, the putative health of the psyche cannot help but follow a path to death. To unravel the puzzle of this narrative, I consider how the Imaginary, the Symbolic, and the Real interact in the sonata. The questions that the sonata poses are whether the subject is willing to leave the Imaginary in order to follow the law-like authority of the Symbolic, and whether the Symbolic can protect the subject from the trauma of the Real. These questions involve a historical dimension that renders the sonata as more than a mere analog to Lacan's structure of subjectivity.

To begin, the Imaginary. Until the point of the recapitulation, we can hear the sonata mounting an ironic narrative about the impossibility of curing a psychic/sexual wound. Borrowing work by Peter Gay (1986), Lawrence Kramer (1998: 14–26) has written about the wound in the formation of masculine subjectivity in the nineteenth century, with particular emphasis on interpreting Schubert's songs. In short, the demands of bourgeois marriage in the nineteenth century often forced the young man to relinquish an erotic first love in order to find a more suitable mate. The result was a "castrating wound" necessary "to consolidate one's masculine identity" (1998: 21). The wounded man often looked back on this first love with a mixture of pleasure and pain, a Lacanian *jouissance*. This concept of the wounded male plays within concepts of sexuality that later take a prominent place in theories of the psyche (30–31). Freud, for example, pushes back the first erotic experience from youth to early childhood: the subject's relationship with the mother. The result is a form of castration in which the psyche gives up the mother, losing her as the first lover. Lacan reworks the wound as the very basis of subjectivity itself; once the subject realizes that he is separate, he apprehends that the erotic potential to fulfill the mother is lost to him. The subject is decentered (*Thou art that!*) and castrated (powerless to fulfill both his own and his mother's desire) at the moment of his formation as a subject. For Lacan, as we have seen, this wound of the psyche manifests itself in symptoms of the Imaginary: symptoms of desire, fantasy, and the erotic.

Brahms's F-minor clarinet sonata enacts a formation of the modern subject and the problem of the Imaginary. From the standpoint of nineteenth-century male identity, the long-ago fulfillment of the second-key area signifies a first love forever lost, an imagined oneness of the psychic world before its fall into crisis. The parallel thirds between the piano and the clarinet are like the harmonious blending male and female voices. As this image of the past breaks off, the third-key area of the sonata commences with a slightly martial and propulsive intent: the subject has denied the first love in favor of a normative masculine identity centered on heroic (later, monumental) action. Moving to the beginning of the sonata—a moment in the present that will look back to the ideal past—the G♭ is a wound: both a remainder and a lack (emptiness) from the past. That wound returns with a vengeance in the recapitulation. But male identity asserts itself once more, and the remainder of the sonata plays itself out in defiance of the empty present. The wound is a symptom of the Imaginary, the realization that an imagined erotic power was lost at the moment the ego took its form.

In addition to the second theme, the development reveals the symptoms of desire and eroticism associated with the Imaginary. For the first half of the development, the place where heroic action is required, the subject indulges in an erotic reverie, ruminating over the theme of the second key, with the motto in the bass of the piano, as the music travels through the magically charged chromatic third from A♭ to E major (Example 1.4). It is only in the second half of the development (m. 116) that the sonata's psyche takes up purposeful deeds, with a more passionate, active, and stern focus on the opening motto in the bass. The piano predominates here, with the clarinet relegated to brief, occasional echoes and portions of the second theme. One surmises that the piano plays the part of the male figure, perhaps of Brahms himself, who takes charge and leaves little room for the feminized voice of the clarinet. The piano takes up the determined theme of the third-key area from the exposition in m. 120, and underscoring an inner compulsion to get things done, the musical persona has an enormous capacity for the modality of *doing* over *being* (see Tarasti 1994: 48–49): the piano covers the various registers with Brahms's version of virtuosity, centered on octaves and thick textures. The development unravels the feminized and sentimental eroticism of the second theme: C♯ minor, the key during this more active section, is the enharmonic modal negation of D♭ major, the second key of the exposition. The music reaches the structural dominant for C♯ minor, but at the moment of resolution, the piano wrenches the tonal center to F♯ minor as it brings in a return of the opening motto. The agency of this passage is a delicate matter. Has the piano as persona exerted a harmonic power that ironically ushers in the minor Neapolitan of the home key? Or has another agent (the Greek chorus? the feminized clarinet?) taken control instead? Whatever our vision of the agency, the effect of the monumentalized version of the opening motto renders a mythic pathos to the music.

We have returned to the symptom in its most disturbing form. The music suffers from this enlarged version of the symptom despite the efforts of the development's second half to rid the psyche of the wound from the Imaginary. This ver-

Dev. Part 1

Example 1.4. Brahms, Clarinet Sonata in F minor, I (development)

sion of the opening motto in the minor Neapolitan does more than interrupt a process that might have led to a successful conclusion. The re-announced motto is a bit tortured with heavy-handed syncopation and a sudden intrusion of ca-nonic writing in the middle voice (Example 1.2c). Peter Smith has demonstrated that this variant of the opening motto takes the form of a fugal subject with a

Dev. Part 2

Heroic Action

Example 1.4, *continued*

tonal answer (2001: 223–26). The motto now takes on a contrapuntal authority, a show of compositional prowess. At the moment of crisis, Brahms holds on to what he knows: counterpoint.

The turn to contrapuntal mastery is no answer to the symptomatic G♭; instead, it is a sign from the Symbolic. More accurately, it is a sign that the subject has chosen the Symbolic over the Imaginary. The only way to leave the Imaginary is to enter the Symbolic order with its mandates and forms of proper conduct. And no form of musical conduct could be more proper than a show of contrapuntal skill. Thus, during the move to the recapitulation, the G♭ is a symptom from the Imaginary covering another symptom from the Symbolic, manifesting itself as contrapuntal and motivic manipulation.

As usual, the Symbolic has a historical and cultural dimension that analysis must acknowledge. Margaret Notley (2007: 56–62) argues that the turn to chamber music, and the emphases on concision, artifice, and "the arcane aspects" of craft (56), were all signs of Brahms's lateness; the contrapuntal writing, in particular, connected Brahms with the late styles of Bach and Beethoven (59). Within the Viennese culture of the late nineteenth century, though, concentration on the academic sides of musical craft had a political implication, whether Brahms liked it or not. In the 1880s, as anti-Liberal coalitions gained political momentum, Brahms's cerebral technique became a target as a symbol of the problems of Viennese Liberalism (32–35). Brahms's excessive technique, his overly refined ability in the academic style, pointed to the monumentalized individualism of nineteenth-century Vienna, whose promised rewards for those adhering to values of hard work and academic rigor nonetheless were granted to the few at the expense of the many. As Adorno points out, with Brahms "there is no longer anything which is unthematic," and this impulse for developing variation is the sign of the ever-becoming individual (2002: 57). For Adorno this thematic working out of musical ideas is ultimately a positive force, but within late Viennese Liberalism, the question was whether such attention to details in Brahms's craft was a sign of the individual who proceeds at the expense of a greater social good. Academic composition in Brahms is a symptom of a sociopolitical problem, a symptom from the Symbolic.

Brahms's academic rigor hits us full force as the music moves to the recapitulation. After the contrapuntal working out of the opening motto (mm. 130–32), the music lands on the dominant of F♯ minor (m. 134). Over the next two measures Brahms indulges in a fancy bit of invertible counterpoint (Example 1.2c). The melodic line from mm. 133–34 moves down a sixth and into the bass in m. 134: the resulting G♯-F♯-F is enharmonic to the close of the opening motto, A♭-G♭-F. Meanwhile, the bass line from m. 133 moves a fifth higher into the upper voice. The result is invertible counterpoint at the 10th, which brings the harmony back to a D♭ major chord in first inversion at m. 136. From here, Brahms adds a B♮, converting the harmony to an augmented sixth chord that moves directly to the F-minor tonic in m. 138. The entire complex, from fugal treatment of the motto, through invertible counterpoint, to the conversion of a triad into an augmented-sixth chord, involves an academic diligence of the highest order. Brahms simply will not back down from a style of composition that was viewed as a symptom of the bad faith of Viennese Liberalism.

There is a connection between this form of motivic manipulation and the opening motto. Walter Frisch illustrates how the motto proceeds "impulsively and irregularly by the successive 'liquidation' of a brief motive" (1984: 148). The first form of the motive leaps up a fourth and then descends by step (m. 1: Example 1.2a). Successive forms of the opening motive vary the leap up and the number of descending steps. If we seek an *Ur*-form of the motive, though, it would take the shape of a small leap up followed by a descent that begins with a whole tone. With this *Ur*-form in mind, we see that the final version of the motive in the opening motto (F-A♭-G♭-F) uses the chromatic G♭ as the necessary and logical continuation after the leap to A♭. The opening C-F-E♭ (leap followed by a whole step) finds its echoes in the C-E♭-D♭ (leap followed by a whole step) in m. 2 and in the F-A♭-G♭ that closes the motto in m. 4. Thus the symptomatic G♭ with its intimations of death is written into the DNA of the opening motive as the unavoidable consequence of Brahms's academic writing. The appeal to rigor is not a solution to a musical problem but a symptom in itself: a symptom of the subject entering the Symbolic order and accepting its authority. Like the climactic section of the recapitulation, the sonata's motto shows one symptom, the G♭ as a sign of the Imaginary, that hides another, the same G♭ as a sign of entry into the Symbolic.

At the recapitulation, once academicism piles up to form the symptom's greatest menace, the moment of crisis calls for a change of compositional strategy. But Brahms is a true believer. There will be no veering from the formal scheme, no altered harmonic background, no capitulation to the motive's virulence. Instead, Brahms stays the course, following the thematic pattern set by the exposition and making only those harmonic changes necessary to keep the music in the home key. The sole cure for academic rigor as a symptom is to take it up and follow its formal mandate to the coda, where death is the foreseeable consequence.

We have come to a second answer concerning the putative cure of a symptom that nevertheless results in death. When the subject leaves behind the desire implicit in the Imaginary, he makes what Žižek calls the "forced choice" of entering the Symbolic "that will represent him, designate his place in the intersubjective network, function as his stand-in in the Other—in other words, in which he will be alienated" (2008: 87). The choice to enter the Symbolic is really no choice at all. The only way the subject can enter the network of personal relationships is to take on the language and its culture that form the only possibility of that network in the first place. Because the Symbolic is a symptomatic structure—because it always fails to signify the particularities of an individual's life—the subject is alienated from the moment she enters the Symbolic. This forced choice begins with the subject saying "'No!' to this darting game of intersubjectivity in which desire gains recognition for a moment only to lose itself in a will that is the other's will" (Lacan 2006a: 320). The hero dies even if the symptom is cured because he gave up what was his in order to speak in the language of the Other. Thus "death as a means can be recognized in every relation in which man is born into the life of his history" (319). Even if the patient convinces himself that he has cured his symptom, he is in the province of death, because he took on the forced choice of *giving up* himself in order to *make* himself in the model of the Symbolic.

Brahms's sonata stages death along the three registers of subjectivity. First, the subject must lose himself by denying the desire of the Imaginary. Although the music looks back with sentiment on the Imaginary, it manages to break free when the symptom raises itself to its highest stature at the end of the development. Second, the subject must lose himself again in the act of entering the Symbolic, which can never make full allowance for his particularity. And for Brahms, this entrance demands a double price. Not only must the music follow a mandate of academicism and bourgeois workmanship that was the mark of Viennese Liberalism, but also the music must stay the course even when the political situation reveals the lie of that liberalism. At the end of the sonata movement, the subject mourns the inevitable loss of a Symbolic order that we all enter through loss to begin with.

Death is the limit of what the subject might understand of his own historicity (Lacan 2006a: 318). But the Real is ever before us as a reminder of the letter that always finds its addressee. We can hear those reminders in the strangely fearsome return of the opening motto at the end of the development, and in the overdetermined signifiers for death in the coda. Overcoming the wound of the Imaginary and making the forced choice to enter the Symbolic without veering from its authority are no guarantees. If the patient dies even after a cure is found, it is because the circuit of desire finally closes itself in the Real, bringing the subject to the only route out of the Symbolic: the instant of death.

Why Is Interpreting the Latent Content Not Enough?

If there is a methodology at play in these analyses, it is akin to Freud's process of uncovering a dream's *latent content,* which is a transformation of its *manifest content* (1965: 311–416). Through condensation, displacement, and a whole range of rhetorical tropes—metonymy, metaphor, synecdoche, irony—the literal and often brief content of a dream hides a wealth of dream thoughts, such that "it is in fact never possible to be sure that a dream has been completely interpreted" (313). Such a methodology, which moves from the manifest to the latent and recognizes that the music-as-dream is open to interpretative abundance, is not the one that Cone pursues. Edward T. Cone did *not* invent the musical symptom after all.

Strictly, this chapter has not invented the musical symptom either, because the symptom involves more than the two elements of the manifest content (the musical surface) and the latent content (some hidden kernel of signification). In order to arrive at a proper notion of the symptom and its analysis, we would have to acknowledge that "there are always *three* elements at work: the *manifest dream-text* [the musical surface], the *latent dream content* or thought [the music's kernel of signification], and the *unconscious desire* articulated in a dream [in the music]" (Žižek 1989: 6). By *unconscious*, Žižek means something quite literal; the unconscious is that part of thought that escapes thought. The unconscious is a form of thought external to thought itself, or what Lacan calls the Symbolic (the Other). For the Other to work, there must be some non-knowledge of it on the part of the subject. The symptom, then, works in the space between what the subject knows and what he cannot know, refuses to know, or pretends not to know.

What the subject refuses to know is the power she gives to the Symbolic without wondering if the Symbolic really has the power to take what it demands. What the Symbolic demands is that the subject learn the language of the Other (language itself), in order for order to reign. But the moment we take on the language of our culture, we bend our thought to the conventions of the Symbolic. And these conventions will fail whatever particularity we might possess. Even deeper, the very thought that the subject has a particularity (or, in the everyday phrase, "we are unique") is an idea given to us by the Symbolic itself as a recompense for the loss of our particularity. We give the Symbolic power over our thought by taking on language because it demands that power; and the Symbolic makes that demand because we have acceded to it in the first place. This is why the choice to enter the Symbolic is a forced one. It was no choice at all. As Marx phrases it in an analogy: "One man is king only because other men stand in the relation of subjects to him. They, on the other hand, imagine that they are subjects because he is king" (1990: 149 n.22). Even when one side of the equation realizes this truth, the relation remains because the subjects in the king's rule refuse to acknowledge the very social structure that binds them. They refuse to acknowledge what they already know.

This is what it means to follow the dead letter of the unconscious (the Other), and to discover "the imperative of the Word as the law that has shaped him [the subject] in its image" (Lacan 2006a: 322). But even realizing what might be called this ideology of the subject, we are powerless to change it. Thus, ideology is not the "false consciousness" that we must uncover in order to live freely; ideology is the act by which we make the reality in which we must live. Did Brahms know that he was following an ideology of Viennese Liberalism that not only failed its promise but also brought on a lateness to the bourgeois class that refused to give it up? The answer to this question, unknowable as it is, will not undo the processes by which any subject (Brahms included) accedes to the dead letter of the Symbolic order and follows the course of thought laid out for him. Whether Brahms, or Beethoven, or Schubert knew that the language and culture they learned was a demand to obey the language and culture they learned, they proceeded *as if* they did not know. In Lacan's model, this is all we can ever do. And this desire not to know in order to make the Symbolic function is what drives the manifest and latent content of a dream: it is the third term of the symptom.

2 The Acoustic Mirror as Formative of Auditory Pleasure and Fantasy: Chopin's Berceuse, Brahms's Romanze, and Saariaho's "Parfum de l'instant"

> The human child, at an age when he is for a short while, but for a while neverthe-
> less, outdone by the chimpanzee in instrumental intelligence, can already recog-
> nize his own image as such in a mirror.
>
> —Jacques Lacan, "The Mirror Stage"

The title of this chapter alludes to Lacan's lecture "The Mirror Stage as Formative of the *I* Function." As discussed in chapter 1, for Lacan it is at the mirror
stage that the young child first recognizes herself in the mirror or the gaze of
the mother. And Lacan doubtless would have enjoyed the double entendre in
the English translation of his essay's title, where the word *I* (*Eye*) and its reference both to the ego of the child and to the gaze of the mother/mirror signify the
ego's formation. Lacan associates the mirror stage (the Imaginary) with Freud's
term *Imago,* which refers to "*an identification,* in the full sense analysis gives to
the term . . . that takes place in the subject when he assumes an image," or what
we would call in common terms a *self-image* (2006b: 94). Later French theorists,
especially those concerned with cinema, proposed that if there is a mirror stage
involving a visual formation of the ego, there may also be an acoustic stage, in
which the young child is enveloped by the voice of the mother. This sonic analog
to the mirror stage has accrued various terms: the *maternal voice,* the *sonorous
envelope,* and so on. But the most common of these is the *acoustic mirror,* which
comes from the title of an influential book by Kaja Silverman (1988). The acoustic
mirror has implications for the psychology and phenomenology of listening, as
well as the hermeneutics of music. To understand these implications, this chapter will consider the acoustic mirror and its connection to the three registers of

the Lacanian subject. In addition, an understanding of the acoustic mirror will offer a way of rereading recent work on what Vladimir Jankélévitch considered to be music's ineffable qualities. Finally, to aid in illustrating the phenomenological, philosophical, and hermeneutic effects of the acoustic mirror, the chapter will refer to three pieces: Chopin's Berceuse, op. 57 (1844), Brahms's Romanze, op. 118, no. 5 (1893), and Saariaho's "Parfum de l'instant" from *Quatre Instants* (2002).

Why Does Music Speak to Us?

The second crisis of the subject's formation (the first being birth) happens at the mirror stage, when "the *I* is precipitated in primordial form" before it becomes reconstituted in the matrix of the Symbolic (Lacan 2006b: 94). That is, the infant has the first inkling that she is separate from those around her; she suffers the "shattering of the *Innenwelt*" (inner world) to make way for the *Umwelt* (outer environment) that is the necessary first step toward acquiring language (97). At first, this primordial *I* is the cause of jubilation on the part of the child; but the recognition of the self as separate and unified in an image in the mirror must face the reality that the body and mind are fragmented, disorganized, and totally dependent on the mother, against whom the child defines itself.

If the mirror stage is a crisis precipitated through the visual field, then the acoustic mirror is its aural counterpart. To be strictly correlative to the mirror stage, though, the acoustic mirror must orchestrate a drama in which the young child realizes that the voice of the mother is directed at the child, sparking the same shattering of the inner world and the same recognition that the mother and child are separate. The child must also realize that the murmuring and babbling, the pleasurable euphony that surrounds him, includes two voices: that of the mother, who directs her voice at the child, and that of the child, who has until now added his voice to the enveloping sound without understanding that it belonged to him all along. But where the mirror stage balanced the jubilance of a unified image with the predicament of the fragmented self, the acoustic mirror involves a different set of difficulties for the developing subject. The child comprehends that a voice is directed at her, that the directed voice demands a response, and that her ability to respond in kind is unequal to the agility, musicality, and timbre of the mother's voice. If we accept the acoustic mirror as the strict correlative of the mirror stage, then it must include the same set of consequences involving an "alienating identity" that will mark the subject's "entire mental development" (Lacan 2006b: 97). The subject will always feel inadequate to respond to the demands implicit in the voice of the (m)other. Yet the subject will feel that the other's voice is directed at him and that it demands the very response that can never be given adequately.

Lacan argues that because of the crisis of the mirror stage, the structure of human knowledge is "paranoiac" (96). The mirror stage inscribes the gaze on the subject: the child realizes that she is the object of the mother's eye. The gaze in the structure of the unconscious is what makes us feel that we are being watched, even when nobody is near us. We are in an empty room, and yet we feel as if we must look around to check whether someone is watching. We look at a painting or a doll with the eerie feeling that it gazes back at us—a convention of subjectivity familiar in narratives ranging from the tales of E. T. A. Hoffmann (the lifeless eyes of Olympia that drive Nathaniel to madness in "Der Sandman"), to the *Chucky* horror movies, to the more subtle film *Suddenly, Last Summer,* in which Catherine Holly (Elizabeth Taylor) is institutionalized in a room with a framed quote from the Book of Genesis, "Thou, God, seest me." From the Lacanian point of view, these notions of sightless eyes gazing on us, and of an all-seeing god policing us, are symptoms from the mirror stage.

Seeking effects in the acoustic mirror that correspond to those of the Imaginary, David Schwarz finds representations of musical gazes in various pieces. During a discussion of the Beatles' "I Want You (She's So Heavy)," for example, Schwarz argues that when pop music fades in, it sounds "as if it were aware of the listener, as if it were listening to *him/her*" (1997: 31). The result is a listening gaze. In a later analysis of Schubert's *Ihr Bild,* Schwarz borrows from Schenker in claiming that a repeated B♭ in the song prompts the listener to "'stare' acoustically at the music as the narrator in the poem stares at the image of his beloved" (74). These examples are better understood as assemblages of the mirror stage and the Symbolic order. The possibility of a paranoiac response to music's listening gaze is built into the structure of subjectivity. But especially in Schwarz's discussion of "I Want You (She's So Heavy)," we see how carefully John Lennon manipulated the recording to make a wall of sound that would become oppressive and blur the boundaries between hearing and being heard (23–29). Lennon used musical signs, a part of the Symbolic with its conventions, to heighten the paranoia already built into the subject via the acoustic mirror.

But there is a more general form of musical address resulting from the acoustic mirror. The listening subject can hear music *as if* it were speaking to her, regardless of special features like a fade-in, a repeated note, unisons, echoing passages, or walls of sound. Hearing music as if it addresses us has a long history, including the turn to music and rhetoric in Joachim Burmeister's *Musica Poetica* (see Rivera 1993), and the expansion of that idea in eighteenth-century thought (see Bonds 1991). Here again, though, we find a focus on features *in* the music that dispose the listener to recognize conventions of musical speech, the interaction of the acoustic mirror with the Symbolic order, which seeks to hide subjectivity in the conventions of language and other semiotic systems.

Before searching through musical features to find the symptoms of the acoustic mirror, we need to acknowledge that the structure of subjectivity itself prompts us to hear music as if it addresses us. Charles Fisk beautifully describes this form of musical address as he experienced it in childhood. Discussing Chopin's B-Minor Prelude, Fisk recounts how he always heard a pair of C-major arpeggios in the left hand as two calls that "feel lonely and unrequited" (2012: 182). After conjecturing that the harmonic and melodic material might have captured a child's imagination, Fisk turns to a more subjective (in the strong sense) explanation:

> But I am also tempted to think that my attraction to these preludes stemmed from an emotional need. . . . Through my mother's playing—even though it, like her, was somewhat reserved—I could sense a register of emotional life that I could not usually access in other ways. As a consequence, the imaginary sound-world of music did not merely fascinate me; it also furnished me with an extension of my nurturing environment, a haven in which an imaginary other recognized and empathized with aspects of myself that were finding no other avenue of expression. (183)

Fisk has no Lacanian motivations in this account, but the language of Lacan is suggested nonetheless. First, there is the coincidence that Fisk hears his *mother* playing the Chopin prelude. What had been the mother's voice is transformed into the piano's voice. Second, the passage twice uses the term "imaginary," describing first a musical sound world and then an other who recognizes him. If the mother's gaze brings on the Imaginary register as a thinking in images, then the mother's voice brings on the Imaginary as a thinking in sound. We are left with a world of images (mirror), and a world of sound (acoustic) that, as we will see, fuel desire and fantasy. Third, Fisk's short narrative uses the word "other" to characterize the music. In Lacan's terms, the first other is the (m)other, whose gaze forms the primordial *I*. But since the mother is off limits, especially after we enter the Symbolic order, the subject finds metonymic substitutes for her that promise a fulfillment we can never really experience. Each substitute, the *objet petit a*, is an object of our desire that stands in for the mother. Finally, the Lacanian elements find their interconnections in Fisk's confession that his mother's playing furnished him with a nurturing environment. Where the voice of the mother was, there music shall be.

Although Fisk's discussion is personal, it reveals a subjective structure common to all of us who must pass through the family romance from the prelingual stage, through the mirror stage, and into the Symbolic. Having formed the paranoiac *I*, in this case through the acoustic mirror, the subject apprehends music as if it were addressed to him. This phenomenon is a form of Lacan's famous statement that "a letter always arrives at its destination" (2006h: 41). As soon as we hear music (or open a letter, find a message in a bottle, read a book, hear a person call), we accept it as a message to us merely because we are in the right place at the right time. And, as it happens, we are always in the right place at the right time. This form of receiving a message is what Žižek calls *Imaginary (mis)recognition* (2008: 12). The illusion that music speaks to us is the consequence of the Imaginary register. We attend to the music as if it addresses us because we happen to be where the music is: "*Whosoever* finds himself at this place is the addressee since the addressee is not defined by his positive qualities but by the very contingent fact of finding himself at this place" (13). Chopin did not compose his preludes for Fisk, or me, or anyone alive today. But when we hear Chopin, or the music of any other composer, we attend to it as if it were addressed to us.

And this form of address, as we shall see in later chapters, is one that demands a response.

Why Is the Mother's Voice a Fantasy?

I have discussed the acoustic mirror as if it correlates directly to the crisis of the mirror stage. But in the literature, the term *acoustic mirror* tends to be used for the entire period of childhood development leading up to the formation of the primordial *I*. As Kaja Silverman argues, this period before the crisis of the mirror is the focus of a powerful cultural fantasy that turns on the image of the young child held safely within the singing of the mother's voice and the swaying of her body (1988: 72). Chopin's Berceuse, op. 57, captures both of these fantasy objects in the gentle but unvaried rocking of the left hand and the hushed, vocal right hand. The piece plays on what Guy Rosolato called the "maternal voice" (*la voix maternelle*) (1974: 81). Rosolato also called the maternal voice the "sonorous womb" (*la matrice sonore*), although English scholars, who seem uncomfortable with the female anatomy, have tended to use the more staid term "sonorous envelope." Rosolato argues that the young baby discovers in the maternal voice the first model of auditory pleasure (*le premier modèle d'un plaisir auditif*) and that music finds its roots and its nostalgia here as well (*la musique trouve ses racines et sa nostalgie*) (81). Because the mother—body and voice—are forbidden to the subject once the "specular *I* turns into the social *I*," any effort to invoke the maternal voice belongs to the realm of fantasy and desire that Lacan linked to the Imaginary (2006b: 98). As such, beauty is both "formative and erogenous" in Lacan's model (96).

Chopin's Berceuse is a nostalgic re-creation of the early auditory pleasure to which Rosolato refers. The simple rocking of tonic and dominant harmonies for nearly the entirety of the piece makes it easy to forget that we are hearing a series of variations: we relive the fantasy of maternal swaying (Example 2.1). The first variation at m. 7 is reminiscent of the musical *babble* with which young babies engage the mother without realizing that they are both the source and the focus of the sounds around them (see Moog 1976; Holahan 1987; Gordon 2003; and Reynolds 2006). In real life, musical babble begins as random vocalizations responding to the mother's voice. As the child grows older, however, the vocalizations become more accurate in imitating the mother (Gordon 2003: 41–42). Chopin cleans up the musical babble in the first variation; the two voices nearly harmonize, though a number of piquant dissonances keep the musical surface from falling into a banal series of sixths and thirds. We can identify with the child in the Berceuse, who lives in what psychoanalyst Louise Kaplan calls *oneness* before a second birth (Lacan's mirror stage) gives the child a sense of *separateness* (Kaplan 1978). If the child had a point of view, harmony and discord would be meaningless. Simply being within the oneness of the sonorous womb is enough. Chopin's Berceuse gathers figurations throughout the variations, until the right hand becomes a blur of pleasurable sound, invoking what Robert Hatten would call *plenitude,* a state of "contented fulfillment" (2004: 43).

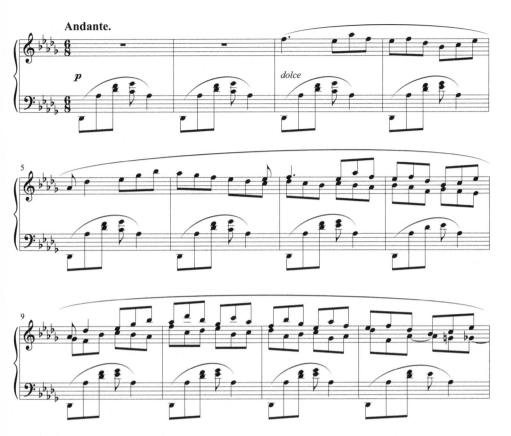

Example 2.1. Chopin, Berceuse, op. 57 (opening)

At only one point near the end of the Berceuse does a move toward the subdominant threaten to break the harmonic spell (Example 2.2). A conventional
reading, ensnared in the Symbolic, would see the move toward the subdominant
as indexical to a moment when the child begins to fall asleep. Soon enough, the
music closes on a simple rocking of the tonic alone before coming to a close. But a
Lacanian reading takes the move toward the subdominant as that new harmonic
element in the constant entwining of tonic and dominant harmonies: an element
that threatens to break the spell of the sonorous womb. It is as if the child is just
beginning to hear with a sense of wonder, just on the brink of an articulation
that might break the oneness. The child is close to understanding that the sonorous womb around him is actually directed *at* him as the voice of the mother. But
Chopin closes off the threat of separateness with a return of the opening melody
over the simplest harmonization imaginable: a repeated tonic chord. We do not
witness the shattering of the inner world.

Chopin's Berceuse plays a part in what Silverman calls the "powerful cultural
fantasy" of the sonorous womb, which turns on the image of the child held within

The Acoustic Mirror 45

Example 2.2. Chopin, Berceuse, op. 57 (coda)

the safe environment of the mother's voice (1988: 72). To be clear, the image is a fantasy because there is no way for us to cross the boundary from the Symbolic back to the period before the first formation of the ego. The culture imagines this early period to be one of fulfilled pleasure because the Symbolic has fixed its eye and ear on a fantasy that comes from the mirror stage in the first place. When

Julia Kristeva imagines the life of the young subject before the formation of the ego, her descriptions largely stay clear of this cultural fantasy. This early period of childhood, which Kristeva calls the *chora,* is marked by drives that "are always already ambiguous, simultaneously assimilating and destructive . . . [and] a place of permanent scission" (Kristeva 1984: 27). Far from a vision of wholeness, the *chora* is a stage of development in which "charges and stases lead to no identity (not even that of the 'body proper'). . . . [It] is no more than the place where the subject is both generated and negated, the place where his unity succumbs before the process of charges and stases that produce him" (28). For Kristeva, the wholeness that we project onto the prelingual stage is no wholeness at all. Instead, drives, scissions, stases, charges, and discontinuities are the stuff of the pre-ego. The prelingual child is both created and destroyed by drives that find no semiotic system to produce a unity that we can recognize as a fully formed subject.

From Kristeva's point of view, informed by Lacan, we can theorize the mirror stage as the site of a double fantasy. First, from this stage the child will discover that the embrace of the mother is something that will be forbidden once the Symbolic comes into play. As such, the subject seeks a substitute for the mother in the *objet petit a;* and those displacements, and metonymies for the mother, cannot give the subject a satisfied fullness. Second, once the subject enters the Symbolic, he looks back on the period before the mirror stage as one in which oneness, wholeness, and fulfillment were the substance of life, such that any subsequent moment entails loss, and any glance back to that time is a moment of nostalgia for something that never existed. We were never whole before or after the mirror stage. We simply fantasize that this was the case.

Chopin's Berceuse, then, is a nostalgic fantasy of the mother, her voice, and the plenitude that we imagine to be lost. But we do not need a berceuse to explore the maternal voice as fantasy. Schwarz describes the auditory experience of listening in a concert hall where the music appears to be all around us. In this "all-around" pleasure, we lose our sense of bodily boundaries and "become one" with the music. Borrowing a term from Freud's *Civilization and Its Discontents,* Schwarz writes that this pleasurable listening gives us an "oceanic" feeling (1997: 7). Looking at Freud's passages about the "oceanic" feeling, we learn that the term came to Freud through correspondence with Romain Rolland, who connected the oceanic to a religious energy that is channeled into the various churches (Freud 1961: 11). But Freud discounts Rolland's explanation, first because he cannot find the oceanic feeling in himself, and second because it implies a falling out of the world, an "intimation" of a wholeness and connection stemming from an "immediate feeling" that is an impossibility in what Freud calls the "fabric of our psychology" (12). Freud's explanation for the oceanic feeling is that it comes from a desire to return to a time before the father put a stop to the "limitless narcissism" of early childhood (21). For Freud, too, the oceanic feeling is a fantasy of return. Thus the maternal voice can find its fantasy object in a phenomenology of listening or a mode of musical signification. In either case, we must not believe that we have recaptured a lost wholeness when we become one with the music.

The Desire to Return

After the stage of the acoustic mirror, the inarticulate babbling that was once part of the imagined pleasure of the sonorous womb must become the articulations of a semiotic system. In short, the child must acquire language and enter the Symbolic order, the law-like forms of communication that separate us forever from whatever wholeness we think we had. There is no going back. Even if we could reexperience the oneness of the pre-primordial ego before the mirror stage, the only way we could represent it to ourselves or others would be through the very Symbolic order that separated us from that imagined oneness in the first place. Thus, for Lacan, as for Silverman, our desire to re-create the image of wholeness is a fantasy, and anything we accept as a totem of that wholeness is a fantasy object, the *objet petit a*.

The famous red-pill/blue-pill scene from *The Matrix* illustrates the impossibility of returning to the sonorous womb. When Žižek writes about *The Matrix*, he argues that the ideology of our situation is not that we are enclosed in a virtual, mediated reality (the Symbolic) from which we should try to break free. The ideology is the very belief that outside the enclosure of the Symbolic "there is some 'true reality' to be entered" (2008: 244). In *The Matrix* the crux of the ideology that we might leave the Symbolic begins in the scene where Morpheus offers Neo the truth of his existence—a scene that Žižek, oddly, never discusses. All the Lacanian elements of the mirror stage are here. After taking the red pill, Neo sits before a broken mirror: the Lacanian sign for our decentered and fractured subjectivity. As Neo exits the matrix, the mirror becomes whole, as if his subjectivity returns to the oneness that was once his province. Swallowed out of the matrix, Neo lands in a technological womb. But the return is not pleasurable. Neo's first feelings are of entrapment, anxiety, and the urge to escape. Having acquired the Symbolic order of the matrix, he really can't leave it at all. Any return to the maternal womb is no moment of bliss but of panic, which we see in Neo's desperate attempts to break out of the gelatinous orb that surrounds him. Accompanying the scene, the sound track includes a hyper-intense version of the noise early computers made as they connected to the internet via dial-up: no humming, tonal echoing, or harmonious blending here; just a technological nightmare of sound gone awry. We cannot go back, except through fantasy substitutions.

Neo's nightmare vision of a return to the oneness of the mother and child is close to Michel Chion's conception of the acoustic mirror. Chion, a composer and theorist of music for the cinema, argues that the maternal voice is a sign of entrapment (1982). At first, we might take this alternative conception of the acoustic mirror as the symptom of oppositional thinking in any signifying system; as such, the maternal voice is either comforting or terrifying. But I think that Silverman nicely argues that Chion's descriptions of the maternal voice come not from the standpoint of a child but from a "subsequent temporal and spatial vantage . . . in short, [from] a fully constituted subject" (1988: 74–75). That is, Chion is not imagining the experience of the young child within the maternal voice but of the adult subjects who somehow find themselves transported to a time where they are helpless within the maternal voice. Thus the opposition is not between the maternal voice as comforting or terrifying but between the maternal voice and the paternal word. After our entrance into the Symbolic order via the paternal word, the maternal voice signifies the discursive impotence of interiority, while the paternal word signifies the potency of exterior discourse.

Implicit is a sexist position, in which music as maternal voice, pleasurable through the loss of boundaries, should be denied in favor of music as paternal word, pleasurable through the articulation of boundaries at multiple levels. We articulate music from its context and from ourselves in the contested phrase "the music itself," and we articulate its internal boundaries in structures. The pleasure of becoming one with the music, of losing our physical boundaries in the all-around sound, is disqualified as the proper way of attending to music. From a Lacanian perspective, though, neither the maternal voice nor the paternal word can claim authority as the better mode of listening. If we listen to music as maternal voice, we risk believing that oneness can ever be ours again. But if we listen to music as paternal word, we accept the Symbolic order as law-like, even though it is a symptomatic structure that cannot capture our being-in-the-world. Both kinds of listening ensnare us in an illusion, though Lacan offers no way out. In Žižek's terms, all we can do is enjoy our symptom, whether it comes from the acoustic mirror and listening as pleasure, or the symbolic order and listening as structuring and denial.

Why Is the Ineffable a Fantasy of Return?

Listening to music can be a fantasy of return. The problem is not to cure that fantasy but to recognize it, because the desire to return can hide behind other ideologies, like the long-standing thought that music lies in a realm about which we cannot speak. This ideology is one that plays a part in recent work on Vladimir Jankélévitch's philosophy of music. It is easy to respond to Jankélévitch's writing with consternation. First, there are those passages where an obtuse literalness worms its way into his thinking. Early in *Music and the Ineffable,* for example, he tells us "a sonata is like a *précis* of the human adventure that is bordered by death and birth—but is not *itself* this adventure" (2003: 14). Like the scene in *One Hundred Years of Solitude,* where José Arcadio Buendia announces with amazement that the world is round like an orange, Jankélévitch tells us what we already knew. Second, Jankélévitch decries the metaphors we use to speak about music and claims to follow Plotinus "in multiplying and destroying the metaphors one by one" (118). But his own writing is filled with metaphors that he allows to stand without the destructive impulse. "When the massive initial phrase of Faure's sixth *Nocturne* emerges right before the end of the piece, out of the A Major shaft suspended like vapor along the entire range of the piano once, *after* the sustained pedal point, the pedal is taken off little by little, then this great nocturnal phrase meets our recognition of it like a distant and faithful friend"

(97). Two metaphors appear in this short passage, but rather than destroy them one by one, Jankélévitch reaffirms and elaborates the metaphor about the faithful friend: "And in truth, the fraternal past had never abandoned us" (97).

Then, there are the apparent contradictions in Jankélévitch's thought. He urges us not to talk about music but argues that it elicits endless talk (72). He tells us that "musicians who permit the sirens of oblivion and the Rusalkas to sing" do not fall prey to the languor of enchantment because "real music humanizes and civilizes" (3–4). Apparently, music spins its civilizing web without the help of *logos*.

Finally, there is a misunderstanding in *Music and the Ineffable* about what is involved in hermeneutics. We suspect that Jankélévitch is against interpretation: the "gnostic" or "hermeneutic order of knowledge" that he opposes to the "drastic" or composing, playing/singing, and hearing (77). This drastic/gnostic opposition is familiar to us from Carolyn Abbate (2004), who also translated Jankélévitch's *Music and the Ineffable* into English. When Jankélévitch refers to hermeneutics, however, he offers only caricatures.

> To decipher who-knows-what cryptic message as perceptible, to place a stethoscope on a canticle and hear something else in it and behind it, to perceive an allusion to something else in every song, to interpret that which is heard as the allegory of a secret, incredible meaning: these are the indelible traits of all hermeneutics, and are first and foremost applied in the interpretation of language. Anyone who reads between the lines or believes himself to have gotten the hint suggests that he is also penetrating hidden thoughts and hidden intentions. (11)

No serious student of hermeneutics believes that it is the task of interpretation to decipher anything. Cryptic messages and hidden codes are the stuff of a boy scout's secret decoder ring. They have no place in hermeneutics or its cognate discipline, semiotics (see Klein 2005: 51–76). Carolyn Abbate sadly repeats this misunderstanding in the opening sentence of her introduction to *Music and the Ineffable*: "Music is no cipher; it is not awaiting the decoder" (2003: xiii). As for the search for hidden intentions and thoughts, these are the comforting and well-worn methodologies of interpretation for those who refuse to grow up. Whatever gnostic tradition Jankélévitch abhors, it is not hermeneutics.

Still, Jankélévitch entices us with fresh observations rendered poetically, which arouse the suspicion that behind his apparent anti-intellectualism, there is something in his thought akin to that of his precursor, Henri Bergson, whose insistence on intuition was what Gilles Deleuze called "a fully developed method, one of the most fully developed methods in philosophy" (1991: 13). Regarding Hugo Wolf's *Mörike-Lieder*, for example, Jankélévitch writes: "Because there never was (in all likelihood) a question at all, this particular 'question' risks being eternally suspended, just like Schumann's 'Warum?' in the *Fantasiestücke*: forever interrogative" (2003: 19). And for those who know enough musicians, the following reads like a wise empirical reminder: "For music, just as it does not make us wiser, does not make us better; that is, music does not have the power to chronically or constantly ameliorate our moral existence, and a life in music does not necessarily imply excellence in the realm of virtue" (125). (So much for the civilizing power that Jankélévitch granted to music earlier in his book.) Another passage reveals that despite an impoverished conception of hermeneutics, Jankélévitch can strike the right tone when he considers musical meaning. He writes that music gives us the meaning of meaning, which is something that even life itself cannot do without "a lethal absurdity"; we learn that "music reveals the meaning of meaning in concealing it, and vice versa renders this meaning volatile and fugitive in the very act by which it reveals it" (46). Finally, if we dare to think that Jankélévitch is the anti-Adorno, there is this aphorism, which echoes Adorno's book on Mahler: "The serious gentleman, listening with his eyes closed, is in fact thinking about the office" (100). For all of his apparent problems, Jankélévitch is someone we must take seriously.

Some who do take Jankélévitch seriously have given us ways of thinking in and around the apparent problems of his philosophy. Both James Hepokoski (2012) and Judy Lochhead (2012) recognize the Bergsonism of Jankélévitch's thought, which Hepokoski reads as an anti-intellectual position that refuses to accept the disenchantment of modernity, and which Lochhead reads as a distrust of reason and its ability to capture experience. Steven Rings argues that Jankélévitch's writing about music serves a deictic function: it is a "linguistic performance" that encourages us to experience music in particular ways (2012: 220). Rings illustrates his thesis by trying to hear the opening of Fauré's Nocturne in B Minor, op. 119, as Jankélévitch describes it. The result for Rings was that he "experienced a moment of epiphanic intensity" that was "accompanied by the physiological effects typical at such moments—among them, mild goose bumps" (222). Although I doubt that Jankélévitch's project was really one in which he hoped we would hear as he did, Rings does succeed in uncovering the way to reconfigure *Music and the Ineffable* as a project concerning the fantasy of the acoustic mirror and the boundary between it and the subject's formation in the Symbolic order.

Goose bumps. Schwarz begins a discussion of the acoustic mirror with the phenomenon of goose bumps and the way they play on the boundary between our adult body and our more archaic body from before the mirror stage, when the internal/external distinction was blurred (1997: 1–8). Feeling goose bumps as we listen to music is the mark of a fantasy of return to the period of the sonorous envelope, when we imagine that we were one with things. From the Lacanian perspective, the question that is crucial to understanding Jankélévitch is how closely we can approach that archaic body of the sonorous womb. If the mirror stage marks both the rise of the Imaginary and the fall of the subject's oneness with things, then Jankélévitch's question, rephrased in Lacanian terms, is whether we can recapture our direct experience before the time of the mirror stage once we have discovered the secret that we are alienated from ourselves by the very Symbolic order that allows us to participate in discourse with others.

Jankélévitch's project is a Proustian one: to wipe away the sediment of language as convention and uncover the secret essence of things (Gallope 2012: 238–39). He whispers: "Music, as a vague and diffluent discourse, situates itself beyond discreet categories like comedy and tragedy: it is situated instead in the depths of lived existence itself" (2003: 65). And elsewhere: "So Bergson's pure perception or N. O. Lossky's intuition establish themselves not just in the immediate proximity of things but face to face with the real *just as it is, at the real*" (32). To be clear, *at the real* is not so far away from Lacan's *the Real* as one might imagine, since the Real is what the Symbolic cannot capture: "*What did not come to light in the symbolic appears in the real*" (2006f: 388). Jankélévitch hopes to approach what the Symbolic cannot capture, and his means of approach is through the sonorous womb, the last moment when the subject was immersed fully in the Real. The Proustian connection becomes clearest when Jankélévitch practically quotes *In Search of Lost Time:* "Now, it can happen that this lost time, like time spent strolling or walking aimlessly, can be time won back, time immediately rediscovered" (67). The problem in this project is how to regain the direct experience of things in the face of our ever-mediated perceptions of the world.

Our entry into the Symbolic is a double one: we enter the Symbolic, and it enters us. Our thought, conscious and unconscious, is the stuff of the Symbolic. This is what Lacan means when he writes throughout his oeuvre that *the unconscious is the Other's discourse.* We speak to the Other (the Symbolic) with the discourse of the Other. And we experience our being-in-the-world through that discourse. But since we speak in the language of the Symbolic, we cannot claim to speak of an immediate experience. The double bind of this problem is that even if we could return to the prelingual mirror stage and the sonorous womb, any experience we had there would need to be translated into the Other's discourse, which would render it mediated again. The problem is well known, even outside Lacan's categories of the subject. About this prison-house of language, for example, Foucault writes: "To know is to speak correctly, and as the steady progress of the mind dictates; to speak is to know as far as one is able, and *in accordance with the model imposed by those whose birth one shares*" (1994: 87; emphasis added). Jankélévitch's problems, then, are to place music outside of culture, to find a way to experience music away from the conventions of culture, and to express those experiences in language that is already incapable of capturing what he hopes to say.

Jankélévitch tries to solve the first problem simply by claiming that music, as a non-linguistic form, is open to direct experience. Restating this thesis in Lacanian terms, music's true form belongs to the period prior to both the mirror stage, the formation of the primordial ego, and our entry into the Symbolic, where language mediates experience. Placing music in a special transcendent realm is a familiar strategy of nineteenth-century philosophers. But in this case, Jankélévitch is part of a tradition of phenomenology that extends from Bergson to Kristeva. Bergson's famous linking of music to time as duration (*durée*) indicates that direct experience, which is non-spatial, is possible in music because we can attend to its ever-becoming, its qualitative properties. Jankélévitch's writing often returns to this Bergsonian theme. Among many Bergsonian passages in *Music and the Ineffable,* we read: "We live music, as we 'live' time, as a fertile experience, with the ontic participation of our entire being" (2003: 95). This tradition of placing music prior to the mirror stage reaches to Kristeva, who claims that music belongs to a pre-Imaginary and prelingual stage of development: the *chora* (confusingly, she also calls it *the semiotic*) (1984: 24). Kristeva explains that "the *chora* precedes and underlies figuration and thus specularization, and is analogous only to *vocal or kinetic rhythm*" (26; emphasis added). This vocal (musical) property of the *chora* is unmistakably maternal throughout Kristeva's writing.

But if music for Jankélévitch belongs to the *chora,* the realm of direct experience before the mirror stage, we still cannot speak of it without the layers of convention and culture that steer us away from pure experience. "Directly, in itself, music signifies nothing, unless by convention or association" (Jankélévitch 2003: 11). Because music has its conventions of meaning that draw us out of direct experience, "one is led to ask whether our ears, far from being organs of hearing, are not rather more the cause of our deafness" (26). The second problem, then, involves learning to fall into music, or, in Jankélévitch's terms, to remain open to musical *Charm* (always capitalized in Abbate's translation). A refusal to submit to musical Charm in the name of a *logos* that pretends to explain away what music does to us is a failure to see that the technicalities and discourses around music do not bring us closer to its secrets but push us into empty banalities. "The phobia about consent, the fear of appearing bewitched, the coquetry of refusal, the resolve not to 'submit,' are the social and sociological forms assumed by alienation, just as the spirit of contradiction is a form of mimicry. Maniac antihedonism is the mark of the technician and is akin in its frivolity to a love for Viennese waltzes" (102). But even if we do submit to musical Charm and turn our backs on the dry technicalities of musical discourse, we have to face the problem of the endless talk that music elicits. Jankélévitch must address a third problem, which is how to write about music when the writing itself comes from a Symbolic order that necessarily fails to capture the particularity of experience. We have already seen Jankélévitch's answer to this third problem, which involves *multiplying and destroying* one by one the metaphors we use for music. If we try this tactic ourselves, we see how difficult a task Jankélévitch sets for us.

As an example, I turn to the two chords that open Debussy's Violin Sonata: a G-minor triad in closed position, followed by a C-major triad, a fourth higher (Example 2.3). In an article on parallel voice-leading in Debussy's music, David Lewin normalizes these two chords by reinterpreting the high G4 in the C-major triad as an "octave leap" from the root G in the G-minor triad (1987b: 59–61). Thus the real upper voices move from B♭-D to C-E♮, creating smooth, stepwise motion. As always with Lewin, his hearing of the opening is clever, allowing for long-range connections across the first movement of the sonata. But from Jankélévitch's point of view, such a rehearing is a way of wiping away direct experience in order to turn the particularities of Debussy's music into conventions. The musical *chora* is transformed into the Symbolic. From this perspective, such a hearing will not do.

How can we describe what we hear without recourse to convention? We might hear the second chord responding in kind (in closed position) to the first, but this, too, is a convention, in this case involving musical agency and the common question/answer metaphor. We might say that the second chord brightens the

Lewin's Reading of the Opening Two Chords

Example 2.3. Debussy, Violin Sonata, I (opening)

hue of the introduction, but this hearing relies on the convention of minor/tragic/ dark versus major/non-tragic/light. We could say that the second chord questions the thesis of the first chord, but this reversal of the question/answer convention only reinscribes itself into a Hegelian dialectic that is always steeped in the Symbolic. We might notice that despite its closed structure, the G-minor triad has a quality of movement in stasis, like George Seurat's "La rivière Seine à la Grande-Jatte," with its sailboat and rowboat moving in opposite directions, lending us the illusion of speed in stopped motion. Does the C-major triad respond in any way to the G-minor one, or can we not say that they approach each other on the same musical canvas, soliciting in us a sense of vertigo that comes from realizing that both we and our surroundings are moving?

In this brief attempt to describe the experience of listening to the opening of Debussy's Violin Sonata, I have followed the only thing close to a methodology that Jankélévitch allows: to multiply the metaphors one by one and then to disintegrate them as soon as they materialize. This process could continue indefinitely, but I have cut short the metaphors with a device common in Jankélévitch's writing: a metaphor in the form of a question. These questions are not rhetorical; Jankélévitch does not offer them in order to answer them himself. Instead, the questions simply hang in the air. They are a convenient stopping point that underscores how far we have come from a conventional reading while acknowledging that we cannot reach the direct experience we hope for.

Jankélévitch's questions also have a function within Lacan's formulation of subjectivity. The result of passing through the mirror stage is that we are alienated from ourselves: we are a symptom. Within the Symbolic, reality is a fantasy construction that masks what cannot be known, what we imagined we once experienced as direct contact with the world. A bit of the Imaginary persists as something that resists the Symbolic (Hoens and Pluth 2002: 5). As Žižek claims, though, what holds for reality also holds for ideology. "Ideology is not a dreamlike illusion that we build to escape insupportable reality . . . but to offer us the social reality itself as an escape from some traumatic, real kernel" (1989: 45). The Symbolic, the conventional, is the escape from the knowledge that we are always already alienated. This situation places the subject in a double bind, because we cannot escape the ideology of the Symbolic—there can be no unmasking scene where truth reveals itself (Žižek 1989: 25)—but we equally cannot return to the *chora* and reclaim any form of direct experience. Neither *logos* nor *melos* can claim to show us the truth of life or to lead us out of enchantment. We are always enchanted, whether in the fantasy of the Imaginary or in the ideology of the Symbolic. Still, the subject has a need to integrate herself into the Symbolic, to cure the symptom of mediated experience itself through an appeal to the Other. And this appeal takes the form of a question, to which the subject hopes for an answer from *an* other as a representative of *the* Other: a question that can reconstitute the subject from the emptiness of mere signs. "But what, in fact, was the appeal the subject was making beyond the emptiness of his words [*dire*]?" asks Lacan. "It was an appeal to truth at its very core. . . . But first and from the outset it was the call of emptiness itself, in the ambiguous gap of an attempted seduction of the other" (2006a: 248). In the end, Jankélévitch expresses his thought in the form of a question that hopes for a response from the Other, which might reconstitute music as a metaphor from the Imaginary and make it (and the ego) whole out of the emptiness of signs.

James Hepokoski wonders about whose ineffability Jankélévitch is talking about before concluding that since our experiences of music are the products of enculturation (the Symbolic), any "disparaging of interpretive conversation about music . . . must be regarded as a rearguard, regressive posture" (2012: 230). But Jankélévitch's project, however impossible to achieve, is not about discounting interpretation but about finding a way around the truth that the subject's being "has never been anything more than his own construction [*oeuvre*] in the imaginary" (Lacan 2006a: 249). And if the work that Jankélévitch does in multiplying and erasing the metaphors for music seems the game of a narcissist, it is also the way of understanding what constitutes both music and subjectivity. "For in the work he does to reconstruct it *for another,* he encounters anew the fundamental alienation that made him construct it *like another,* and that has always destined it to be taken away from him *by another*" (249). Including Kristeva's theory of the *chora,* which precedes the mirror stage, we have three levels of subjectivity in Jankélévitch's thought: the *chora* (the site of music and oneness), the Imaginary (the site of our first alienation that fuels a fantasy of return), and the Symbolic (the Other to whom we make an appeal for the meaning of our alienation). Jankélévitch's writing begins in the Imaginary as an intimation that we are alienated from music. He attempts to capture the *chora*, about which no speech is adequate. And he returns to the Symbolic, where every effort is made to avoid a construction that is *like another* so that it cannot be taken *by another*.

Fear of the Maternal Voice

Jankélévitch stages a crossing of boundaries between the Imaginary and the Symbolic, where music is the *objet petit a* that promises to restore lost time, the metonymy for a lost wholeness of the subject, and where the erasure of metaphors promises to approach that wholeness in the Symbolic while denying the possibility of success from the start. Jankélévitch distrusts *logos* as a convention that bars us from the reality of things. He also distrusts those who refuse to lose themselves in music. For Jankélévitch, "technical analysis is a means of refusing to abandon oneself spontaneously to grace, which is the request the musical Charm is making" (2003: 102). Jankélévitch is suspicious of those who are afraid to lose themselves in the maternal voice.

Sometimes music will stage a similar crossing between the Imaginary and the Symbolic, although it often takes the reverse form of Jankélévitch's project: music will approach the maternal voice only to withdraw from it. In Brahms's Romanze, op. 118, no. 5, for example, we move from the Symbolic in the opening section to the fantasy of the maternal voice in the middle section, only to return to the Symbolic in the closing section, although (to be clear) this crossing uses the signs of the Symbolic throughout. The first section plays with a number of topics: conventions of musical discourse that announce the Symbolic (Example 2.4). There is a chorale topic throughout, and in the material of the first measure and its subsequent returns (mm. 5, 9, and 13) there is reference to a Sarabande topic. The opening measure also includes a descending-thirds sequence, while the final measure in each phrase forms a hemiola. Taken as a whole, the conventions point to a dignified and spiritual journey: a lonely processional, a pilgrim's progress. The problem is that our poor pilgrim keeps going astray, beginning in F major and moving toward D minor in each phrase. The progress meets an obstruction that prompts the fourfold playing of the opening phrase. The music is thus a series of re-beginnings. Although each phrase is a variation of the first, suggesting a motivation to reach a state of plenitude, the opening section lands on a D-minor chord in the last measure (16) before a move to D's dominant suggests that the music will try a new tactic.

That new course comes in the Romanze's middle section, which is a series of continuous variations on a simple four-measure harmonic pattern (Example 2.5). Kevin Korsyn's famous article on the anxiety of influence makes a connection between this middle section and Chopin's Berceuse, where Brahms faces the anxiety of influence through the swerve of *tessera*, or completion, which is evinced in the way that he extends a five-note motive from the Berceuse across the theme and into its first variation in the Romanze (1991: 26). Another way

Example 2.4. Brahms, Romanze, op. 118, no. 5 (opening)

to read the anxiety of the Romanze, though, is to hear the middle section as a fantasy of the maternal voice, which the music wishes to evoke while refusing to maintain long enough to forestall a return to the Symbolic in the opening material.

Like Chopin's Berceuse, the middle section of the Romanze features a set of continuous variations that reaches a plenitude over a rocking bass line. Already in the second measure, the duet texture in the right hand suggests the voices of the mother and child in the sonorous womb. The fantasy is profound here since the voices harmonize so perfectly. Curiously, though, Brahms's four-bar theme concludes on a V_2^4 of V that refuses to resolve conventionally to a V6 chord in the next variation. It is as if the music makes an effort to ward off the conventions of harmonic progress. The G♯ in the last measure of the theme is a stain on the fantasy of the maternal voice, because it suggests forward progress in time, out and away from the security of the sonorous womb and toward the alienation of the mirror stage. An alternative interpretation hears the G♯ as a Lydian alteration, conjuring a long-ago musical practice prior to the conventions of functional tonality. Unlike the Berceuse, whose simple rocking between tonic and dominant harmonies allowed the listener to become lost in the growing plenitude of the

Example 2.5. Brahms, Romanze, op. 118, no. 5 (middle section)

maternal voice, there is a sense of a magical avoidance of destiny each time the G♯ in the Romanze moves to the next variation.

Like Chopin's Berceuse, the variations conclude with a reflective move to the subdominant via a V7 of IV. Rather than allow this fantasy to continue, a simple transition of trills brings us back from the maternal voice, sending us to the here and now, the moment of our full formation in the Symbolic. The shivering thrill of those trills takes on a dark hue when a B♭ sends the music to D minor, as if we exit this fantasy with a sense of loss. The simple transition marks another double bind in subjectivity: to exit the fantasy of the maternal voice is to reexperience the alienation that is our peculiar inheritance, but to remain with the maternal voice is to risk losing ourselves in the anxiety of entrapment without the means to speak, even if only with the discourse of the Other. The Romanze opts for assuaging the anxiety of losing oneself in the pleasure of the maternal voice by returning to the opening section, which completes the piece after only two phrases, the second of which reaches a full cadence in F major that counters the many turns to D minor in the first section. A plagal cadence closes the Romanze with a sense of spiritual acceptance and fulfillment, as if the subject has taken the right action at last.

In terms of subjectivity, the opening of the Romanze stands with the paternal word, the middle section looks back to the maternal voice, and the final section returns to the paternal word, satisfied that it has foreclosed the fantasy object from the past. But there is no way to close the circuit of the fantasy object. Even if the psyche were allowed to pursue the *objet petit a,* the unfettered subject would find that the desired object is in reality an obstacle that prevents the closed circuit of satisfaction in the first place. In preventing the circle of pleasure from closing, the *objet petit a* causes displeasure in the subject, although that displeasure is simultaneously the source of enjoyment (*jouissance*), a pleasure in pain that comes from a drive to find the object that will forever bend away from our grasp (Žižek 2008: 55–56). The *objet petit a* is not external but internal to the subject: it is a fantasy and an obstacle that is constitutive and that can be neither obtained nor denied. What constitutes Brahms's Romanze is the constant swerve, a bending in space toward D minor in the opening section. But even when the music loses itself in D major during the middle section, the recurring G♯ acts as an obstacle that prevents fulfillment here as well. Take away the swerves toward and away from D and what is left of the Romanze? A few measures of entirely conventional, entirely routine material. The negative substance of the music lies in its attempts both to avoid and to capture the *objet petit a.*

When the Romanze returns to the paternal voice (the Symbolic) in the closing section, it merely replays the forced choice that every subject makes. Our only path to socialization is through the Symbolic that forces us to give up the incestuous object of our desire (that is, the mother as first other). That object, though, only becomes incestuous at the moment we "make the choice" to enter the Symbolic, at which point we realize that the mother is off-limits. We also come to know that we were never really one with the mother: it was all a fantasy of oneness that was upheld by an early form of subjectivity that failed to realize its separateness from the mother in the first place. What we seek, then, is something that we never had, that which only came into being as we became socialized. The choice is forced because the only alternative is to remain unsocialized, which is a mode of freedom that we call *psychosis.*

Living in the Imaginary

In review, to be strictly correlative to the mirror stage, the acoustic mirror must be a point at which the child recognizes his own voice as separate from that of the mother. In this chapter, I have made a distinction between the mirror stage and the terms *sonorous womb,* or *sonorous envelope,* which refer to a period before the mirror stage, a period when the child is one with the voice and body of the mother. Kristeva calls this stage the *chora,* and her conception of this period of development includes themes of drives, intensities, scission, rhythm (from the mother's body), and music (from the mother's voice). Kristeva's vision of the *chora,* then, is far less a fantasy of oneness than a portrait of life unsocialized and untamed by the Symbolic. Whichever way we view this period of development, once the subject enters the mirror stage, drives and desires begin to focus on fantasy objects that stand in for the prime prohibition of ever being one with the mother. In the *objet petit a* subjects seek what they think they have lost, what they never really had, and what they can never attain.

These themes surrounding the Imaginary—the sonorous womb, the acoustic mirror, the fantasy of the (m)other, the *objet petit a* that promises fulfillment while prohibiting a closure of the circuit of desire—all play a role in some of Kaija Saariaho's works since the 1990s, from *Château de l'âme* (1995) to *Lonh* (1996) to her first opera, *L'amour de loin* (2000), through echoes of that opera in *Cinq reflets de L'amour de loin* (2001) and *Quatre instants* (2002). All of these works feature static sound spaces that surround the singer(s) and/or the audience. In *Lonh,* for example, "the three-dimensional electronic soundscape envelops the listener in a virtual garden" (Moisala 2009: 43). The words *envelops* and *virtual garden* in Pirkko Moisala's description of *Lonh* already suggest that the music explores a return to the powerful cultural associations of the sonorous womb. It is not only that the characters in Saariaho's stage works are in a musical fantasy space, but also that the audience is enveloped in that space.

Saariaho's stage works of this period involve texts that echo the tropes of desire, the acoustic mirror, and the problems of the Imaginary. *L'amour de loin* especially plays on the theme of finding in the other the *objet petit a* that nevertheless refuses the subject's grasp. Briefly, the opera involves three characters: Jaufré, a troubadour; Clémence, a countess living in exile in Tripoli; and the Pilgrim, who acts as a messenger between the two. Clémence falls in love with Jaufré "from afar" after reading his poetry, which the Pilgrim brings to her. Jaufré falls in love with Clémence "from afar" and makes a journey with the Pilgrim to be united with her. But on reaching Clémence, Jaufré dies, leading Clémence literally to shout in despair. In an analysis of the opera, Yayoi Uno Everett argues that the lovers in *L'amour de loin* displace their desire "from the idealized Other to each other" (2013: 330). The lovers project fantasies onto one another, while the Pilgrim acts as the vehicle that can draw together the circuit of their desire. But since the circuit can never be closed, the only possibilities are that the two lovers never meet or that one of them must die before they can be united. As Everett rightly points out, despite the implicit reference to Wagner's *Tristan und Isolde*, the narrative of *L'amour de loin* avoids romantic notions of transcendence or completion in death (331). Instead, the death of Jaufré underscores a rift in subjectivity, as Clémence expresses a primal cry of pain that comes when the *objet petit a* bends from her grasp.

A similar theme plays out in Saariaho's song "Parfum de l'instant" from *Quatre instants*. Like the libretto of *L'amour de loin,* the poetry for these songs is by Amin Maalouf. The poem for "Parfum de l'instant" follows with a translation.

Tu es auprès de moi
Mais je ferme les yeux
Pour t'imaginer

Nos lèvres se frôlent
Nos doigts s'emmêlent
Nos corps se découvrent
Mais je ferme les yeux
Pour rêver de toi

Tu es le parfum de l'instant
Tu es la peau du rêve
Et déja la matière de souvenir

You are before me
But I close my eyes
To imagine you

Our lips touch
Our fingers entwine
Our bodies discover one another
But I close my eyes
To dream of you

You are the perfume of the moment
You are the skin of the dream
And already the material of remembrance
                (Translation by the author)

Looking first at the poem, we see the crisis of the mirror stage already in the first stanza: "You are before me / but I close my eyes / to imagine you." This is a curious statement that nonetheless captures those moments when we are with one lover who stands as a substitute for another. Among the series of substitutes, the primal lover is the mother. The stanza also points to the impossibility of closing the circuit of desire. Even when the lover is before the speaker of the poem, s/he is a projection from the Imaginary.

Example 2.6. Saariaho, "Parfum de l'instant" (opening)

The next stanza expands this theme of presence and absence. For the second time, the poem refers to closing the eyes, indexical to the visual aspect of the mirror stage, while the word *dream* pairs with *imagine* from the first stanza, directing our attention again to the Imaginary, where images of the unconscious stand in for primal desire. The lovers are entwined, yet the voice of the poem dreams of a fantasy image, the desire for the *objet petit a* that the addressee cannot fulfill. The final stanza brings home the unreality of the lover and suggests that the *you* of the poem, the addressee, may be someone other (literally Other) than the lover. This is a problem to which I will return after considering Saariaho's musical setting of the poem.

In discussing the song, I make reference to a live performance by Karita Mattila that is available on YouTube (see Saariaho). Saariaho wrote *Quatre instants* for Mattila, and the performance is part of a gala concert celebrating the fiftieth birthday of Esa-Pekka Salonen, who conducts the Swedish Radio Symphony Orchestra in the video. The basic strategy of the song is that the orchestral accompaniment picks up pitches from the vocal part, surrounding the singer and the audience with static and shimmering sound worlds, a sonorous womb. In this way, the music forms the acoustic counterpart to the mirror stage enacted in the

Example 2.7. Saariaho, "Parfum de l'instant" (later section)

poem. The vocal part uses a limited set of pitch classes, a single hexachord (D, E♭, F♯, G, A, B♭) that tends to hover in a single octave above middle C (D4, E♭4, etc.), although the voice does reach into the fifth octave at times, and twice it lands on a climactic and extended A5. Although the orchestra fills in pitches that complete the aggregate, its primary function is to echo the pitches of the vocal part. For example, the first two pitches of the singer's opening line are G4 and F♯4, while the last pitch is D5; this same trichord forms the orchestral response in m. 4 over a pedal C♯, creating a fractured echo of the vocal part (Example 2.6). The orchestral rhythms are repetitive and minimalist, forming glistening and non-progressive textures. Saariaho employs similar techniques throughout the song. In the second stanza, for example, the voice centers on A♭4, B♭4, D5, and E♭5, while the orchestra surrounds the vocal part with another sonorous and diaphanous texture involving repeated patterns that borrow those same pitches (Example 2.7).

The song never finds its way out of the fantasy of the maternal voice, staged through the static rhythms and pitches that surround the vocalist and audience. As a whole, the song bears the characteristic marks of Saariaho's mature works: brilliant layers of color, sensuality, and a mysterious, dream-like atmosphere (Moisala 2009: 28–29). In this performance, Mattila is a fantasy object herself. Dressed in a black single-piece suit that partially reveals her breasts while compressing them, Mattila is simultaneously an image of oneness and a fantasy substitution for the mother. In Deleuze and Guattari's terms, she is a *body without organs* that is reterritorializing itself around the breasts and (during performance) the mouth: an apt totem for the mother and the child (1987: 172). Although she may signify the promised wholeness of a fantasy object, during her performance she makes gestures that imply a motivation to pull herself together, as if her body verges on scission. When she sings the words "Je ferme les yeux pour rêver de toi" (I close my eyes to dream of you), she encircles her body in her arms, the subject of her own embrace, as if attempting to make whole the fractured self. And her eyes in the performance, which often open and close in exaggerated ways, point to the Lacanian mirror, with its emphasis on vision. She makes a gaze, as she is the object of our gaze. She is whole, and she is fractured. She is the object of desire as she seeks the object of her own desire, reminding us that what the young child took as the promise of wholeness in the body of the mother was not only the source of desire but also a mistaken notion that the mother herself was ever whole. We are all fractured and decentered in the Lacanian vision of the subject. Neither the mother nor her fantasy substitutions can return us to a lost unity, because that unity itself is a fantasy from an imaginary past.

Turning to the final stanza, the words disclose a difficulty running through the poem: just who is the *you* whom the singer addresses? The question brings us back to Lacan's famous aphorism that a letter always finds its addressee. Lacan's claim works in the three registers of the subject: the Imaginary, the Symbolic, and the Real. Within the Imaginary, our first impulse may be to think of the addressee as a lover, who is oddly absent and present simultaneously: the always-missed object of desire who stands in for the mother as first lover. This possibility comes to the fore in the last stanza, where the putative lover is addressed as incorporeal: a perfume, the boundary of a dream, the material of remembrance. Keeping within this register of the Imaginary, another possibility is that the singer/speaker addresses us directly, because, as we have learned, the mirror stage creates the subject as the one to whom the other addresses herself. We are unreal, unwhole, the objects of the Imaginary, the material of fantasies and dreams for those around us.

Within the Symbolic, the singer addresses the Other itself. She imagines the Other as ever present, always embracing her, the very substance of her existence. Yet the Other is not real. We cannot touch it, nor can we name the particles of its substance. The Other, too, is a perfume, a skin of the dream. The Other only has power over us because we make the forced choice of entering the Symbolic by taking on language and becoming socialized. But the voice of the poem is coming close to unmasking what cannot be unmasked: that the Symbolic as the "Other who is supposed to know" is dead. Like the famous Freudian dream in which the father does not know he is already dead, the subject can only acknowledge the unreality of the Other as a vehicle for self-reproach (Freud 1965: 466).

Placing "Parfum de l'instant" within the context of the surrounding songs in *Quatre instants,* we see that self-reproach is a theme running through the whole work. In the first song, "Attente" (Awaiting), the woman likens her situation to being in a boat set adrift, unable reach the far shore where her lover awaits. The text has obvious connections to the theme of separation in Saariaho's *L'amour de loin.* It is in the second song, "Douleur" (Anguish), that we see the self-reproach typical of the subject who has realized the forced choice involved in entering the Symbolic. Here, the woman recalls with horror being united with her lover. She sings of wishing to avoid gazing upon him, walking toward him, embracing him, while her body has refused to obey her. She burns with remorse at her encounter with her lover ("Le remords me brûle"). And the song ends with a powerful and primal high note that reminds us of Everett's interpretation of the finale of *L'amour de loin,* where Clémence's final outcry is a "crisis of identity associated with *jouissance*" (2013: 330). The key words repeated a number of times in this second song are "brûle" (burn) and "obéi" (obey), indicating that the nameless woman of the songs burns because she has failed to obey; or, from the view of the Symbolic, she burns because she can only obey. In describing a performance of this song by Mattila, Tim Ashley of *The Guardian* offered the interpretation that the woman burns with remorse because her lover has "sexually assailed" her (quoted in Moisala 2009: 48). This is a possible reading, although nothing in the song mentions sexual assault. A Lacanian reading recognizes that there are two things the Other demands: obedience and the denial of enjoyment. Once we enter the Symbolic, the only source of enjoyment (*jouissance*) we are allowed is the very denial that is demanded of us. We burn to fulfill our desires outside the eyes of the Other who, we discover, is the dead letter of the law that nonetheless binds us (Žižek 2008: 143). But we can only fulfill our desires if we try to take back the forced choice of entry into the Symbolic and return to the period before the Imaginary. Thus, the third song, "Parfum de l'instant," returns to the fantasy of the sonorous womb.

Turning to the Real, the woman in "Parfum de l'instant" addresses the stain on discourse that is the substance of the Real. This possibility comes to the fore particularly with the words "Tu es la peau du rêve" (You are the skin of the dream). Even our dreams speak in the language of the Other (the Symbolic), but they also present us with the problem of the Real, which is everything that does not work in the Symbolic. The woman of the poem has refused to remain in the Symbolic, as we see in "Parfum de l'instant," and prefers to return to the stage of the Imaginary and before. By the fourth song, "Résonances" (Resonances), we see the effect of going past the Imaginary into the *chora* itself, the realm of the Real. The lines of this song are taken entirely from the lines of the previous three poems. Like the *chora*, this poem is riven. The shards of subjectivity, like the prophecies of the Cumaean Sybil, are scattered by the winds. Our form of address to the Real is to the Other, the one who is supposed to know. But in reality, it is not we who address the Real, but the Real that addresses us. In doing so, the Real spurs us to find the secret of its message.

The Imaginary, the Symbolic, and the Real are all symptomatic structures in Lacan's thought. In terms of Jankélévitch's troubled opposition between the Drastic and the Gnostic, then, we can in no way have a Drastic experience of music that isn't already a fantasy from the acoustic mirror. Any attempt to return to the *chora*, the only possible site of pure experience, risks tearing us apart as in the final song of Saariaho's *Quatre instants*. Music as the vision of the ineffable will not release us from the Symbolic and give us back what we think we have lost. Our only choice is to recognize that music is marked with the symptoms and crises that are the substance of the modern subject. All we can do is to take the course of interpretation that will lead us to understand what constitutes us, even though a full understanding will always bend away from our grasp. And that course, whether through the fantasy of the acoustic mirror or the law-like structure of the Symbolic, is one that will spur us to the moment of our death.

3   Debussy and the Three Machines of the Proustian Narrative

What an abyss of uncertainty, whenever the mind feels overtaken by itself; when it, the seeker, is at the same time the dark region through which it must go seeking and where all its equipment will avail it nothing.

—Marcel Proust, *In Search of Lost Time: Swann's Way*

Does the Past Have an Agency?

Once we are socialized in the Symbolic, there is no exit. But if we cannot go back to an earlier stage of our subjectivity, can an earlier stage come to us? In seeking an answer, our first impulse may be a turn to Freud, for whom the interpretation of a dream is the way to the undiscovered kingdom of our past. "We are thus driven to admit that in the dream we knew and remembered something which was beyond the reach of our waking memory" (Freud 1965: 45). Our forgotten past also speaks to us through the Real in the form of symptoms, a topic that I take up in chapter 4. But Freud's model for uncovering the past through dreams and symptoms was not the only one developed during the crises of early modernism. Proust, too, viewed the past as something lost that could be regained, although the mechanism for its retrieval was different from that of the Freudian method. Proust's model of time redeemed is the topic of this chapter. The stage is the music of Debussy. And the relationship between Proust's vision of the past, Debussy's music, and Lacanian subjectivity will be manifest in Kristeva's concept of the *chora*. Although it is clear that through the Freudian, Lacanian, or Proustian models, the past can speak to us, it is not clear that we can rediscover a past that goes back far enough to revisit a subjective stage prior to the Imaginary. The *chora*, then, will be of particular importance to the later portions of this chapter. Through Proust, Debussy, and Kristeva, we approach the question of whether the past has an agency capable of speaking to us beyond the divide of the mirror stage.

Debussy first. To take up this problem properly, we need to set aside a convention of hearing certain music as the representation of an image or scene. Debussy's "Reflets dans l'eau" is not just about water. "Des pas sur la neige" is not just about footsteps in the snow, although it does open with an intimation of such steps. "La Cathédrale engloutie" is not just about a cathedral sinking into the sea. These musical works are concerned with a private experience of time regained that reaches an eternal moment before the truth of mortality. The narrative path of these pieces suggests kinship with a recurring theme of time and remembrance in Proust's *A la recherche du temps perdu* (hereafter called the *Search*). To understand one form of that path, I borrow from work by Gilles Deleuze, who wrote about memory, eternity, and crisis in Proust's *Search,* calling them the *three machines* (2000: 145–60).

It is unlikely that there is anything like a line of influence cast from Proust to Debussy. Instead, the argument must involve a more impersonal crossing of texts, an intertextuality that relies on Stephen Kern's claim that during the decades up to World War I the culture of central Europe was preoccupied with the problems of time and space (1983). In light of the increasing establishment of a uniform and public time during that period, philosophers and artists like Edmund Husserl, Henri Bergson, and his cousin Marcel Proust grew concerned about the loss of a private experience of time. The phenomenology of time in Debussy, then, must be read within this cultural context. And the crises involved concern industrial time, the power of memory to form us in ways we may not realize, and the knowledge that every realization will be lost in the dust of mortality. I begin by reviewing the theme of time regained in Proust's novel before turning to Deleuze and the three machines. Then, I proceed to a discussion of Debussy's music, beginning with "Reflets dans l'eau," after which I consider the time/space problem in subjectivity during early modernism and its extension to postmodernity in what Fredric Jameson calls "the end of temporality" (2003). Finally, I investigate whether Proust's model of the past really does allow the *chora* to speak to us from a time prior to the Imaginary.

What Is Proust's Conception of Time and Memory?

Proust's *Search* is a musical text, not only because music plays such a large role in the lives of its characters, but also because, as Jean-Jacques Nattiez has shown, the themes of the novel reappear in transformations like leitmotivs (1989: 21–22). Reading the *Search,* we do have a sense that its themes unfold musically, often contrapuntally, appearing first only as intimations, but transformed and enlarged throughout the nearly 5,000 pages of the novel. And the number of these leitmotivs is breathtaking. Harold Bloom lists the *Search*'s abundant themes in alphabetical order as "aestheticism and beauty, brothels, the dead (who annex the living), dress, the Dreyfus Affair (and its immersion in anti-Semitism), friendship, habits, inversion (homosexuality, both female and male), jealousy (above all!), literature itself and the gradual evolution of the narrator into a novelist, lying, memory (as prevalent as sexual jealousy), sadomasochism, the sea, sleep, and time (about as omnipresent as jealousy, and memory)" (2000: 181). Curiously, Bloom never mentions music (the form to which the novel aspires), and he focuses on the single theme of sexual jealousy as the most important of the *Search*. One surmises that the Freudian background of Bloom's brand of literary criticism influences this choice of the *Search*'s main theme. But Proust is not a Freudian thinker. His model of memory and time is more ecstatic and less fraught with the Oedipal peril than Marcel's obvious attachment to his mother in the novel might attest.

Despite the complex weaving of themes in the *Search*, the two most examined ones concern us here: time and memory. And the all-too-obvious entry to these themes involves the famous scene of the madeleine, where Marcel takes a sip of lime-flavored, madeleine-soaked tea as a shiver of "exquisite pleasure" grips him (Proust 2003a: 60). Marcel writes that he ceases to feel "mediocre, contingent, mortal" (60). Realizing at once that the tea's power comes from some forgotten part of his past, Marcel "must lean down over the abyss" of his memory ten times before he recalls that his Aunt Léonie would offer him a bite of a madeleine soaked in lime tea when he was a child (63). With that successful recovery of lost time, the town of Combray around his aunt's home comes back to Marcel in every detail: "In that moment all the flowers in our garden and in M. Swann's park, and the waterlilies on the Vivonne and the good folk of the village and their little dwellings and the parish church and the whole of Combray and its surroundings, taking shape and solidity, sprang into being, town and gardens alike, from my cup of tea" (64).

The scene of the madeleine is the exemplar for what critics call *involuntary memory* in the *Search*. But we must be clear about what is involuntary and what is not. In the *Search*, it is a sensation—a sip of tea, a snippet of melody, a scrap of color—that involuntarily calls forth an instant of pleasure connected with the past. We cannot seek this sensation; the sensation must seek us. Once it does, the sensation fails to evoke, at least involuntarily, the fullness of a memory, which requires a cognitive effort to recover: Marcel's multiple glimpses into the abyss of his memory. For Proust's cousin, Bergson, the effort of memory offers us the only way to freedom, because it allows us to step outside the chain of stimulus and response in order to recognize that time is a quality instead of a quantity: "Between brute matter and the mind most capable of reflexion there are all possible intensities of memory or, what comes to the same thing, all the degrees of freedom" (1912: 296). In Bergson's model, we plunge into the past as an act of freedom: "We place ourselves at once in the past . . . as into a proper element" (Deleuze 1991: 56). But Proust finds the recovery of the past to be a difficult task. Further, a cognitive effort to revive the past without the prompting of involuntary memory is quite different from that effort after some sensation prompts the shiver of pleasure. A cognitive effort alone is akin to the present casting a line into the past to find a slice of time that we already know exists. But an involuntary memory is akin to the past casting its line into the present to awaken our sense of lost time.

The scene of the madeleine has been the subject of borrowing, allusion, and even parody in other artworks. One of the more recent of these borrowings occurs in the climactic sequence of Disney's animated feature *Ratatouille* (2007). Near the end of the movie, a notoriously antipathetic food critic, Anton Ego, comes to the restaurant Gusteau to see if the new chef, Linguini, really lives up to his rave reviews. Unbeknownst to the characters in the movie, a rat named Remy has been responsible for Linguini's prowess in cooking. Just as Ego appears in the restaurant, the kitchen staff discovers the rat behind Linguini's success, and they depart in disgust, leaving Remy, a pack of fellow rats, and Linguini to run the restaurant. Short-handed, Remy decides to make ratatouille for Ego, even though it is considered a peasant's dish. When Ego takes the first bite of the ratatouille, he stops short as a sensation of pleasure captures him. The camera zooms into his eye, as if entering the past through his mind, and we see an episode from the critic's childhood. We see a rural setting behind an open door as we gaze upon Ego, who is now a young boy sniffing following some unknown emotional distress. As he sits at the kitchen table, his mother places a plate of ratatouille before him. The young Ego eats the dish with growing pleasure as his childhood hurt disappears. The camera zooms back to the present, and the usually dispassionate critic drops his pen in amazement to eat the ratatouille with growing gusto, forgetting to take notes about the meal.

Much of this scene parallels Marcel's experience of the madeleine in the *Search*. And some of the details concerning Ego are too good to be true. Although the name Ego in this case is intended to express the commonplace meaning of *self-importance*, it is hard to ignore the Freudian/Lacanian implications when the critic returns to his childhood via a felicitous coincidence of the palate. The conventional zooming into the eye as a vehicle for memory conjures the mirror stage associated with the primordial formation of the ego: a stage that the young Ego would have had within close grasp during his childhood episode. The fantasy of the mirror stage is present, as well, in the appearance of Ego's mother, who looks into her son's eyes with sympathy. When Ego drops his pen after the memory disappears, he has moved from a gnostic attitude about food to a drastic one. He is literally speechless, reliving a fantasy before words formed him in the Symbolic. In Proust's terms, he has entered the rapturous and secret essence of experience. The music follows a similar path, moving through a symphonic climax as Linguini brings the ratatouille to Ego and turning to an allusion to French folk music while the critic relives the past. When Ego returns to the present, the music invokes a slightly ecstatic sonorous womb of sound that wipes away the cultured symphonic music from before, replacing it with a simple melody in the flute: an attempt to eliminate the Symbolic while using conventions of the Symbolic nevertheless.

Ratatouille's climactic sequence approaches a sentimentalized version of Proust's scene of the madeleine: what Martha Hyde would call *reverential imitation,* involving a work of art that follows the model "with a nearly religious fidelity or fastidiousness" (1996: 206). Not fastidious enough. For all of its parallels to Proust's *Search,* the scene involving Ego and the ratatouille swerves from its model in a crucial way. When Ego tastes the dish from his childhood, the sensation of pleasure brings him to the primal memory without delay. His taste regained involves no cognitive effort, no peering over the abyss of his memory to find the source of the pleasurable shiver. And because he finds the memory so quickly, we can imagine that the memory was always there for him, ready for the right delicious bite of food to send him to his youth. Ego knows that his mother comforted him with food. He knows, too, that no dish in his present experience has succeeded in capturing the feeling of his youth. When he finds that dish at last in Remy's ratatouille, the circuit of desire is closed, the *objet petit a* has been found. Or so he thinks. Having found what he was looking for all along, Ego's character, and the movie, falls into a fairy-tale nostalgia where nothing new can startle us. Without knowing it, Ego's memory has been ratted out.

Marcel's experience is more profound than Ego's, not only because the memories he regains are truly lost prior to the phenomenon of involuntary memory, and not only because the shiver of pleasure prompts a cognitive effort in the recovery of time past, but also because what he recovers is an enlarged and ecstatic version of what was hidden and unimagined in his life as he was living it. Even after recalling the fullness of Combray, Marcel fails to understand why he takes so much pleasure in the sensation of involuntary memory. Not until the end of his life, and the final volume of the *Search*, does Marcel realize that with the recovery of the past "the permanent and habitually concealed essence of things is liberated and our true self . . . is awakened and reanimated" (2003c: 264). In the present, we are overwhelmed with so many perceptions and thoughts, so many objects and situations whose meanings we cannot fathom. Only when our actions and perceptions are reclaimed as the once lost past do we understand their meaning, their essence. But we must not confuse this reclaimed past as some scene from our past presenting itself as it really was. The remembrance of things past via Proust's model awakens in us "the complicated state of time itself" (Deleuze 2000: 45). In the awakened memory, Combray comes back to Marcel in an ecstatically charged version. Thus the Shakespearean title that the first English translation gave to Proust's work (*Remembrance of Things Past*) was wrong in more ways than one. It is not things, or scenes, or situations, or people that we recover in Proust's model but time itself and, by extension, our *Self* itself, which, in both Proust's and Bergson's models, we experience only when we know the essence of time as a quality of being. Thus, this reclaimed past is the product of an impulse to make sense of time. Proust inverts the usual model: time does not help us make sense of our otherwise jumbled lives; our jumbled lives help us make sense of time.

Since this fuller understanding of the phenomenology of time comes to Marcel only near the end of his life, his success is tempered by the regret that he will not live to finish the novel that records his efforts. This theme of regret, even in the face of time regained, runs throughout the *Search*. In the final line of the first volume, *Swann's Way*, for example, Marcel tells us "the memory of a particular image is but regret for a particular moment; and houses, roads, avenues are as fugitive, alas, as the years" (2003a: 606). The recompense for this regret is another realization that I discuss in a later section of this chapter.

What Are the Three Machines of Time Regained?

The themes of time and memory in Proust's *Search* leave us with a narrative paradigm that begins with an involuntary memory and moves to a cognitive effort that results in an ecstatic recovery of the past, after which there is a moment of regret. Deleuze reframes this paradigm as "the three machines" of the *Search,* which are (1) reminiscences/essences/time-regained (memory); (2) the repossession of lost time (eternity); and (3) catastrophe/aging/death (regret) (2000: 148–49). Deleuze's point of departure is the idea that "the modern work of art is a machine and functions as such" (145). We can think of modern art in terms of signifiers searching for their signifieds, or in terms of texts to practice our hermeneutic skills, or in any terms we like, but the *purpose* of modern art, for Deleuze, is to do something to us: modern art produces an effect in us that causes us to read ourselves, understand the world, or make art of our own. As such, we must use Proust's book as a kind of toolkit, producing truths that come from the effects the book has on us. And the making of ourselves into ourselves by responding to the *Search* is akin to making art: we make the book that is us. That is why it is pointless to make fine distinctions between Marcel the author and Marcel the character. In the case of the *Search,* Marcel (character) is Marcel (author) who made himself (author) in the act of making himself (character).

Since the modern work of art produces effects in us, Deleuze thinks of the interaction in terms of a machine. When the *Search* is working, we are figuratively plugged into it as we read. A vocabulary of machines is common in Deleuze's work, especially in his collaborations with Félix Guattari. Deleuze's references to machines, assemblages, and consolidated aggregates appear contrary to the concern with industrialization and modernity that marks Proust's novel. The metaphors around machines also play into the fear of the automaton that began with the French Revolution, appeared in the works of E. T. A. Hoffmann, and reappeared in French modernism, especially in Bergson's *Essai sur les données immédiates de la conscience* (retitled in English as *Time and Free Will*) (see Abbate 1999). Deleuze counters the fear that we are little more than machines by uttering the secret that we *are* little more than machines. Afraid that the automaton and the human are one and the same? Take that, E. T. A. Hoffmann: they are the same. Worried that subjectivity is nothing more than the symptom of a culture's discourse? No arguments here. Concerned that the notion of freedom is lost if the body is no more than a machine, Bergson? Well, since Deleuze is a Bergsonian, he might say that the illusion of freedom belongs to a proper understanding of time as a quality, and that it is not the body-as-machine that we should worry about, but how the body-as-machine plugs itself into the time machine, the time-as-quality machine.

Deleuze's metaphor of the machine is more than a postmodern irony that turns our deepest fears on their head by showing us that they were neither deep nor set aright in the first place. The machines are not of the industrial variety; "they surpass any kind of mechanics" (Deleuze and Guattari 1987: 511). A Deleuzian machine is not something you can touch or see. But you can feel its effects. Such a machine is a combination of cultural, or physiological, or physical, or natural elements that produce these effects. "Abstract, singular, and creative, here and now, real yet nonconcrete, actual yet noneffectuated—that is why abstract machines are dated and named (the Einstein abstract machine, the Webern abstract machine, but also the Galileo, the Bach or the Beethoven, etc.)" (511).

Although Deleuze never mentions it, there is a Lacan machine in which parts—the Imaginary, the Symbolic, the Real—work together to produce effects that we call *subjectivity*. These parts of the Lacan machine belong to different orders of classification, or what Deleuze and Guattari would call *plateaus*. The Imaginary is already the consequence of the premature birth that forces the young child to remain with the mother for so long. The Symbolic, though, is a different machine: the language of a culture that sets the rules of the game and enforces a law of conduct and of thought. The Real is the ghost in the machine that points to what does not work in the Symbolic. Thus we have a consequence (Imaginary), a language (Symbolic), and a ghost (Real) working together to make the Lacan machine. When we are plugged into the Lacan machine (and we have no choice in the matter), it produces certain effects. For example, the Imaginary fuels desire, while the Symbolic tells us what we are allowed to desire at the same time as the Real points out that the desires of the Symbolic were never ours in the first place. Once plugged into the Lacan machine, the subject's desires are set into a motion that swirls through the parts of that machine.

Here we are dealing with the Proust machine, which is an assemblage of elements that create an effect in which we understand time through three other machines called *memory, eternity,* and *regret.* These three parts are themselves machines because they also consist of parts. When Marcel recalls the past (memory), for example, it is not a simple matter of turning on the neurons of his aging brain. Proustian memory involves an object, or person, or act (tasting the madeleine); it involves a shiver of pleasure; and it involves the cognitive effort (peering over memory's abyss) to recapture lost time. That is why Deleuze refers to the *three* machines of Proust's *Search*. It is necessary to be plugged into all three of these machines for the *Search* to work its proper effect on us. One person reads Proust and feels the ecstatic shiver of pleasure along with Marcel; such a person is plugged into part of the memory machine. But another person reads Proust and feels nothing at all; such a person is not plugged into Proust's memory machine. It is not a matter of saying that the person plugged into Proust is better than the one who is not. We are all plugged into multiple machines. In cinema's terms, these machines are like *The Matrix,* and in Lacan's terms, they are like the Symbolic. The difference is that for Deleuze, machines are a multiplicity of multiplicities, a collection of parts made of a collection of parts. There is no one machine that makes up a culture. That is why it takes a thousand plateaus (or more) to understand being in the world.

The three machines of Proust's *Search* create an ethos about time that I address later. For now, I turn to Debussy to show how his music sometimes involves the same three machines as Proust's *Search*. I start with "Reflets dans l'eau" from *Images I*, reading it rather woodenly at first, as a parallel to the scene of the madeleine. But from this first reading, I branch out to hear the parts of the Debussy machine in his other works.

"Reflets dans l'eau"

Debussy's "Reflets dans l'eau" opens with a clear, metrical pattern, establishing a well-ordered temporality that projects an aura of objective representation without uttering the secret of its own subjectivity (Example 3.1). Beneath the asymmetrical arch of the chords in the right hand, the merest intimation of a melodic agency emerges in a three-note motive, whose hint of pentatonicism signifies a persistent back-to-nature in Debussy's music. As always with Debussy, we hear the opening twice in a non-developmental technique that Adorno heard as another signifier for nature, or, more properly, the erasure of a human agency, or a type of agency involved with being instead of doing (2004: 189; see Hepokoski 1984). But when Adorno makes the connection between Debussy's music and nature, he does so as a critique, because nature stands in for a desire to return to some pre-cultural paradise. Developing this critique, we can argue that from Adorno's point of view Debussy responded to the problems of modernity by retreating from them. Adorno recognizes, though, that behind the appeal to nature the "music retains something of the subjective experience of time" (2004: 189). There is no retreat possible; the objectivity of the natural scene is always already surrounded by the hue of subjective experience.

By m. 16 the pentatonicism is more conspicuous as the left hand traces an ascending pentatonic scale, while the right hand descends in open fifths, conjuring Debussy's orientalism, which points again to a *negative capability* (see Keats 2009: 60) with humanity erased from the scene—another attempt to capture an experience of time without a subjective phenomenology. The music projects an undisturbed detachment from culture that is nevertheless cultural all along. Adorno is correct on this point. Debussy's music tries to evoke an objective sense of time and nature without realizing that subjectivity cannot be erased. Still, the ordered and regulated temporality in the opening section of "Reflets" is untroubled and sacred. Similar musical material will return once near the center of "Reflets," and it will conclude the piece as well.

Between the opening material and its two returns, the music moves through a different motive and experience of time. Preceding the first turn to the contrasting motive is a cadenza, resulting in a formal structure of A-cadenza-B-A'-B'-A". This static picture of the piece fails to capture what really goes on in "Reflets." The music starts a narrative path that leads to a crisis before it starts that path again and succeeds with an apotheosis before concluding where it started. The whole is a narrative of try, try again, suggesting a parallel to Marcel's various attempts to understand memory and time.

The cadenza begins in m. 20 as the music unmasks its subjectivity to reveal an inner, private sense of time (Example 3.2). The first suggestion of the temporal shift comes shortly before the cadenza, where what David Lewin calls a "ruffling motive" disturbs the musical surface in mm. 18 and 19 (1987a: 238). Launching itself through transpositions of the Tristan chord, the cadenza ecstatically reaches the piano's upper stratosphere before suspending time on a single repeated arpeggio at m. 23. The sudden thrilled breakthrough of the cadenza is like that first

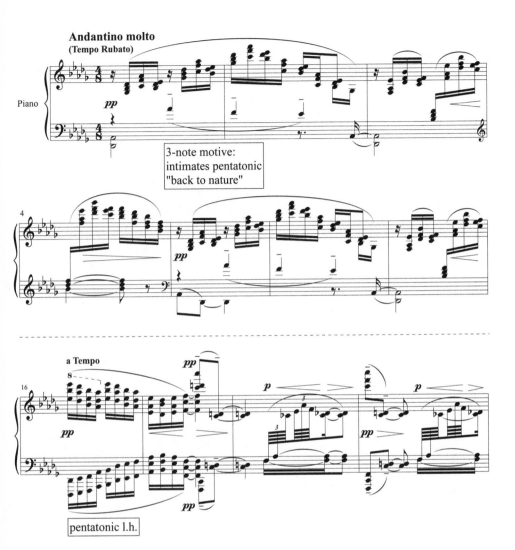

Example 3.1. Debussy, "Reflets dans l'eau" (opening)

shiver of pleasure that Marcel experiences after tasting the madeleine-infused tea. And if we want to be obstinately thorough in seeking intertextual correspondences, the Tristan chord that started us on our way is like some experience from the musical past casting forth a line to the present, while underscoring the sensuous pleasure of this new turn of events. The static sense of time at m. 23 prepares us for the entrance of a new motive, which will become the center of the musical action for much of the remainder of "Reflets." This new motive, which I call the "lost time" motive, serves as an indistinct memory that will become clear and bright in a moment of Proustian eternity later in the piece.

Debussy and the Three Machines of the Proustian Narrative 75

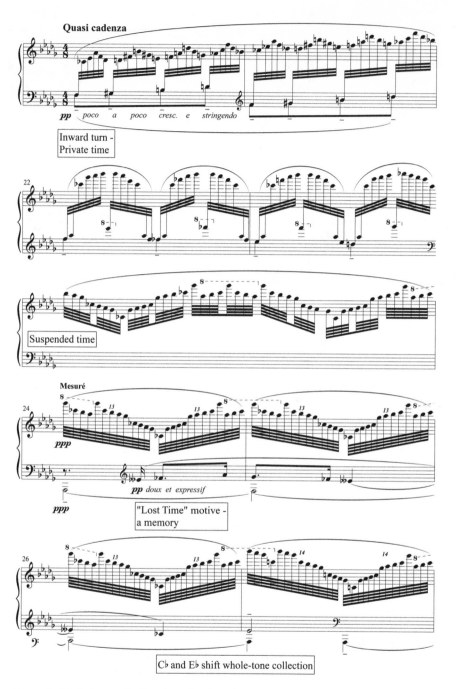

Example 3.2. Debussy, "Reflets dans l'eau" (cadenza)

Example 3.3. Debussy, "Reflets dans l'eau" (crisis)

The "lost time" motive (in the B sections) unfolds in two waves in "Reflets," with each wave following the narrative trajectory of the three machines: memory, eternity, and regret. The second wave is more expansive than the first, reaching an apotheosis in E♭, away from the home key and too far from the end of the piece to mark a culminating triumph. During each wave, the motive moves from an indistinct form within a whole-tone setting to a clearer form within a diatonic setting that reaches a moment of crisis. No two forms of the "lost time" motive are the same; its intervallic structure, its harmonic background, and even its length changes with each return. As the motive transforms itself in the two waves, the sense is that, like Marcel, it is going through a search of its own. The "lost time" motive does not develop as an analog to a maker of things or a doer of great deeds (Beethoven) but morphs in an attempt to come into focus, like a memory or a dream that we cannot quite recapture (Proust).

During its first appearance at m. 24, the "lost time" motive is submerged below arpeggios in the right hand, tracing a path through a whole-tone collection that keeps the present at bay while signifying the indistinct, like the first intimation of a memory. As the motive concludes in m. 27, its final pitch, E♭, breaks away from the whole-tone collection, like a memory beginning to come into focus (an E♭ arpeggio will also mark the music's apotheosis later in the piece). The outer sense of time stops while inner experience searches for a long lost secret. By m. 29 the motive gains clarity in a pentatonic collection accompanied by a dominant—a cognitive effort brings the memory into focus. But this early attempt at the eternal moment falters with the crisis at m. 30, where the arpeggios of the right hand terminate on diminished seventh chords (Example 3.3). Although unsuccessful in its effort at recovery, this first wave of the "lost time" motive exhibits an incipient determination to emulate the three machines: the motive begins like an obscure memory that gains momentum toward a clarified realization only to be undercut by a crisis.

During the second wave, the "lost time" motive has more success (Example 3.4). In m. 50 the motive reappears in its indistinct form above another whole-

Example 3.4. Debussy, "Reflets dans l'eau" (apotheosis of "lost time" motive)

Apotheosis - Eternal Moment

minor
subdominant

Wagnerian move to C minor - "Regret"

tone collection. A sudden decrease in the rhythmic momentum at this point underscores the cognitive effort involved, as if time holds its breath while the musical agent works out the details of this lost memory. The motive comes into focus at m. 54 on a major-minor-seventh chord. But where the first wave held firmly to a single major-minor seventh as the anchor for retrieval, this wave moves through three such chords that refuse to carry out their conventional function. Like direct modulations through chromatic mediants, the sudden shifts from one major-minor seventh to another signify a magical change of perspective, underscored by the rapturous arpeggios. The last major-minor seventh, on G♯, is enharmonic to the structural dominant of the home key. We recall that this is the sonority on which the first wave failed to accomplish its search. If the home key is the objective reality around us, the first order of things, the present condition, similar to Hepokoski's and Darcy's reading of the primary theme in sonata forms (2006: 65), then this search for lost time must not send us to D♭. Such a return would simply bring us back to the here and now instead of sending us to an ecstatic memory that was once lost. Here in the second wave, the putative structural dominant in m. 54 discharges its function by reaching past D♭ and landing on E♭ major at m. 56, whose breakthrough moment opens up an apotheosis one measure later.

The apotheosis in m. 57 presents the "lost time" motive in its most diatonic form, signifying a clear realization as the music finds its moment of eternity. The recovery is like a literal musical memory because the arpeggios preceding the apotheosis feel in the hands and sound in the ear like Chopin's so-called "Ocean" etude (op. 25, no. 12). And when the "lost time" motive sings out in m. 57, the music has found another Chopin moment, because the chords in the right hand and the arpeggios in the left recapture a texture that the motive had yet to find. In all of its previous statements, the "lost time" motive was hidden in the texture, or covered by the right hand, or played in the extreme upper register. At last, at the apotheosis, Debussy relinquishes control to allow the memory of Chopin to come to the fore. And, like the rising up of Combray, the revelation of a Chopin memory is supercharged and overabundant. We do not hear Chopin's music as it was; we hear Chopin's music as it is transformed by the exquisite pleasure of time and memory regained.

Regret is not far behind. From the exalted E♭ major, the music travels a tritone away to A major in m. 65, where the "lost time" motive unfolds with a strong Lydian implication, tinged with a minor subdominant. This loss of the eternal moment is prepared by whole-tone liquidation of the diatonic harmonies in mm. 60 and 63–64. The distant and Wagnerian move from A major to C minor at m. 67 signifies a moment of regret, an intimation of mortality. Our gateway to the interior subjectivity searching for the past came with the cadenza and its Wagnerian quote (the Tristan chord), and now our exit from the ecstatic remembrance is via a Wagnerian harmonic convention. The move to the past worked through Wagner (the cadenza) to the deeper past of Chopin (the climax of time regained) and returned to the present via Wagner again. Debussy shakes the Wagnerian aura to find his more profound musical past in Chopin. Once the moment of regret passes, the music reaches the structural dominant for a return to the home key, setting up the final section with its variation of the opening material. This prolonged and static version of the opening allows time to unfold as if the rush of the clock has been banished forever. For now, I forgo further discussion of this new form of time, which results from the interaction of the three machines.

This reading of "Reflets" has pressed the analogy between Marcel's tea-infused madeleine and the workings of time and memory in Debussy's piece. But in the next section, I show that the three machines work throughout Debussy's music. My proposed analogy, then, serves the purpose of showing us the way to think about Debussy in terms of a Deleuzian dream of Proust. Once we see other workings of the Debussy machine, we will return to "Reflets" and its final section.

Machines That Work

The three machines (memory, eternity, regret) are abundant in Debussy's music, although they do not always follow the Proustian order set out in the scene of the madeleine. Generally, Debussy's eternal moments are set as apotheoses away from the home key, often just past the mid-point, at the Golden Section, as Roy Howat has demonstrated (1983). But the Debussy eternity-machine is not the proportion-in-nature machine, as illustrated by pine cones and snails in nature. Debussy's eternity-machine, like Proust's, is the realization that the past can reach out and capture us in a moment when time stops to reveal itself without the taint of industry. Because the moment cannot last, the music must go on for some time past the apotheosis. And since the moment is not of the here and now, the apotheosis cannot take place in the home key; it must be far away to signify the distant past. In "Hommage à Rameau" from *Images I*, for example, the climactic realization bursts forth on a dominant over G in m. 51, near the end of the music's middle section (Example 3.5). Leading to this monumentalized projection of the music's second motive, a pedal on C♯ supports a series of parallel chords traveling through a whole-tone collection (mm. 49–50). The sudden swerve to a diatonic harmony over the G, a tritone away from the pedal C♯, lends this climax its own sense of breakthrough, underscored by the arpeggio that spans the keyboard in m. 52. Whether we hear G as the central pitch or as an indexical sign for the dominant of C major, the apotheosis is tonally distant from the home key, G♯ minor. The eternal moment may endure in our imagination, but it does not last long in the music. Already by m. 54, an F♯ urges the harmony to move on, and three measures later a fancy bit of parsimonious voice-leading brings the music back to the opening material. The coda of "Hommage" features an instant of regret, too, when a hopeful C♯ major chord, the major subdominant, makes a Wagnerian move to an E♯ minor one at m. 69, casting a chilly dread on the closing phrases (Example 3.6).

Sometimes, climactic clarity in Debussy foregos the unrestrained clangor of apotheosis in favor of a more subtle approach. In "Des pas sur la neige" from Preludes I, for example, memory thaws when motivic snippets finally come together to shape a long melodic passage in G♭, the raised mediant of the home

Example 3.5. Debussy, "Hommage à Rameau" (eternity in climax)

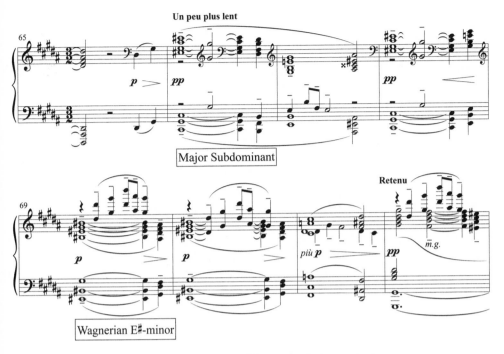

Example 3.6. Debussy, "Hommage à Rameau" (regret in closing section)

key, D minor (Example 3.7). The prelude begins with iconic signs for footsteps that never seem to move forward. But the music is not about footsteps, despite its title; the footsteps point to another meaning. Among a number of readings for this passage, for example, Steven Rings suggests that the "trudging footsteps" are indexical to "a dissolution of conscious focus on the present . . . perhaps caused by a plunge back into thought, or maybe memory" (2008: 195). The Proustian problem of memory lies beneath the surface of Rings's interpretation. Memory is like a frozen landscape that traps us in an altered consciousness. Debussy's frozen footsteps and their indexical signs for memory have a literary counterpart in one of Mallarmé's most famous poems: "Le vierge, le vivace et le bel aujourd'hui" (The virginal, lively, and beautiful day). The poetic voice of this work wonders whether the present will take flight, or, like a once magnificent swan entrapped in an icy landscape in time past, will the day linger in hopeless exile. Like the frozen swan, and the footsteps in the snow, a Proustian thought in the poem wonders whether it can thaw its memory and then return to the present with its potential for action. And the power of memory both to still action in favor of thought and to conjure some ecstatically resplendent past is manifest in the line *Un cygne d'autrefois se souvenir c'est lui/Magnifique* (a swan of former times remembers that it was he that was magnificent). But the swan's memory fails to save him from the frozen prison.

Example 3.7. Debussy, "Des pas sur la neige" (recovery and regret)

The Proustian connection to Mallarmé's poem is even deeper for the coincidence that in *La fugitive* from the *Search*, Marcel quotes Mallarmé's "Le vierge" in a letter to his fugitive lover, Albertine. At first, Marcel writes that if Albertine had stayed with him, he would have bought her a Rolls-Royce and a yacht, which he would have named *Swan*—an oblique reference both to Mallarmé's poem and to the character Swann, whose jealous relationship with Odette parallels that of Marcel and Albertine. Later in the letter, Marcel makes the connection to Mallarmé clear by writing that on the yacht he would have engraved lines from Albertine's favorite poem: "You remember—it's the poem that begins: 'The lively, lovely, virginal today.' Alas, today is no longer either virginal or lovely" (2003b: 614). Even this short passage reveals the machines of memory and regret that form part of the crisis of time in modernism. Marcel's despair over losing Albertine thus connects with the despair of the poem's swan, which has failed to migrate (to move on), becoming entrapped literally in the frozen landscape and figuratively in the memory of its past magnificence (see Goodkin 1989: 292–96). Memory, time, and despair come together in the scene from Proust's *Search,* the swan of Mallarmé's "Le vierge," and the icy footprints of Debussy's "Des pas."

Throughout the first half of "Des pas," the frozen footsteps accompany an upper line that tries to form a melody, as if snippets of memory endeavor to come together. Starting in m. 20, the music has some success as it turns toward Gb and a longer melodic line. When the passage begins, contrary motion signifies an attempt to raise the musical stature. Earlier in m. 5, the prelude had traversed this same musical path, only to land back on the frozen home key, D minor. This time, however, just as the open fifths in the left hand are poised to complete the same journey, they overstep their target, landing on a dominant over a Db in m. 21. This harmonic breakthrough prepares the entrance of a new melodic wholeness in Gb major, the key of the sublime in the nineteenth century. Dominants pile up in harmonic support of the melody, which falls just short of completion at m. 25 before the unwelcome return of the frozen sensibility in m. 26, underscored by the reappearance of a lonely D-minor harmony in m. 27. Soon the translucent melody in Gb returns in a version that is too untroubled to convince us of its reality. Debussy makes plain the remorse in the score with the expression *comme un tendre et triste regret* (like a tender and sad regret). Thus the crisis of time and memory at the beginning of the prelude returns at the end in the form of a regret. And the middle section in Gb, like the swan's memory of some past magnificence in Mallarmé's "Le vierge," only awakens the Deleuzian machine of some failure in the warp and weft of time and action.

Memory, eternity, and regret are machines that work in Debussy's music. They produce an effect with a collection of musical parts that are combined and recombined; they may follow the order of the Proustian machine (memory-eternity-regret), or they may follow their own logic (regret-memory-regret, or regret-memory-eternity-regret, etc.). Sometimes Debussy takes the parts for these machines directly from his earlier music—that is, he forms intertexts. One instance appears at the climax of the first movement of the Cello Sonata (Example 3.8). At m. 21 a rumbling and agitated passage has the aura of a development, during which the cello repeats a brief motive with ever-increasing speed in what I take to be a locomotive topic. During the first decades of the twentieth century, if a Parisian is on a train, as Marcel so often is in the *Search,* he is fleeing to the country: away, out and away, to the flowered fields of Combray, or the pastel waves of Balbec. This musical train performs its indexical function: it points to the coming recapitulation. Here we go. Just before we reach our destination, low G pedals in the piano support a dominant, announcing the coming recapitulation. The G pedal discharges its function onto the spacious and clangorous open fifth in C at m. 29, while the cello sings the opening theme, now transformed from its original minor mode. The music has found its eternal moment, extended by the pentatonic ascent in the piano. Together, the G pedal, the exalted fifth on C, and the pentatonic ascent form an intertext with the staggering climax of "La Cathédrale engloutie" (The engulfed cathedral), whose own musical narrative reaches a moment of sunlit glory.

Example 3.8. Debussy, Cello Sonata, I (development and recapitulation)

The breathtaking return of the opening theme at m. 29 is like a memory of a memory. When we first hear the melody in mm. 1–2, it has an antique élan, particularly in the triplet figure. Marianne Wheeldon, following a line of research on Debussy that involves his heightened sense of nationalism during the war, connects the opening of the Cello Sonata to the composer's intensive study of Rameau and Couperin (2005: 667–71). As Debussy's eighteenth-century forebears take an intense importance in his music, so the allusion to Rameau and Couperin in the Cello Sonata becomes amplified and supercharged in the passage starting at m. 29. As with Proust, this memory of a memory is not the recovery of things as they once were but of things as they have become after they are fueled by time and some unnamed portion of the subject's effort to understand existence.

The return of the first theme in m. 29 engages the machines of memory and eternity. The musical problem is that this apotheosis has reached the wrong key, and the music will soon return to D minor, which ironically pulls the sonata back from its accomplishment. This dramatic irony is matched by a rhetorical one: as the cello plays the opening theme at the music's moment of arrival, it strives for the upper tonic pitch with a portamento that marks its achievement as a poignant struggle. Finally, in a form of postmodern and romantic irony, the piano's intertext with "La Cathédrale engloutie" fragments that earlier prelude, which had staged its own narrative of ascent and decline. The entire passage offers us a glimpse of wholeness, which is already fallen at the moment the music captures it. A transition at m. 37 prepares for the return of D minor. This transition is little more than octatonic noodling in the cello with harp-like chords in the piano, as if signifying the end of a magical dream sequence, or, in terms of the Proustian narrative, a return to the present after the miraculous recovery of the past. Four measures after the reentry of D minor, a *pianto* in the cello makes plain the regret of the closing section.

Of the three machines in Debussy's music, eternity is a machine that works especially well. It is not only that Debussy finds the means to represent eternity, as in a musical painting of water lilies, or to narrate eternity, as in a tale of paradise. Rather, as Deleuze argues for Proust, it is that Debussy *produces* eternity as the effect of a musical machine. If we are plugged into the Debussy machine, the phenomenology of his music's eternal moments is that we feel the effect of hearing an ecstatic time outside time. For an instant, music takes on the transcendent role that the nineteenth century thought to be the unique province of music (though that ideology is now discredited), and the Debussy machine forms an immediacy, the direct experience of a time overcoming the lapse of time, allowing us to go beyond a mere reflection of the divine so as to live within it.

Occupying Time

Why the regret, then? If eternity is a machine that works in Proust and Debussy, why turn its capacity toward crisis and the fall of time? Before approaching a Lacanian view of the matter, I outline three possible answers to this question: the idea of pastoral, the end of temporality, and the tenants of time.

Pastoral. As Raymond Monelle reminds us in his magisterial book on musical topics, pastoral is one of the most ancient of cultural concepts, though its exact configuration changes with history (2006: 185). In its lower forms, pastoral is little more than wish fulfillment and the illusion of a golden age. But already with the Eclogues of Virgil, the dream of arcadia meets the regret of loss. Virgil's Fourth Eclogue sings of a perfect world, where "Justice returns, returns old Saturn's reign, / With a new breed of men sent down from heaven" (n.d.: 24). But by the Ninth Eclogue, Virgil shows us a realm of tranquil sadness: "Time carries all things, even our wits, away. / Oft, as a boy, I sang the sun to rest, / But all those songs are from my memory fled" (48). The loss of all things, including memory, is a discordant thought for a Proustian. These themes of timelessness and loss run throughout pastoral discourse, including Proust's famous if somewhat conventional line: "The only paradise is paradise lost." Within this context, then, the turn toward regret after the eternal moment in Debussy's music is a sign in a convention of pastoral discourse that knows in advance its own profound myth. If we are lucky enough to invoke the eternal moment in the recovery of time and memory, we are either imbuing the past with a fullness that it never really had, or we are indulging in a reverie of a future-past, in which we imagine that the romanticized once-upon-a-time will find its truth and reality in an era yet to come. Regret is the realization that this idealized form of time is nothing more than false consciousness.

The end of temporality. Fredric Jameson proposes that the first modernists negotiated two types of temporalities (2003). The first was the agricultural temporality of the farms and villages, a deep time governed by patterns of biological, meteorological, and cultural cycles. The second was the urban temporality of the bureaucrat, the industrial timetable, the train schedule, and the coordinated effort. The two temporalities, of course, play within pastoral discourse, as well, with its own oppositions of rural and urban. But the rural/urban opposition was associated with the time/space opposition in early modernism. Marcel spends the first half of the *Search* in the rural sections of France—in Combray and Balbec—but by the end of the *Search* he is trapped in Paris, literally an invalid, whose only experiences are those of his former self through the efforts at time regained. Marcel progresses from the fullness of time to the enclosure of space. The modernists witness the displacement of the rural for the urban, the flowered field for the city block, the content for the form, time for space. Do not confuse time with space, Bergson enjoins us in *Essai sur les données immédiates de la conscience.* But Bergson is too late. The great novels of the early twentieth century—*The Magic Mountain, Ulysses,* and *In Search of Lost Time*—all place the majesty of time at the center of our consciousness, because, argues Jameson, the modernists witnessed the kingdom of time vanish into the implacable advance of space. Thomas Mann writes of his *The Magic Mountain* that "time is one of its themes," and, as if to connect his novel to Proust's work, he asks the reader to read his book twice, so one can "really penetrate and enjoy its musical association of ideas" (1969: 723). But Mann also realizes that the type of time he wrote about belonged to "an epoch, the pre-war period of European history" (723). Mann was writing about a lost time. Adorno also acknowledges and laments the loss of time as a quality, arguing that music reminds us that we have lost duration, and that we fend off this problem "with the important man's superior assertion that he has no time, which lets slip its own ignominious truth" (1992a: 73).

Bergson viewed early cinema with its disjunctions and lapses as a threat to time, because cinema is the problem of time transformed into space, particularly the space of the enclosure. Spatial metaphors for contemporary fears have become acute in our movies and TV shows. In *The Matrix,* Neo's mind is enclosed in a computer, his body attached to a machine, the perfect industrial nightmare. Most of the scenes in the television series *Battlestar Gallactica,* set in the confines of a post-apocalyptic spaceship, have a claustrophobic mania about them. *Snakes on a Plane,* the *Saw* movies, *The Silence of the Lambs, Flightplan, Panic Room,* the *Raiders of the Lost Ark* franchise, the *Aliens* franchise, to name a few, all have their extended scenes of enclosure, confinement, imprisonment. The problem of time in the early modernist period has become the problem of space for us. And time is no longer a problem only because, in the Proustian sense, it truly is lost to us. Thomas Friedman captures the culture's spatial preoccupation in the titles of his two books, *The World Is Flat,* and *Hot, Flat, and Crowded.*

Within the context of the time/space opposition, we can read the regret in Proust and Debussy as a form of farewell to time itself. Such a reading has particular resonance for Debussy's Cello Sonata, whose second movement conjures a cinematic time, as Rebecca Leydon has argued (2001). The regret in the first movement, then, is like the last will and testament of time before the entrance of space in the narrative of the sonata. Regret is a sign of the end of temporality.

The tenants of time. Proust stages the time/space opposition in *Time Regained,* the final volume of the *Search.* At first, regret shades the conclusion of the novel as Marcel suspects that he will not live long enough to record the recovered experiences of his life. Even after the realization that his ecstatic memories are transient, however, Marcel still embraces time as the final redemption of life. In the last pages of the novel, every reference to time is capitalized, like so many bells ringing and overlapping throughout the page.

> We occupy a place, always growing, in Time. (2003c: 528)

> This notion of Time embodied, of years past but not separated from us, it was now my intention to emphasise as strongly as possible in my work. . . . (529)

> And I felt, as I say, a sensation of weariness and almost of terror at the thought that all this length of Time had not only, without interruption, been lived, experienced, secreted by me, that it was my life, was in fact me. (530–31)

Reviewing his experiences, Marcel feels a sense of vertigo at the sudden insight that his life has hidden so much time. The final hope of the novel is just this thought that people occupy a place in time so considerable "compared with the restricted place which is reserved for them in space . . . for simultaneously, like giants plunged into the years, they touch the distant epochs through which they have lived, between which so many days have come to range themselves—in Time" (2003c: 532).

For Deleuze, Marcel's realization that we are the tenants of time, filling a temporal span vaster than any spatial one, is the final product of the third machine, regret. After we come crashing down from the enraptured memory, the clash with the present pushes the past back to an incredible remoteness, as if a lifetime is a geological period, or, in Proust's terms, a distant epoch. So much wasted and lost time, which is written into the *Search* as the intimation of mortality, becomes the galaxy far, far away after the instant of time regained. Regret is the ma-

Example 3.9. Debussy, "Reflets dans l'eau" (closing section)

chine that works us back into the fullness of time. We must not think, though, that in finding the truth of an epoch that lives within us, we have found a promised unity that usually eludes us. "Time is not a whole, for the simple reason that it is itself the instance that prevents the whole" (Deleuze 2000: 161). We are still a multiplicity, like time itself. But we learn through Proust that our temporal selves are the undiscovered kingdom vaster than the spatial one.

We can hear a musical correlate to Marcel's realization at the end of Debussy's "Reflets dans l'eau," after the catastrophe of the Wagnerian signs of mortality. Through the end of "Reflets" the opening motive is laid bare by the gradual falling away of the accompanying arpeggios (Example 3.9). By m. 81, all that remains is the opening motive reconfigured as a bell topic in the upper register with accompanying chords deep in the bass. Debussy makes the expression clear with his marking *harmonieuse et lointaine* (harmonious and distant). With an anti-Bergsonian swerve, we can map the far away onto the long ago, feeling the full sense of time as a duration more profound than space. The long aftermath of an apotheosis in Debussy's music, then, is an enactment of the geological age of time within us. Within that expression of time in the closing measures of "Reflets," there still lies the echo of regret in the rolled chords on the flat submediant in mm. 81–82 and 85–86. The three machines thus form an assemblage in the final measures of "Reflets": memory (the return of the opening motive as if from long ago), eternity (the profound depths of the catholic bells), and regret (the rolled chords on the flat submediant). Together, these three signs give us the sense of the profound *durée* of human experience.

Successful Artwork, or Return to the Imaginary?

Reading Proust. Critics cannot help themselves. Reading Proust is a life-changing event. Roland Barthes acknowledges Proust as "*the* reference work, the general *mathesis,* the *mandala* of the entire literary cosmogony" (1975: 36). Bloom, for whom no writer can measure up to Shakespeare, practically gushes over Proust's "greatest strength," which is his power of characterization: "*In Search of Lost Time . . .* actually challenges Shakespeare in its powers of representing personalities" (1995: 395). Even Adorno, who rarely admits to falling for an artist or an artwork, must admit that he is smitten by Proust: "I would like to say in advance that I cannot speak about this book in the role of a critic. For the past thirty years Proust has been too important an element of my spiritual existence for me to have the detachment to do so, and the quality of his work seems to me to be such that the critic's claim to superiority would amount to impudence" (1992b: 313). In Deleuze's terms, Proust is a machine that works for Adorno; he can find no fault with the *Search.* When Adorno mentions Proust's importance to his "spiritual existence," he lets slip the possibility that he is enchanted, unable to see the same faults in the *Search* that he generally finds in every other artwork. The cure to that possibility is evident when Adorno makes clear that Proust's success in the *Search* adheres to a consistent theory of the project of literature and music, starting in the nineteenth century.

Briefly, Adorno values individuation in the artwork-as-subjectivity; and that individuation comes from particularities resulting from a rational necessity that fights against the very ideology that makes the artwork possible in the first place (see Subotnik 1978: 42–45). Concerning the more narrow concept of breakthrough (*Durchbruch*) in music, the artwork stages a critique of social totality by an "unforeseen event" that renders "apparent what a work's artistic logic has excluded in terms still consistent with that logic" (Buhler 1996: 129). This aesthetic project becomes clearer if we give Adorno a Lacanian child by transforming his terms into those of the three orders of subjectivity. The artwork, which Lacan finds to be ensnared in the same Symbolic order as the subject, has no other recourse than to work within the language of the Symbolic. If the artwork is like a subject, it can no more exit the conventions of its culture, the social totality, than can any of us. Still, in order for the artwork to find some form of individuality, it must seek out a particularity that uncovers the lapses in the Symbolic while using the terms of the Symbolic at the same time. Like the Real, the artwork must use the signs it has at hand to show what cannot be thought within the Symbolic.

Particularities. When Adorno considers what draws him to Proust's work, it is the writer's attention to detail, the particularities to which he turns. No great architectonic force unifies these particularities; rather, "it is against precisely that, against the brutal untruth of a subsuming form forced on from above, that Proust revolted" (1991: 174). Proust dwells on the details without worrying how to make them adhere into some totalizing form, because time itself will take care of that problem. "The *durée* the work investigates is concentrated in countless moments, often isolated from one another" (175). As Bergson tells us over and again, time is not a line; it is a multiplicity. Proust's insight was to pull apart the multiplicity of time as "an intellectual splitting of the atom, trying to lay open the most minute elements of the real and show them as force fields in which all the power of life is crystallized" (Adorno 1992b: 313). This single-minded adherence to looking deep into the order of things is Proust's way of pushing against the ready-made thought. His writing finds a home at the limit of thought and "holds out the promise that the order of nature is not the ultimate order" (Adorno 1991: 183).

The order of nature is precisely what makes Debussy's music the path not to follow in Adorno's aesthetics. Debussy represents a reactionary move, a back-to-nature whose simple harmonies inspire the mass culture of Tin Pan Alley (Adorno 2002: 442). As the route to mass culture, Debussy's music cannot withstand the pressure of the conventions that make us. In Lacanian terms, his music uses the signs of the Symbolic with no hope of seeing beyond the Symbolic. But the problem with this view is that Adorno never understood popular music, or what he commonly called "jazz" (whether it was or not), on its own terms (see Gracyk 1992). In addition, it is ironic that when Adorno writes of the *Search*, he recognizes "a musical impulse" that results from the same "vegetal proliferation" that he finds in the music of what he considers to be great composers, like Berg (1991: 174). Putting together Adorno's fascination with Proust's particularities and his observation that the *Search* has a musical impulse, we arrive at a deep focus on the workings behind the Symbolic that make writing a form of music.

If writing can be musical, then Adorno's analysis of Proust rings with the pre-echoes of Kristeva's theory of poetic language. Briefly, Kristeva considers two modalities of enunciation: the *semiotic* (a term that she uses differently than does the field of semiotics) and the *symbolic* (1984: 23–24). Taking the latter term first, the symbolic is what a semiotician would call a *sign*, a signifier whose signified is a matter of convention and thus, for Lacan, is part of the Symbolic order. What Kristeva calls the *semiotic* is a nonverbal signifying system that she associates with the *chora*: the energy, desire, scissions, and fractures of the prelingual subject (as we have seen in chapter 2). One such semiotic system for Kristeva is music

(24). The two systems of signification, semiotic and symbolic, work in a dialectic. But it is the semiotic that is the focus of Kristeva's work: revolution in poetic language. When language manages to escape the conventions of the Symbolic (in Lacan's terms), it is "enigmatic and feminine, irreducible to its intelligible verbal translation; it is musical, anterior to judgment, but restrained by a single guarantee: syntax" (29). The semiotic and its connection to the *chora* form "literature as a rhythm made intelligible by syntax" (30). The theory is a transformation of Adorno's reading of Proust; the musical and particular elements of the *Search* manage to escape the Symbolic (they are semiotic in Kristeva's terms), while keeping within a syntax that disallows the total freedom that might lead to utter unintelligibility. Proust manages to achieve individuation by allowing the *chora* to enter his language, his focus, and his very refusal to adhere to the standards of formal structure; yet the particularities make a whole and satisfying artwork. As the saying goes, it is not that Proust's *Search* is too long; it is that the *Search* is not long enough.

Inverting the equation, however, does not allow Adorno to acknowledge the success of Debussy's music. Language may become revolutionary because it aspires to the condition of music, but music does not become revolutionary by aspiring to the condition of language. Yet to hear Debussy as Adorno read Proust leads to the possibility that music, too, can focus on particularities and make way for a musical music, an untamed music, that enters the interstices of thought. Debussy's "Reflets dans l'eau," then, is really a single reflection, or a collection of reflections on the particularities of reflection itself. After the cadenza begins, Debussy stops time on the repeated arpeggio before gradually, almost painfully, altering the chord, tone by tone. And the first crisis of the music is more than the crisis of a memory lost; it is the catastrophe of losing a particularity at the moment it is within our grasp. The same cadenza lies outside of musical time: a single unmeasured unfolding of tones that refuse to be corralled in the conventions of the Symbolic. The cadenza releases the untamed *chora* as music.

In the climax of Debussy's Cello Sonata, the same particularities fill the music in a multiplicity of time regained. An eternal moment includes the frenetic thought patterns leading to ecstatic realization (the train motive at the end of the development), the opening of a vista (the landing on C major), a remembrance of the past (the reference to "The Engulfed Cathedral"), the sudden heart-breaking thought that all might be lost (the cello straining to its high note), the pealing of bells (the open fifths in the piano at the moment of the recapitulation), a majesty of accomplishment (those same bells), and the acknowledgment of a defeat to come (the entrance of B♭ into the sunny world of C major). Time, thought, and memory are an assemblage that Debussy weaves into a few measures of musical material, revealing the particularity of experience. In Kristeva's terms, the music forms a dialectic between the semiotic and the symbolic.

Or are we deceived? Is being smitten by Proust or Debussy merely a wish to return to the Imaginary? Especially with Debussy, do we suffer from an enchantment with an acoustic mirror that makes whatever we have to say about the matter both an illusion and a desire for the return to an idealized moment in our subjective development before the forced choice of language and the Symbolic? This question is the one that Kristeva tries to answer with the *chora*. If we are entrapped in the Symbolic, then how does language renew itself, take on new forms, and wend its way through the unthinkable? Kristeva's answer is that an older self, an ancient self in Proust's terms, speaks to us and through us. It is our peculiar heritage to listen to that ancient self—a knock from the past, a sip of madeleine-soaked tea, a Wagnerian ruffle that hides a Chopinian redemption—and find those particularities of the self that can revolutionize experience.

4   Chopin Dreams:
The Mazurka in C♯ Minor
as *Sinthome*

Life, as they say, plays with cards up its sleeve;
but when one snatches at them, they've disappeared,
and one grips something else,—or else nothing at all.

—Henrik Ibsen, *Peer Gynt*

One Dance or Many?

The mazurka is a curious multiplicity. We soon learn that it is not one dance but three: the *mazur,* which takes its name from the Polish region of Mazovia but may have its origin in Kujawy; the *oberek,* which possibly takes its name from the Polish word *obracać* (to spin) but comes from the Mazowsze region; and the *kujawiak* from the Kujawy region. In addition, Jim Samson includes the *powiślak* and the *światowska* among the dances subsumed into the mazurka (1985: 110). Concerning the three main dances, the *oberek* is the fastest, the *mazur* is slower but still lively, while the *kujawiak* is the slowest and most expressive melodically. Turning quickly to Chopin, we can distinguish these three dances in the Mazurkas op. 68, nos. 2 and 3, which were published posthumously and, as juvenilia, presumably adhere more closely to Polish folk models than do his later mazurkas (Example 4.1). The middle section of op. 68, no. 3, with its drone (a Polish bagpipe) and lively Lydian melody (a high-pitched shepherds' pipe), is an *oberek.* The opening section of the same mazurka, with its slower tempo and characteristic dotted rhythm on the first beat, is a *mazur.* The beginning of the Mazurka op. 68, no. 2, with its much slower tempo and expressive melody, is a *kujawiak.* In addition, the melody features a piquant augmented second in the first measure due to the raised fourth degree in the minor mode: another characteristic of some Polish folk music. This mazurka also includes a recurring trill, highlighting a notated accent on beat three; and again, there is the familiar dotted rhythm on the first beat, which drives to an agogic accent on beat two.

Despite the relative clarity of the dances within Chopin's op. 68, knowing that the mazurka includes three main dances does not ease the task of disentan-

A. Mazurka op. 68, no. 3, middle section (*oberek*)

B. Mazurka op. 68, no. 3, opening (*mazur*)

C. Mazurka op. 68, no. 2 opening (*kujawiak*)

Example 4.1. Chopin, Mazurkas, op. 68 (types of Polish dances subsumed into the mazurka)

gling them. Polish ethnography on this matter usually begins with Oskar Kolberg's monumental *Lud*, a multi-volume collection of Polish fairy tales, proverbs, and over 12,000 folk songs collected between 1861 and 1890. Chopin saw an earlier collection of Polish folk songs transcribed by Kolberg, although he was unimpressed, probably because the piano accompaniments were too unimaginative (Thomas 1992: 317n.33). For all of its breadth, though, *Lud* is not as helpful as we might hope. Sometimes Kolberg lists a folksong by dance type, but often he merely designates a region of Poland (Swartz 1975: 250). Confronting the problem from a different angle, Aleksander Poliński attempted to define the three main dances by patterns of accentuation (1914). Confusingly enough, though, Poliński claims that the *oberek* is distinguished by its *slower* tempo with accents on the last part of the second measure, unless the dance has a more festive mood, in which case the main stress falls on every third beat. For all of Poliński's care in differentiating the three dances, Anne Swartz finds that when comparing his classification system to the melodies in Kolberg's collection, "the dances which suit the definitions are the exception rather than the rule" (1975: 250). Turning again to Chopin, if we wish to see something like an authoritative attempt to trace the three dances through his mazurkas, then Wiaczesław Paschałow's book on the composer's Polish influences is the place to start (1951). Still, Chopin's music often frustrates our attempts to identify the various dances unequivocally. A Chopin mazurka is a curious multiplicity of multiplicities.

We cannot make a taxonomy that will keep separate the various forms of the mazurka, because the dances are not essences but what Wittgenstein calls a "family of resemblances." When Wittgenstein tries to find a commonality between everything we call a "game," for example, he finds only various resemblances like those between members of a family: "build, features, colour of eyes, gait, temperament, etc. etc. overlap and criss-cross in the same way. . . . But if someone wished to say: 'There is something common to all these constructions—namely the disjunction of all their common properties'—I should reply: Now you are only playing with words" (1997: 32, §67). If we wish to find something common to all mazurkas or their subsumed dances, we are playing a losing game. Sometimes an *oberek* is fast, with drones and a Lydian melody, people dancing in a circle, and an air of intoxication. And sometimes it is not. A dotted rhythm on the first beat may appear in a *mazur*, or it may bring to life a *kujawiak*. A strong accent may land on beat three or on beat two. The cross rhythms may appear in the drone of an *oberek*, or they may accompany a *mazur*. Short repeated phrases might occur in any of the dances, or they may not. And if we wished to say that there is some disjunction that can separate the common properties of every *oberek* from every *mazur* and *kujawiak*, we would have to admit that we are only playing with words, blinding ourselves to the nature of signification. Ultimately a sign is empty; when it points, like the scarecrow in *The Wizard of Oz*, it does so in many directions.

What a mazurka does, then, is to territorialize, deterritorialize, and reterritorialize the various family resemblances in the *oberek*, *mazur*, and *kujawiak*. As Deleuze and Guattari explain, a territory is not only a place, like Mazovia, but also an act that forms an assemblage of items (customs, desires, signs, etc.) that work together (1987: 508–10). An *oberek* is a musical territory within the Mazowsze region of Poland, another territory. The assemblage of the *oberek*-as-territory includes a *dudy,* a *fujarka,* a brisk melody, people dancing in a circle, a chance to gather, laughter, joy, etc. When Chopin first writes a mazurka, the *oberek* takes a line of flight from this territory: it becomes deterritorialized as it leaves behind the *dudy, fujarka,* and the people of the country gathering so that it can find a place at a piano in a parlor in Warsaw. When Chopin leaves Poland for France (via Germany), he, too, is deterritorialized; he takes a line of flight that breaks apart the assemblage of Polish culture to create a new assemblage and a new territory in Paris. Chopin's *oberek* is territorialized in the Mazurka op. 68, no. 3; it is separated by a clear musical boundary from the *mazur* before and after. But Chopin also can deterritorialize the *oberek* in a mazurka; its characteristics take a line a flight away from the confines of a complete section and blend in with other dances, so that we find it difficult to pinpoint the *oberek* at all.

Chopin's Mazurka in C♯ Minor, op. 30, no. 4 will be our case in point. The piece is in four sections with a coda: A-B-C-A-Coda. Among these, the B section makes the clearest bid for one of the three main dances subsumed into a mazurka (Example 4.2). With its dotted rhythm on the first beat in the left hand of every measure, and with its expressive melody at a moderate tempo in the minor mode, the B section must be a *kujawiak.* As the music moves to the C section, the tempo becomes more animated (literally *con anima*), the mode shifts to major, and although the accents fall primarily on the first beat, by mm. 74 and 76 they fall on the second beat: a *mazur,* yes? Or maybe a waltz at first that only becomes a *mazur.* The A section includes shifting accents, a melancholic melody in the minor mode, and a drone: all indexical to the *kujawiak.* But the rolled chords that form the droned left hand lend the music a balladic tone (Chopin's op. 7, no. 3 is the only other mazurka to use rolled chords as an accompaniment). And the unusually disturbing introduction sends the A section past any conventional expression of Polish sentimentality. If we think, then, that this mazurka hopes to announce some kind of authentic Polish expression, we might recall Lacan's statement that whatever message we send comes back to us in inverted form (2006h: 41). If we hear this mazurka's message as "I am Polish," one answer must be "No, you are not." This mazurka has been deterritorialized into something else.

The task, then, is not to disentangle the various dances within a Chopin mazurka in the hope of defining a precise kind of Polishness in the piece, or in an effort to unlock a secret code for the music. There *is* no secret code. Instead, the task is to understand that as the various Polish dances become deterritorialized in a Chopin mazurka, they form different assemblages with different meanings, forms of desire, and functions.

In this chapter, I consider the Mazurka in C♯ Minor as a piece that has been deterritorialized from the Polish roots we might seek. The mazurka is reterritorialized as something akin to a dream, open to interpretation as a form of subjectivity and, more importantly, as the site of symptoms. From a Lacanian point of view, as we saw in chapter 1, the very notion of music as a dream, as a site of

Introduction of the mazurka

A Section of the mazurka

B Section of the mazurka

Example 4.2. Chopin, Mazurka in C# Minor, op. 30, no. 4 (excerpts from various sections)

C Section of the mazurka

symptoms, necessarily means that interpretation cannot stop at the first reading. Therefore, this chapter proposes a number of readings for the mazurka. At first, these readings may appear to follow a well-known methodology in the hermeneutics of recovery. That is, the readings start from the Parisian culture around Chopin and his Mazurka in C♯ Minor as a way of organizing particular meanings both in and around the music. But each of the readings can only go so far; to force the mazurka to fit any of its cultural contexts is to overlook signs that point to other contexts. It is necessary to understand up front that no single meaning vies with the others for priority; nor do the various meanings come together into something like a unified whole. The readings do not run from something shallow

Coda of the mazurka

Example 4.2, *continued*

to something deeper—an opposition that we could only accept in order to reveal its inadequacy. Rather, the readings overlap, or even hide one another. Finally, although I have used the word *context* to describe a process of interpretation, a more accurate term would be *symptom,* which, as we have seen, is a problem both in a social order and an individual (a subject) within that order. From Lacan's point of view, the symptom is not something we seek to cure but rather attempt to understand through cycles of interpretation that nevertheless cannot reach a fixed point. Thus the various readings of the mazurka will each fall apart until they approach the Real, and the music becomes what Lacan called a *sinthome,* a form of symptom that defines the subject, making a person who they are. A fuller exposition of the *sinthome* will come later in this chapter.

One Symptom or Many?

The Lacanian symptom is a curious multiplicity. As we have seen, Lacan's notions of the symptom evolved throughout his career, broadly following what he viewed as the three registers of subjectivity: the Imaginary, the Symbolic, and the Real. Chapter 2 dealt with symptoms of the Imaginary, which involve fantasies of the mother, desire, and the *objet petit a.* Symptoms of the Symbolic involve a sign from the unconscious that demands interpretation; it is the "signifier of a signified that has been repressed from the subject's consciousness" (Lacan 2006a: 280). As a sign, the symptom is a "nodal point [*noeud*] of signification," whose signifieds range widely within the Symbolic (Lacan 2006e: 166). Lacan illustrates this idea with the word "curtain" (*rideau*) and offers a range of meanings from the conventional object at a window, to the "limit of my domain," to the "screen for my meditation in a room I share with someone else," to a word I shout to halt my boredom at a play ("Curtain!"), to "an image of meaning *qua* meaning, which must be unveiled if it is to reveal itself" (2006e: 167). In search of a symptom's meaning, one never reaches a stopping point, except in setting aside one symptom to consider the meaning of another. In this chapter, I use Lacan's later thought, in which a symptom is a message from the Real addressed through the unconscious to the Symbolic. And, as we saw in chapter 1, we will discover that whatever it is that the Real wants to say to us, its message is a series of partially hidden ideas that the Symbolic ultimately cannot capture, since it cannot signify the fullness of life, thought, and the strangeness of consciousness itself.

When we approach a symptom of the Real, like Peer Gynt peeling away the layers of an onion, we eventually discover that each meaning of the symptom falls away to reveal another until there is nothing left. At the core of subjectivity, there is no core. In the end, it is the symptom that gives the subject the only thing close to an essence that can prop him up. A symptom of the Real is like those bogeymen in horror movies; they just never die. Was there anyone who didn't guess that the Alien was in Ripley's escape shuttle at the end of *Alien*? And if we take the Alien seriously as a symptom from the Real, what does it signify? The first answers come readily enough. The crew in the movie rides a spaceship called *Nostromo*, Italian for boatswain or (more broadly) shipmate. The connection to the Alien is obvious enough: like the symptom, it is the companion who has been with the crew all along. But *Nostromo* is also a novel by Joseph Conrad, in which the title character becomes consumed by nightly efforts to recover a treasure of silver, ingot by ingot, which others believed to be lost forever. Since the spaceship *Nostromo* in *Alien* is on a return trip to Earth in order to bring precious minerals to a mega-corporation, the connection to Conrad's novel is evident. The Alien, then, is also a corporate greed that has moved from the colonialism of Conrad's time to a new colonization of the vastness of space itself: a form of capitalism run amok to its limitless limit.

But we have only unraveled the first layers of the symptomatic Alien. Its manner of reproduction through the oral cavity until it bursts through the chest like some phallus bent on the greatest violence speaks of homophobic fears and the brutality that the sexual act can take. Ash, the name of the science officer who we later discover to be an android, plays into the question of the automaton and its fraught relationship to our ideas of personhood: a recurring problem in our culture since at least the nineteenth century. The Alien thus becomes an unleashed remainder: the dark and uncanny difference between organic and inorganic life.

In the various sequels to *Alien*, some of these themes of the symptom are revived, while new themes also come to indicate more layers of meaning. In *Aliens*, a representative of the Weyland-Yutani mega corporation, Carter Burke, makes evident the theme of capitalism run amok in his efforts to bring an alien back home at all costs. Both the name Yutani and the multiplicity of the aliens in this sequel are indexical to the fear of an Asian molecular sublime that threatens Western values. The bogeyman theme uncovers itself in the form of Newt, the young girl who is the sole survivor of the colony that Ripley and her armed companions have come to rescue. The point is clear. The Alien is not one symptom but a series of partially disclosed and overlapping symptoms. As if to make Lacan's point that the symptom is the only thing that props us up, by the end of the *Alien* franchise, *Alien: Resurrection*, Ripley has been cloned using strands of alien DNA, lending her strength, acidic blood, and a dispassionate view of humanity: Ripley has become her symptom.

Like the Alien, the symptom from the Real is both inside and outside; it reveals itself in varied forms and appears to come from the unconscious. But since the unconscious is itself a product of the Symbolic, any symptom is both a problem for the sufferer and a manifestation of a problem in the culture. When we uncover a symptom of the Real in a movie, a piece of music, a novel, or any text, we are seeking to reconstitute the Symbolic order of the particular artwork. And within that order we are also seeking what fails to work. Whatever does not work within the Symbolic of the artwork is a symptom that requires more than one reading, more than one set of associations. Turning at last to Chopin's Mazurka in C♯ Minor, we will need to undertake a number of readings until we reach what cannot be read, what refuses integration into the Symbolic. At that point, the Real will reveal that there is no final interpretation for the signs it uses to address the Symbolic. Subjectivity will show itself to be empty, like the sign itself.

Orientalism or Nationalism?

To know what a mazurka meant in the Symbolic order of Chopin's Paris, a good place to start is Liszt's chapter on that dance in his *Frederic Chopin* (1963). Although Liszt's essay tends to meander, the basic argument begins with the declaration that "the feminine (and effeminate) element becomes clearly conspicuous" in the mazurka, especially by comparison to the polonaise (64). From here, Liszt describes the various dance steps of the mazurka in Poland, where we learn that the main motivation for the dance involves the man proudly claiming his partner "like a conquest," presenting her "for his rival's admiration before whisking her away in a whirling, voluptuous embrace that does not conceal the defiant expression of the victor and the blushing vanity of the prize" (66). The chapter moves to a long pronouncement on the charms of Slavic women, who, not surprisingly, Liszt compares to the "half-Egyptian, half-Parisian," whose powers of attraction come from their "Asiatic languor, by the flashing of houri-like eyes, by the indolence of the sultana, by the revelation of inexpressible tenderness, by gestures that caress without encouraging" (73). In short, Liszt's evocation of the Polish woman as exotic other could hardly be clearer if he had traveled a century forward to read Edward Said's *Orientalism*.

Liszt's essay concludes with an anecdote in which "one of the most distinguished women of Paris" is overcome with emotion after hearing Chopin play the piano in an intimate setting. When the woman asks whence comes the "remarkable emotion poured into his compositions like ashes of the nameless in splendid urns and finest alabaster," Chopin responds with the single Polish word *Żal!* (79). Beginning with the word's literal translation (regret, grief, rancor), Liszt creates an entire philosophy around *żal,* which, he claims, moves from tenderness and resigned regret to malice, revolt, and a vengeance that feeds on "sterile bitterness." The concept even extends to Chopin's sweetest music, Liszt argues, which embraces a divine endearment "natural only to women of semi-Oriental lands" (80). Throughout the passage, Liszt always capitalizes *żal* and appends an exclamation point in his fervor over the word, as if he has disclosed the secret power of Chopin's music.

Thus, Liszt manages to align both sides of the mazurka—the vigorous and the melancholic—to oriental exoticism. But Liszt was expressing nothing new with this alignment. Parisians had associated the Poles with the Orient since at least 1831, the first year of the so-called Great Emigration (sometimes called the Great Migration), when large numbers of Polish people fled to Paris after the fall of Warsaw to the Russian czar, Nicholas I. Many of the French were sympathetic to the Polish cause, even rallying for war against Russia, though the French government refused to grant military aid. Still, Parisians considered Poles to be "strange creatures with Oriental faces . . . and Asiatic outfits" (Atwood 1999: 47). They viewed Poland as a land "on the misty reaches of eastern Europe . . . shrouded in Oriental exoticism and peopled by a race of Tartars whose ancestors rode across the steppes of Asia with Genghis Khan and Tamerlane" (58). With the Parisian taste for the exotic, mazurkas and polonaises became quite popular, whether or not the music could make any real claim to ethnographic authenticity. In writing about the meaning of Chopin's mazurkas, then, Liszt was telling the Parisians something they already believed; he was writing within the Symbolic.

We can read Chopin's Mazurka in C♯ Minor as embracing the signs that Liszt has laid out for us. The A and B sections of the mazurka clearly evoke the sense of melancholy and regret that Liszt calls *żal.* The sweet thirds accompanying the first melody become signs of "Asiatic languor" (in Example 4.2, note the augmented second in the alto of m. 12). By contrast, the C section, which finds the major mode, enlivens the music and reaches a climax at mm. 73–74, follows Liszt's depiction of a dance in which the male partner proudly displays his female companion "like a conquest." The music even finds a bit of swagger in the characteristic dotted-rhythms at the climactic moment, as if the male has reached his fullest stature. Within the Symbolic order of his time, Liszt failed to see the irony that the male conquest of a Polish (read "Oriental") woman paralleled the Russian conquest of Poland, or, more accurately, he was blind to the logic of orientalism as a form of conquest itself.

If we do read Chopin's mazurka *à la* Liszt, though, we find a number of parts that refuse to fit. The music remains in its regretful melancholy for a long time: both A and B sections are rank with it, remaining glued to C♯ minor with only brief forays to tonicize E major in the A section, and G♯ minor in the B section. The B section is particularly stuck, repeating a two-measure melodic fragment over an unchanging dotted rhythm in the bass. Yes, a mazurka often includes repetitions of short phrases, and, as Jeffrey Kallberg argues, repetitions early in a mazurka direct us "to the aura of dynamism that Chopin tried to instill through propulsive literal repeats" (1988: 22). But this instance is marked for its insistence. Twice the fragment sputters on a trill that almost brings the music to a stop (mm. 39–40 and 55–56; the first instance is in Example 4.2). If this mazurka were from a time several decades later, we could read the halting trill as analogous to a machine that can't start properly: a sign of technology and its problems, which the early modernists faced. Finally, what do we do with the unsettling introduction to the mazurka, whose first sonority is a diminished triad outside the home key? We might force a conventional connection between chromaticism and the exotic, but the opening four measures are too darkly hued for such an interpretation. In short, there is something else hiding behind the symptomatic *żal,* orientalism, and conquest in this unusual mazurka.

The three terms of the first reading—*żal,* orientalism, conquest—do form another association involving the very emigration that brought the Poles to France in the first place. The web that Liszt weaves around *żal* (grief, nostalgia, anger, revenge) was common to the Polish diaspora. In Paris, the Poles experienced grief and nostalgia over a lost homeland, anger at its conquest by Russia, and a sense that vengeance would restore Poland to its former glory, even to stand as a symbol for the independence of all nations (see Bellman 2010: 114–23). The narrative arch of these emotional responses finds repeated resonance in Adam Mickiewicz's poetry, which in recent years has inspired a number of interpretations of Chopin's music, the ballades in particular, as narratives of Polish loss and redemption (or failed redemption) (see Berger 1994; Swartz 1994; Zakrzewska 1999; Goldberg 2004; and Bellman 2010). Liszt himself mentions that Chopin's mazurkas sometimes resound with "faint fanfares, like glory's distant recollection" (1963: 78). And Chopin was known to improvise on the so-called "Dąbrowski Mazurka" (also known as "The Hymn of General Dąbrowski's Polish Legions," or "Poland Has Yet Not Perished"), which later became the Polish national anthem. Bohdan Zaleski, a poet and close friend of Chopin, recalled an improvisation by Chopin on the "Dąbrowski Mazurka" in which the music moved from "voices pleasant and painful from the past" to a conclusion on the tune of the famous mazurka "in all tones, from militant to children and angels" (quoted in Goldberg 2004: 70).

Reading the mazurka in these terms does make sense of certain parts of the music. The A section, for example, features an accompaniment of expanded rolled chords that, as we have seen, stand out from Chopin's other mazurkas. Chopin's usual practice in signifying the drones of the Polish folk dance is to use simple open fifths in the left hand, as in the mazurkas op. 6, nos. 2 and 3, op. 17, no. 4 (middle section), or op. 24, no. 2. Otherwise the most common accompaniment figure in Chopin's mazurkas is a waltz pattern or a set of repeated chords. The rolled chords in the Mazurka in C♯ Minor give the music a balladic tone, as if we are hearing one of Mickiewicz's epic poems about the fall of Poland. The music has found something old; it tells of its own nostalgia. As for "glory's distant recollection," we can hear the animated C section with its expanded texture and dotted rhythms in the major mode as an image of military splendor, undimmed before the breaking of Warsaw. Within such a reading, we are forced to relive the death of Poland as the gloomy A section returns to complete the mazurka. And a descent to the grave has its musical correlate in the chromatically descending dominant sevenths that begin in the coda (Example 4.2, mm. 129–32), while the final C♯ minor chord in the low register of the piano leaves no room for hope.

The return of the opening section is what doesn't work in this reading. Although there is plenty of room for nostalgia and regret at the beginning and end of such tales, the artistic conventions among the Poles in Paris included some reference to the hope for a renewed and free Poland, generally expressed near the end of a poem or musical narrative. In Book Twelve of Mickiewicz's epic *Pan Tadeusz*, for example, a cimbalon virtuoso named Jankiel improvises a song that begins with the nostalgia of a lost Poland but concludes with the triumph of "March Dąbrowski" (the "Dąbrowski Mazurka"). Bellman argues that Mickiewicz's inspiration for this scene might have come from hearing Chopin improvise on Polish themes (2010: 130–31). In the Epilogue of *Pan Tadeusz*, Mickiewicz returns to the regret of a fallen Poland: "Oh Mother Poland! So freshly entombed / One has not strength now to speak of your doom!" But he also makes room for the promise of a free Poland yet to come:

> Some day—when lions of vengeance have spoken,
> Trumpets are silent, and the ranks have broken,
> When the foe utters his last cry of pain,
> Is still, and nations know freedom again; . . .
>
> Their swords discarded, unarmed shall sit now
> Our knights! They songs now shall gladly allow! (Mickiewicz 2004)

Chopin permits no such promise. Even in his other works with putative inspirations around the Great Emigration—notably his first and second ballades—a tragic end is preceded by furious passages that follow the conventions of storm or battle scenes: the hero goes down fighting. But no heroic struggle leads to the entombment that marks the end of the Mazurka in C♯ Minor. In addition, we still have the symptoms that plagued the orientalist reading: the cryptic introduction, the prolonged melancholy, and the sputtering trills.

Before we set aside the orientalist and nationalist readings of the mazurka, we should make note of what they mean within a Lacanian paradigm that views the music as akin to a dream with its multi-layered symptoms. Within the Symbolic order of Chopin's Paris, both the orientalist and nationalist readings of the mazurka are perfectly legitimate. These readings point out symptoms not only in Chopin (as exotic other and as displaced patriot) but also in the Symbolic order itself. More accurately, the problems of orientalist thought (involving attraction to the exotic other and a need to capture it) and of nationalist loss (involving nostalgia, regret, and vengeance) mark places where the Symbolic does not work.

And since consciousness forms itself in the Symbolic, and even the unconscious is the discourse of the Other, any symptom we read in the music of Chopin, or the poetry of Mickiewicz, or the novels of George Sand, is simultaneously a problem in the Symbolic and in the personal history of Chopin, or Mickiewicz, or Sand. This is one of the things that Lacan means when he writes that the analyst teaches the subject to recognize that "his unconscious is his history": a history that is both large in the Symbolic and small in the particular workings of that order within the subject (2006a: 217).

The problem is that our first readings of the mazurka as orientalist or nationalist turn out to be rather disappointing. *Of course* Chopin and his Polish contemporaries knew that they were viewed as exotic, and that they were displaced from their home: these problems harassed them every day. But these symptoms as they appear in the mazurka are meant to hide other symptoms more difficult to face. Those problems make themselves known in the places where the mazurka resists the first interpretation. Those resistances are goads to more interpretation.

How Polish Is It?

To embark on other interpretations of Chopin's mazurka, I here widen the cultural net and become less concerned with what a mazurka meant as a Polish dance and more concerned with what it meant as a dance that happened to come from Poland. We will find that while the connection to exoticism remains, other associations are uncovered. Our point of entry is nineteenth-century ballet, where the mazurka often stood as one of a collection of national dances that signified the exotic, or colorful, whether or not it had any logical connection with the scenario. In a recollection about the St. Petersburg Bolshoi, for example, prima ballerina Yekaterina Vazem recalled that when Marius Petipa staged the French opera *Paquita* (1846) in Russia, he inserted a *Mazurka des enfants* in the last act, even though "it seemed incongruous to perform a Polish national dance in Zaragossa" (Vazem and Dimitrievich 1988: 39). Here the mazurka becomes what Deleuze and Guattari call a *placard,* a matter of expression that is possessive and appropriative, constituting "a having more profound than being" (1987: 316). The Polish dance is a form of alterity that is nonetheless familiar and obligatory, an other to be appropriated as a form of expression. It is not a matter of acquiring Poland itself as a form of desirable other but of taking an attribute and making it a form of expression. In music, this form of expression may be a topic that is imported yet recontextualized. In nineteenth-century ballet, the mazurka as a musical topic begins to lose its indexical relationship to Poland to take up a more generalized meaning as one of a collection of dances that mean alterity, nationalism, non-Western, and so on.

Among the later ballets to highlight the Polish dance was Delibes's *Coppélia* (1870), whose overture is in the style of a mazurka, featuring characteristic dotted rhythms on the first beat. After a brief introduction in the horns, whose material bears a striking resemblance to Wagner's Valhalla leitmotif, a mazurka enlivens the remainder of the overture. Early in Act I, the people of the small village

Example 4.3. Tchaikovsky, Mazurka from *Swan Lake*, Act III

that forms the setting of *Coppélia* dance a mazurka as well. The importance of the mazurka in the overture and Act I has little to do with its Polishness; there is no indication in E. T. A. Hoffmann's "Die Puppe" or "Der Sandmann," the two stories conflated in *Coppélia*, that the setting is in Poland. In addition, *Coppélia* includes little of the uncanny that Freud read in Hoffmann's tales. Instead, we are treated to a comic version of Hoffmann's work, in which poor Franz's love for the doll Coppélia is undone by his girlfriend, Swanilda, who discovers that Coppélia is mechanical, takes her identity to embarrass Franz, and wins back his love. In this context, the mazurka signifies Swanilda's grounded sense of reality. That the dance is Polish is important only to the extent that it points to the village, the countryside, the peasant. And the *Valhalla* horns preceding the mazurka in the overture point to a nobility away from Wagner's mythical domain and toward the realm of the townsfolk.

A mazurka also has a prominent place in Act III of Tchaikovsky's *Swan Lake*, which depicts the ball where Prince Siegfried must choose a wife. Just before the act's finale, the ball concludes with a number of national dances: a czardas, a Spanish dance, a Neapolitan dance, and a mazurka. Following the mazurka, Siegfried professes his love for the Black Swan, Odile, while the White Swan, Odette, witnesses his vow with desperation. It is the mazurka that forms the climax of Siegfried's growing love for the wrong swan. Tchaikovsky's mazurka for this scene includes the characteristic dotted rhythm on beat one (Example 4.3), although tambourines in the orchestration jeopardize the ethnographic authenticity of the dance. Still, the mazurka is overloaded with indexical significations: it has become aristocratic, it brings the ball to a crescendo of sentiment, and it serves as an aphrodisiac that helps to blind Siegfried to the true identity of the Black Swan. Siegfried is overtaken by the mazurka. The scene practically follows Liszt's description of a dance in which the male takes his partner as a conquest, although, in this case, it is Siegfried who turns out to be the vanquished once Odile's true identity is revealed. The allure of the mazurka has overwhelmed Siegfried's ability to see the truth.

Tolstoy's *War and Peace* gives us another glimpse of Russia's attraction to the mazurka. In volume 2, part 1, chapter 12, which takes place in 1806, Tolstoy renders a scene where Natasha dances for the first time at a "real ball," organized by the dance instructor Iogel at the Bezukhov home (Tolstoy 2007: 334). Natasha is Iogel's best pupil; as the orchestra begins to play "the newly fashionable mazurka" (334), he shows his pride in her skill by choosing her to dance with him as the lead couple. Iogel dances "softly, delicately, in his little boots," while Natasha follows with "timidly but carefully performed" steps (335). Natasha attracts the attention of Denisov, who sits among the old ladies, telling stories. But Nikolai, Natasha's brother, coaxes her sister to invite Denisov to dance, since he is "famous even in Poland for his skill in dancing the Polish mazurka" (335). In contrast to Iogel, Denisov dances with élan and abandon. "Only on horseback and in the mazurka did Denisov's small stature not show. . . . On the downbeat, he gave his lady a victorious and jocular sidelong look, unexpectedly stamped his foot, bounced off the floor springily, like a ball, and flew along in a circle, drawing his lady after him" (335). His dancing includes the characteristic Polish steps: stamping of feet, clanking of spurs, and flying in circles. "Even though Iogel did not acknowledge this mazurka as authentic, everyone admired Denisov's skill, choosing him constantly, and the old men, smiling, began to talk about Poland and the good old days" (336). Denisov has fallen for Natasha. After dancing, he does not leave her side for the rest of the ball. Later in the novel, though, Natasha will refuse Denisov's marriage proposal.

Tolstoy shows us two mazurkas in this scene. The first, danced by Iogel and Natasha, is a refined and aristocratic version with delicate steps carefully placed. Lacking the usual stamping of feet and clicking of heels, this mazurka is deterritorialized in the Russian ballroom. As a result, it becomes no more than a dance from Poland, stripped of its surroundings: another placard of expression that has been torn loose from its indexical meanings. The second mazurka, danced by Denisov and Natasha, is reterritorialized with the assemblage of Polish dance steps and gestures, its vigor and folk style. Iogel's refusal to acknowledge Denisov's mazurka as authentic is both ironic and true. Denisov does not dance the Russian version of a mazurka, which has become authentically aristocratic under Iogel's cleaning up of the folk moves. Instead, Denisov dances the Polish mazurka, whose authenticity belongs to another territory (Mazovia) entirely, evoking an authenticity that Iogel refuses to see. But Denisov's reterritorialized version widens the indexical meaning of the mazurka. We see that he gains stature only when he dances the mazurka or mounts a horse, the latter of which has a broad network of significations for valor, strength, and vitality in the nineteenth century (see Monelle 2000: 45–65). Denisov's Polish mazurka indicates vigor (of the people), spirit, exuberance, and a bit of immoderation. Before the mazurka, Denisov lounges with the old ladies at the party. After the mazurka,

Example 4.4. Chopin, Mazurka in C♯ Minor (conclusion of section C and return of introduction)

Denisov comes to life. More accurately, the mazurka brings him to life: the life of the party. The connection to the theme of *Coppélia* is clear: a puppet comes to life in the sight of the mazurka danced by the people of the village. It makes no difference if that village is Polish. The mazurka brings people to life.

Brought to life. Chopin's Mazurka in C♯ Minor comes to life, too, during its C section. Beginning in m. 65 the mazurka takes on a sense of harmonic direction that it lacked until this moment (Example 4.2). Its new sense of harmony is especially contrasting to the B section (mm. 33–64), which simply toggled between dominant and tonic harmonies in C♯ and G♯ minor. The C section, appropriately marked *con anima*, breaks away from the gloom of virtually the entire mazurka to this point and establishes B major. For the first time the accompaniment takes on the characteristic *oom-pah-pah* of a mazurka or a waltz: the music has become a real dance instead of a telling or a showing of one. A new melody stretches beyond the shorter one- and two-measure motives that repeat themselves throughout the rest of the mazurka. A sense of purpose is underscored by an ascending sequence through a cycle of thirds that brings the melody from B major (m. 65), through the mediant, D♯ minor (m. 69), to the dominant, F♯ major

(m. 73), with each step initiated by its own dominant, propelling the music to its new goal. The climax of the section and of the entire piece runs through mm. 73–74, where the music fills out the texture and announces the famous mazurka dotted-rhythm on the downbeat of each of the two measures. But the rhythm goes beyond its sign of conventionality to become an announcement of vitality and élan. Like Denisov, the mazurka takes on a sense of heroism and dignity that was absent until this point. The mazurka has come to life.

The vital moment does not last long. In mm. 75–76, as the melody descends and the harmony reaches the local tonic, B, the music relaxes from its high point. But a four-measure transition, again featuring the dotted rhythms, allows the mazurka to replay the entire passage involving the ascending sequence and climax in mm. 81–92. Although the music recaptures its moment of noble grandeur in mm. 89–90, this time we have a greater sense of loss when the music falls once again to B major in m. 92. A second pass through the transition in mm. 93–96 fails to reenliven the music, and we find ourselves again at the curious opening passage, which closes off any sense that the mazurka will continue to bring itself to life (Example 4.4).

We can take the B section preceding the coming-to-life of the mazurka as a placard: ironically, a matter of expression acquired from the genre of the mazurka but emptied of its usual signification. As a placard, a deterritorialized version of one of the mazurka's attributes, the unrelenting dotted rhythm of this section takes on a new meaning, especially when we recall the sputtering trills that trip it up (Example 4.2). The whole section is like a wind-up toy that hits a few snags as its mechanism runs its course (recall that Coppélia is a mechanical doll). The section is a symptom pointing to the problem of the automaton, which acts as a foil to the mazurka-come-to-life of the music's climax. The whole mazurka, then, moves through life (the climax), death (the coda), and the place in between (the B section and its automaton). The music occupies the boundary between life and death before it spills to one side and then the other. This refusal of the B section to fall on one side of the life/death opposition brings us to an association that will set up new interpretations for the symptoms of the mazurka.

Poetry or Pathology?

You keep syphilis hidden, hoping that its unhurried course will go unnoticed. You hide from the terror of cholera and its deadly swiftness. But you display tuberculosis, the most fashionable disease in Chopin's time, because it marks you as a desirable other (see O'Shea 1990; Daniel 1997; and Dormandy 2000). The physical signs of the consumptive were unusual thinness and pale skin, both of which characterized Chopin in his early years in Paris. In northern Europe, those signs were associated with poetic insight, beauty, and a magnetic virility. Women would diet on sand to emulate the pallid aspect of the consumptive and gain a heightened allure (Dormandy 2000: 91). Poets with consumption could anticipate a reputation as a visionary. "I should like to die of consumption," said Lord Byron to a friend, "because the ladies would say, 'look at that poor Byron. How

Example 4.5. Chopin, Mazurka in C♯ Minor (Neapolitans at close of section A)

interesting he looks in dying'" (quoted in Daniel 1997: 32). Chopin's own death sadly matched Byron's sardonic comment. As Chopin lay dying, his apartment became the center of the whispered buzz of high society. A contemporary cartoon about Chopin's final days depicted a crying woman and a caption that read, "The Only Countess in Whose Arms Chopin Did not Die" (Eisler 2003: 198). A poetic death to match a poetic disease.

The poet with tuberculosis—and there have been ever so many—writes on the familiar themes of the grave, the doomed maiden, the transience of youth, the ruin. How could syphilitic Schubert resist tubercular Hölty's lines from "Todtengräberlied," uttered by the titular gravedigger?

> Jener Kopf mit Haaren
> War vor wenig Jahren
> Schön wie Engel sind.

> That head with hair
> was a few years ago
> beautiful as angels are.

Tubercular characters in the arts, like their kindred poets, are too numerous for a full account, but they often share the themes of morbidity, physical beauty, or unusual insight. Does Marcel's heightened awareness of time and memory come from his life as a consumptive? Does Violetta's pallor intensify Alfredo's love for her? Is a vampire a reconfiguration of the signs of tuberculosis? All the elements are there: the wan aspect, the unusual animal magnetism, the knowledge of mysteries and the beyond, the margin between life and death. Even the thirst for blood has its inverted form in the bloodletting that was a common treatment for consumption. Thomas Daniel reports that one of the "most bizarre" treatments for tuberculosis was drinking the blood of freshly slaughtered animals, which was hoped to strengthen "the resistance of tuberculosis patients to the disease" (1997: 168). Is it a lucky coincidence that Mickiewicz once referred to Chopin as George Sand's "evil genius, her moral vampire . . . who torments her and may well end up by killing her" (quoted in Bellman 2010: 140)?

The tubercular artist occupies the boundary between life and death, sending us visions that contradict the happy possibilities of the Enlightenment. Kallberg has documented how Chopin's contemporaries heard his music as otherworldly, ethereal, and melancholy, though he argues that these descriptions materialized from his "idiosyncratic manner of performing" (1996: 63). But Chopin's physical symptoms reinforced the symptom of the tubercular as the visionary. Not all the otherworldly voices in Chopin are the stuff of faeries.

The Mazurka in C♯ Minor shows the symptoms of consumption and its meanings in Chopin's Parisian culture: pallor, thinness, melancholy, morbidity, ethereal poeticism, and sexual allure. One of the clearest signs comes in mm. 21–27, where the music gets stuck on a spectral Neapolitan through several repetitions of a two-measure cadential progression (Example 4.5). The first Neapolitan in m. 21 proceeds conventionally to a dominant and then tonic in m. 22. But as the Neapolitan returns in mm. 23, 25, and 27, the music lingers over it with everexpanding arpeggios before proceeding harmonically. By m. 27, the music refuses to leave the Neapolitan as it stretches through the first two beats with an arpeggiated cadenza that disappears into the piano's stratospheric D. The mazurka falls out of time as it displays its symptom and peers into its own translucent poeticism, gesturing up and out of quotidian existence.

Leading to the repeated Neapolitans, the opening theme is hushed and morbid; the rolled chords over the C♯ pedal lend the balladic music a gothic gloom. The melody is harmonized in thirds, constant companions that make the first theme overripe to the point of decay. When the accompaniment drops out in m. 12, the thirds descend to land on a quizzical C♯ over A, clashing with the prevailing dominant from the previous measure (Example 4.2). As with the Neapolitans, the theme has fallen out of time, holding still on the weak part of beat two: a trope on the tendency of a mazurka to accent the conventionally unstressed beats of a measure. Rather than give the music a sense of syncopation, though, the held C♯/A sounds uncertain, as if the music questions where it might go next. As the first theme starts again, it manages to find a bright place in B major, beginning in m. 17. But this reharmonization of the theme only manages to reach the persistent Neapolitans. The whole first section, then, shows signs of a pale unwholesomeness that nevertheless promises a vision into a realm that only the consumptive poet can reveal.

The mazurka's B section manages to shake off the persistent and coyly sweet thirds of the opening music. Although an anemic aspect remains, we have a sense that the music might lift the deathly hue, since the accompaniment turns away from the heavy rolled chords and, as we have seen, animates the new theme with the characteristic dotted rhythm of the *mazur* or *kujawiak*. But it is not until the C section that the mazurka finally comes to life, as noted earlier. With the thicker texture, the harmonic motion, the turn toward the major mode, and the spirited melody, we can hear a growing seduction that reaches a point of self-possessed swagger in the climax of mm. 73–74. The music steps back from this show of boldness in mm. 77–80 in order to replay the wind-up to another display of potency. But this second climax fails to recapture the same effect. Where the earlier passage featured held chords in mm. 74 and 76, this later passage includes rests and a *decrescendo*, casting doubt on the success of the theme's advances. All too soon, the dark opening theme returns.

The coda makes clear the theme of death in the complex around the consumptive symptoms. After the returning A section reaches the Neapolitans, the mazurka falls into decay with a series of descending dominant seventh chords (Example 4.2). The mazurka lands on a dark subdominant in m. 133, where it remains until a solo melody descends through that same chord (with an added sixth) to find a final C♯ minor triad in the low register of the piano. A deep melancholy fills the repeated subdominant chord, a thin paleness glimmers through the solo arpeggio, and death comes with the final minor triad.

As with the other readings of the mazurka, the first four measures and their return in the middle and at the end of the piece resist satisfactory interpretation. The mazurka opens with a marked sonority, an apparent diminished triad that comes as quite a shock (Example 4.2). The first harmony moves to an apparent half-diminished chord in m. 3, which does little to settle the unnatural atmosphere. Beneath these chords, the bass winds up with a dotted rhythm whose pitches toggle down and up through half-step neighbor motion. In retrospect, it is the lower note of each bass pattern that represents the real root of the two chords in the introduction. The underlying progression, then, is a fairly simple V7/V to V7, landing on the tonic to begin the first theme. But this rationalization of the progression fails to shake away the disturbing start of the mazurka.

The opening falls in the space between; it lies in the impossible boundary on both sides of life and death. The strange beginning of the mazurka is a symptom that stands both as a message from and a marker to the otherworldly realm. But the problem is that there can be no occupation of the territory between life and death; such a thought is already a product of a Symbolic order that cannot make room for the very idea it tries to represent. We are close now, so close to the trauma of the Real. But before we glimpse the impossible realm, we must acknowledge that the Parisian Symbolic for tuberculosis as the sign of poetic transfiguration was already a lie, a symptom.

In the view of nineteenth-century medicine, disease was not something separate from the life of the patient but a modification of that life. "Disease is a deviation in life," Foucault tells us, and the idea that disease attacks life is replaced by the idea of the "pathological life" (1973: 188). There is the tubercular life, the syphilitic life, the cancerous life, and so on. This view is prevalent even today: there is the cancerous man, the diabetic woman, the dyslexic child, all of whom are treated as if leading a pathological life, a life defined by their illness or abnormality. Such people have *become* their symptoms (in Lacan's terms). The problem in the Symbolic is that such lives have little to do with reality. Chopin's tuberculosis in reality had little to do with the poetic thought that the Parisians saw in such a pathological life. Chopin suffered gastrointestinal problems that restricted his diet. He suffered swollen glands and (often embarrassing) swelling of the nose. He coughed blood and phlegm by the bowlful. By the end of his life, his lower extremities and face had become swollen to a point beyond recognition. He had the barrel chest typical of those with long-lasting lung diseases. His fingertips showed signs of "digital clubbing," a deformity in which the pads of the fingers enlarge like small pillows (O'Shea 1990: 142–51).

Such signs find no place in the Symbolic order of Chopin's Paris. The problem, then, is not that Chopin was occupying a place between life and death, but that his life was a deviation from the norm: a form of suffering that was never very poetic. That deviation finds its correlate in the opening chord of the Mazurka in C♯ Minor. While a music theorist can rationalize the first chord as an apparent one that resolves to a dominant seventh when the bass E moves to D♯, the diminished sonority opening the piece reappears through each of the larger beats in the hemiola of the first two measures. It refuses to remain fixed on the structural D♯ until the last beat of m. 2. And this syntactic rationalization of the chord as a neighbor to a functional secondary-dominant does not help us to discover what it signifies. The diminished sonority and those that follow are the symptoms that resist integration into the Symbolic order. They are signs from the Real, which will never lead to some secret kernel of meaning at the center of the symptom, because there is no secret kernel to be found. They are also the signs that through the mazurka Chopin becomes his symptom in what Lacan called the *sinthome*.

What Is a *Sinthome*?

Chopin suffered from hallucinations, nightmares, and moments of disorientation. His hallucinations began as early as adolescence, and his so-called "Stuttgard Diary," which the composer kept between 1829 and 1831, contains passages of alarming incoherence (Szulc 1998: 46–49). In the final years of his life, Chopin experienced "ghastly nightmares and nocturnal disorientation," probably as a result of his respiratory failure (O'Shea 1990: 146). Thus the physical symptoms of Chopin's tuberculosis were matched by psychological ones; the problems of his body were the problems of his mind. It can be no other way. When Lacan tells us where we can find the truth of the subject's history, he begins with "monuments: this is my body, in other words, the hysterical core of neurosis in which the hysterical symptom manifests the structure of a language" (2006a: 259). Both the body and the mind are caught in the discourses of the Symbolic. Where the body exhibits a symptom, there the mind will be, and vice versa. If there is a split, it is not between the body and the mind but between the body-as-mind, the mind-as-body, and their own curious multiplicities, because we as subjects (body/mind) are fragmented at the moment we enter the Symbolic order. *Thou art that!*

Chopin's hallucinations bring us to the Freudian *Unheimliche* and its desperate obsession to find a wholeness that was never there to begin with. As we saw in chapter 1, one of Freud's explanations of the uncanny involves that class of the terrifying arising from "something repressed that *recurs*" (1958: 394). The twin mechanisms of repetition and repression allow the ego to make space in order to function. But sometimes these mechanisms malfunction. Repetition becomes a compulsion that hopes to keep the ghastly thought away from consciousness; or, repression fails and the terrifying vision returns, fueled by a morbid anxiety from the unconscious. Freud illustrates his theory of the uncanny with stories by E. T. A. Hoffman, notably "Der Sandmann" (coincidentally, one of the two stories that were conflated to make the scenario of *Coppélia*). The stories typically involve automatons mistaken for real people, childhood fears that return in terrible forms, and characters who fall into madness.

We have already seen a form of repetition compulsion in the B section of Chopin's mazurka, where the *mazur* rhythm of the left hand repeats nearly unabated for thirty measures, and a two-measure melodic fragment in the right hand repeats twelve times. The only interruptions in this obsessive cycle are the trills at mm. 39–40 and 55–56, which take on the tremor of anxiety, as if an unwelcome thought threatens to make its uncanny reappearance (mm. 39–40, in Example 4.2, show the first instance of the trills). The repetitions do their psychic work, clearing space for the animated and climactic section of the mazurka, the only breath of free air that the music allows. But the return of the opening section puts an end to the health that the mazurka's climax had promised. Although the B section is a clear instance of repetition clearing space for the ego to work, in truth the entire mazurka is a plague of repetitions. The A section proceeds with two-measure ideas that always come in pairs until the fourfold repetition of the Neapolitan chord in mm. 21–27. The A section does not reach a cadence so much as it repeats a dominant four times in mm. 28–31 before dematerializing on a repeated G♯ (Example 4.5, mm. 31–32). Even the climactic C section has small- and large-scale repetitions of material. It is during a promised third return of the climax, beginning in m. 93, that the introduction reappears to turn the music back to its ghostly aura: the return of the repressed.

The introduction has been a problem in each interpretation of the mazurka's symptoms. In this case, it appears as the unsettling thought that sets the music on its way. But what can the introduction mean? One answer comes to us at the end of the mazurka (m. 133ff.), where the melodic material from the B section is accompanied in the left hand by the neighbor motion and harmony reminiscent of mm. 2–3 from the introduction (Example 4.2, mm. 133–end). Coming from the descending dominant sevenths, and leading to the fatalistic final chord, these measures are signs of death. This final appearance of material from the introduction serves as a master signifier that reorganizes our thinking about the mazurka.

As we saw in chapter 1, a master signifier functions as a kernel around which the subject organizes experience. As Žižek explains, "Every historical rupture, every advent of a new master-signifier, changes retroactively the meaning of all tradition, restructures the narration of the past, makes it readable in another, new way" (1989: 56). Retroactively, then, the coda of the mazurka is the master signifier that reorganizes the signs of each previous instance of the introduction, so that we know at last that the unsettling thought repressed throughout the music was death itself.

In this reading of the mazurka, there is a constant and uncanny series of repetitions, hoping to keep away the thought of death, the very death of the music as a form of subjectivity. But if we take away these repetitions, these symptoms, what do we have left? The answer is nothing. The mazurka is constituted by the very compulsions and symptoms that it hopes to escape. What does not work in the Symbolic, then, is the very thought that the subject could ever be a unified and unequivocal whole. Freud's *Unheimliche* is not just a pathology for the poor subject whose conscious and unconscious mechanisms have failed; the uncanny thought that comes from the terror of mental fragmentation unto the emptiness of death is the very substance (or zero substance) of subjectivity itself. One peels away the various meanings of the symptom to reveal another and another until there is nothing at all. The music as subject has become its symptom.

We have come to the *sinthome,* Lacan's final conception of the symptom, which he discussed in his seminar of 1975–76. The *sinthome* is a form of enjoyment (*jouissance*) that comes from the constant deferral of a final interpretation demanded by the Symbolic. One learns to take pleasure in the very unconscious (Symbolic) that determines us, along with all of its symptoms. Those symptoms become us: they are us. As a message from the Real, the symptom can never reveal its full meaning. It clothes itself in a series of signs that only partially tell us what it wants to say. In the case of Chopin's mazurka, these symptoms have led us through the problems of orientalism (alterity), nationalism (nostalgia), coming to life (the automaton), tuberculosis (the boundary of life and death), and the uncanny (fragmentation of the body/mind). Each interpretation of the mazurka's symptoms has led us closer to the trauma of the Real, but no interpretation will ever bring us to the fullest message of the Real. That message includes a series of symptoms and their various interpretations, but those interpretations, even the significations of death, cannot express fully the message of the Real. In the end, we reach something indecipherable, an enigma, something the subject will never understand or overcome. At this point, the only thing that props up the subject at all is the very symptom that resists interpretation in the first place. But the subject will continue to try to make sense of the symptom even though it will never be cured. At the moment when making sense is all that is left, the subject becomes the symptom. We have reached the *sinthome,* which, following Lacan's penchant for word play, sounds curiously like *sent-homme:* the man (*homme*) who senses (*sent*) or who makes sense. It is an enjoyment in making sense of something that will never fully make sense in the first place. Like any symptom, the *sinthome* is a stain on the discourse of the Symbolic, but it is also a positive condition of that order, because it assures that we choose something over nothing: that we choose to attach ourselves to the Symbolic with all of its problems rather than yield to an emptiness that even the word *emptiness* cannot capture (Žižek 1989: 56). It is the *sinthome* that drives us to understand our history, and our being in the world. The *sinthome* is not concerned with a final meaning but with the production of meaning; it uses the Symbolic, itself a "symptomatic structure," so that the subject will make sense (Hoens and Pluth 2002: 11–13). One does not cure the symptom. One becomes the symptom. The Mazurka in C♯ Minor is nothing more than the very symptoms that we have uncovered in trying to understand it. But take away those symptoms, and nothing will remain.

Who Is the Dreamer?

I am walking along West 57th Street in New York City, although the area looks more like Chinatown than Midtown. But this discrepancy doesn't bother me, because I know exactly where to find Horowitz's apartment. Soon, I'm in a large and ornately decorated foyer, waiting for the doorman to arrive. I'm going to tell him that I've come to hear Mr. Horowitz play the mazurka. In my mind there is only one mazurka: Horowitz played it during his return to Carnegie Hall in 1965. It is the Mazurka in C♯ Minor, which I listened to many times as a child, since my father's habit was to play an LP of the famous concert. I am waiting. A worrying thought tells me that Horowitz is dead, and he might not want an unexpected guest asking him to play the piano. No matter, I decide. Rubinstein lives nearby. I'm certain I know the way to his apartment, too.

I leave the grand foyer, and soon I am in the entrance hall to Rubinstein's apartment. Since the doorman seems unaware that I am here, I decide to take a look around. I find art-deco objects in many of the rooms, although their colors are faded. Because the art is outdated, I conclude that Rubinstein must be very old, and the worrying thought that he too might be dead gnaws in the back of my mind. Soon I find a large room with a piano and rows of chairs lined up as if for a recital. I am relieved to see that Rubinstein is already planning to perform for a small gathering, although no one is in the music room at the moment. Maybe I can blend in with the expected audience. Looking at the chairs, I see that one of them has my name printed on it, although the last name is misspelled. Still, I decide that this will be a good place to sit and wait for the concert to begin. Maybe nobody will notice that I am not the real Michael Kline. At the moment when I take the seat, Mr. Rubinstein enters the room and sits at the piano. He sees me over the top of the music stand but does not seem perturbed that a stranger is in his home. He lifts his hands to begin the mazurka. But as always happens in a dream, the moment his hands touch the keys, the scene fades away.

This dream is one that I had a few days after starting to think about Chopin's mazurka (in the dream, it is the only mazurka). Many elements of the Lacanian interpretation were formed already in the images of the dream. The scene is both exotic (Chinatown) and cosmopolitan (Midtown). The action touches on the theme of the dead (Horowitz), and the return of the dead, or the repressed

(Rubinstein). I am a figure with no real place in the dream (the chair that I occupy is for another: Thou art that!). The compulsion is to hear a message from the dead: Rubinstein inhabits the boundary between life and death. But the message is one I will never know, since I never hear the mazurka played (we cannot know the message of the Real). We might say that at the moment I dreamt the dream, I caught the symptoms of Chopin's mazurka.

In the most exacting way, there can be no Lacanian interpretation of an artwork from a dead artist. The message of the artwork is directed to the artist's Symbolic order as a demand to be heard, to be understood. Implicit in the demand is that the Symbolic will give a response, even if that response is silence. The artist as subject sends a message that comes back to him as the return of the repressed. Thus we come again to one of the meanings of Lacan's famous statement that "a letter always arrives at its destination" (2006h: 41). More importantly, though, the artist as subject begins to understand his own alienation and starts a dialectic in which the series of crises that makes up conscious/unconscious thought will bring about "his particularity and his universality, going so far as to universalize this very particularity" (2006e: 182). What the subject perceives as her personal symptoms (particularities) are also the symptoms of the Symbolic order (universalities), and vice versa. But at the moment of death, the subject falls out of the Symbolic and "materializes the pure Nothingness of the hole, the void in the Other (the symbolic order), . . . the pure substance of enjoyment resisting symbolization" (Žižek 2008: 9–10). At the moment of the subject's death, the Lacanian circuit of interpretation ends.

To take up a Lacanian reading of the dead artist's work, we the living must be caught in the symptoms of the artwork. Following Žižek, we can think of the artwork as akin to a message in a bottle (2008: 11–12). At the moment the artist tosses that message into the sea of time, whoever picks it up becomes its addressee by the very act of picking it up (a form of Imaginary mis-recognition). We accept the letter as ours, even if it is not addressed to us. In this case, again, the letter always finds its destination. We hear the music of Chopin, and we apprehend it as a voice calling to us, demanding our response, as if we represent the Symbolic order to which the music makes its appeal. We have caught Chopin's symptoms, and our only way through is to take them as the prompt to interpretation.

In his *Interpreting Music,* Lawrence Kramer explains the difference between semiotic and hermeneutic approaches to music on the way to announcing "My vote is for hermeneutics" (2011: 21). Mine too. Although semiotics informed Lacan's discovery that the unconscious is structured like a language, semiotics as it is practiced today too often falls into the formation of neologisms and taxonomies that end up telling us what we already know. The choice, though, is not really between semiotics and hermeneutics but between hermeneutics and a desire to maintain a mystified vision of music as a real (no capital R) experience, whose alluring fullness deserves our attention. But this experience of music, lovely and enticing as it is, is an attempt to recapture an Imaginary (capital *I*) stage in our development, when we took ourselves to be whole. We fall into music's acoustic mirror, push away the history that hurts, and accept a vision of music as ineffable and transcendent. But the damage was already done at the moment we learned that there was a word called "music," and we entered the Symbolic order in a crisis that made a happy wholeness irretrievable. Music as the vision of the inexpressible will not release us from the Symbolic and give us back what we think we have lost.

Our only choice is to recognize that music and the music makers are marked with the symptoms and series of crises that are the only substance (the zero substance) of consciousness. We pick up the symptoms of the music, like catching a cold. And then we take the course of interpretation that is the only way to understanding the history of our consciousness. How we answer Chopin's letter to us is to accept its traumas as demands for interpretation that we know in advance will never be satisfied. If we listen to Chopin again and again; if we are drawn to understand some new detail previously overlooked; if we cannot turn away, we become a *sinthome:* the one who *makes* sense. In this way, Chopin's symptoms become our symptoms; his traumatic life and death questions become our questions. Chopin's dreams become our dreams.

Intermezzo: On Agency

> Science turns out to be defined by the deadlocked endeavor to suture the subject.
>
> —Lacan, "Science and Truth"

Agency is a problem, and not only for music. If agency is the capacity of a person or other entity to act in the world, then implicit is the notion of a separate body performing the action. The agent is individual. In human terms, the agent is *an* individual. But already in the nineteenth century, Hegel and Marx began to think of human agency as historical, dynamic, and collective, rather than individual. Marx, for example, refers to capital as if it had agency and volition: "As a capitalist, he is only capital personified. His soul is the soul of capital. But capital has one sole driving force, the drive to valorize itself. . . . Capital is dead labour which, vampire-like, lives only by sucking living labour, and lives the more, the more labour it sucks" (1990: 342). Marx is not playing with words. Capital does not act *as if* it had a soul but *because* it has a soul (an unpleasant one) culled from a collective of individuals. Agency becomes a social structure with forces, and "individual agents are but locations or 'bearers' of such forces" (Green 1998). If we were to seek a controlling consciousness for capital, where would we look? If capital acts through the combined agencies of business, the government, monetary institutions, and so on, can we say that there is a controlling individual who makes the final decision or commands the collective of capital?

Such questions became acute in Foucault's reflections on power and institutions. Foucault's thesis in book after book is that the discourses of institutions in the nineteenth century created types of human subjects. The discourse of the prison created the criminal. The discourse of psychiatry created the insane. And, as Joseph Straus has shown, borrowing from Foucault, the discourse of medicine created the disabled (2006). This formulation does not claim that criminals, or madness, or the disabled only came into being after the nineteenth century. Rather, Foucault's argument is that in the act of studying the criminal, the madman, the disabled, the sexual deviant, and so on, institutions of the nineteenth century used discourses that ended up defining and confining those human subjects under examination. Lacan puts this type of claim in his usual perplexing way: "There is no such thing as a science of man because science's man does not exist, only its subject does" (2006g: 859). There can be no science of man, because science creates the subject (a type of person) in the act of studying what it takes to be man (or, more properly post-Lacan, people).

The discourse of institutions has an agency that creates types of individuals and delimits the boundaries of their behavior; and this disperse agency continues to act in creating subjects today. A recent example is the 2013 update of the *Diagnostic and Statistical Manual of Mental Disorders* (or *DSM-5*), which, among other changes, dropped Asperger syndrome as a classification. With the new publication of *DSM-5*, the Asperger individual ceased to exist. As a Lacanian might phrase it, the subjects with Asperger syndrome act as they do because they have been classified as such, and they have been classified as Asperger subjects because they act as they do. Once the classification is gone, then, so is the Asperger subject. But where can we find the controlling agent that erased the Asperger subject from existence? The cover of *DSM-5* lists the author as the American Psychiatric Association, an institution, and the inside cover attributes authorship to the *DSM-5* Task Force. Is the chair of that task force the controlling agent? Or is there really no controlling agent? Where can we find the agency of this or any other institution?

Tolstoy again. Contemplating the agency of Napoleon's Russian campaign, Tolstoy writes: "The actions of Napoleon and Alexander, on whose word it seems to have depended whether the event [the Russian war] took place or not, were as little willed as the action of each soldier who went into the campaign by lot or by conscription" (2007: 605). In a peculiar way, neither Napoleon nor Alexander willed the events at the battle of Borodino, or at the French army's entrance into Moscow. As Tolstoy explains a bit later:

> There are two sides to each man's life: his personal life, which is the more free the more abstract its interests, and his elemental, swarmlike life, where man inevitably fulfills the laws prescribed for him.
> Man lives consciously for himself, but serves as an unconscious instrument for the achievement of historical, universal goals. (605)

A slight adjustment in this passage would bring Tolstoy's argument in line with Lacan's model of the subject. Where Tolstoy writes of an "unconscious instrument" for which a person "serves," a Lacanian would say that the subject serves the Symbolic, or, more properly, that the subject *obeys* the Symbolic. Further, what a modern subject may take to be the most personal and individual part of the self (their "personal life") is already the product of the Symbolic. Rather than ask how an individual acts in historical, cultural, and interpersonal events, we might ask how those events act in the individual.

If we are to use human agency as a metaphor for musical agency, then, we must be aware of what model of subjectivity results from our conception of music as acting and being acted upon. When Edward T. Cone explains that each agent (performer) in a piece of chamber music experiences their part "under the guidance of the implicit agent, the central intelligence in whose mind all the agents subsist as components," his metaphor invokes a now outdated model of subjectivity that consists of an independent mind capable of controlling its psychological environment (1974: 106). Seth Monahan writes of Cone's model that it is directed toward "experiences of Romantic music and its attendant aesthetic of emotive communication" (2013: 323n.3). Extending Monahan's observation, we could say that Cone's model implies the Romantic composer-as-genius, whose distinctive voice lends him (always him) the very controlling power necessary to collect various agencies into one. Put bluntly, though, subjectivity just doesn't work that way.

When Fred Maus confronts the problem of musical agency, he allows for a more flexible approach to the interacting agencies of notes, themes, performers, composers, and listeners. He writes that we might imagine that the music performs actions, or that the composer presents those actions, or even that the "*performers* are *improvising*," such that there is a "pervasive indeterminacy in the identification of musical agents" (1988: 68). Maus's model is a freer one than Cone's, and the unspoken ideology involves a model of subjectivity that is also more open. That is, human agency is difficult to pinpoint because the human subject is less unified and monologic than Cone allowed; thus, musical agency for Maus follows a different model than it does for Cone.

Monahan admits that Maus's view of musical agency is "incontestable," yet he is compelled (by what? by the Symbolic?) to adjust it, because it paints "a somewhat chaotic picture of our analytical practice, with fictional agents flitting in and out the discursive frame in a kind of interpretive free-for-all, regulated only by the analyst's whim" (2013: 323). We could counter that even the analyst's whim is regulated by a Symbolic order that prizes the idea of objectivity in the first place. Monahan's counter to Maus's work, though, is of a different order than the one above. He lists four "agent classes": the *individuated element* (themes, motives, etc.), the *work-persona* (the entire work, personified), the *fictional composer* (the person that the listener imagines as the composer of the work), and the *analyst* (327–33). In addition, Monahan argues that musical agencies are hierarchical, that lower-level agencies can be subsumed into higher-level ones, and that listeners are adept at moving back and forth from level to level (324).

Monahan works out some brilliant examples, among which is Duke Gonzago's meditation on human agency from Shakespeare's *Hamlet* (338–39). If we are imagining Harold Bloom as the interpreter of this meditation, as Monahan asks us to do, then the lowest-level agent is Gonzago, moving up to the agency of the play itself (*Hamlet*), moving up to the agency of Shakespeare, and concluding with the controlling agency of Bloom. Because the model is hierarchical, we can imagine Gonzago as an agent subsumed under the agency of Hamlet, or Shakespeare, or Bloom. In a later passage, Monahan reconfirms that there can be no hierarchical contradiction in this model: "There is little sense, I think, in regarding Bloom as an 'action' of the fictional Shakespeare, or Shakespeare as the 'action' of Hamlet" (346). Everything is worked out, logical, and beyond reproach from the standpoint of the objectivity we might hope for in hermeneutics. But as with the work on agency by Cone, and Maus, there is an implicit and unspoken conception of the human subject behind Monahan's model. His discourse has created a type of subject.

Before continuing, I would like to point out that I have no quarrel with Monahan's expressed objective to think through how analysts treat musical agency. My intent is to show the ideological implications of his regulating model. Monahan often uses the phrase "chain of command," which is the symptom that can clue us into the type of subjectivity formed through his discourse. Tolstoy refused a "chain of command" as the likely metaphor for agency, and a Lacanian would question it, as well. If the subject is the product of the Symbolic, and if the works of Shakespeare form part of that order, can we not say that Bloom *is* an action of the playwright? More properly, as the analyst we call *Bloom* entered the Symbolic order, he made the forced choice of taking on the English language and its turns of phrase. We could say that Bloom lent the Symbolic his own agency, in order to eradicate what we imagine to be a contradiction in the formation of his subjectivity. From a Lacanian point of view, though, it is more correct to say that the Symbolic impressed itself on Bloom, so that once he took it on, his conscious and unconscious thought became the thought of the Symbolic, including the thought of all those who have entered the Symbolic and remained there in what passes for immortality.

Throughout this book, I have used the concept of the Symbolic as I think Lacan used it: the Symbolic is a monolithic dead letter (language), which forms the subject before birth, demands obedience during life, and continues to be formative even after death. I will now imagine the Symbolic as more multiple than Lacan allows, although it still interacts with individual subjects in various ways that are constrained by language. Thus, Bloom becomes the subject engaged more deeply than others with that part of the Symbolic that we call *Shakespeare*. He reads Shakespeare every day. He reads him all the time. And Shakespeare becomes the agent that acts on him, that is more alive than him. Is it any wonder that Bloom wrote a book about the anxiety of influence? This contradiction in the chain of command also runs at lower levels. If the people who enter our dreams are the others who appear to us as if they have an independent agency (recall the discussion of *Cities of the Plain* from chapter 1), then is it possible that the character of Duke Gonzago might enter Shakespeare's conscious or unconscious thought and act upon him? If Gonzago is a substitute for an other in the life of Shakespeare, is Gonzago an agent subsumed by Shakespeare, or is Shakespeare an agent subsumed by Gonzago?

I am playing with words, and words are playing with me. And it is this play between words and me that uncovers a layer of meaning behind the conventional conception of subjectivity. When we notice the "pervasive indeterminacy" of our language in dealing with musical agency, we may try to set aright what appears out of kilter. In so doing, though, we suture the subject, who, for Lacan, is not whole, unified, and self-determined, but fragmented, decentered, and determined by discourse. The indeterminacy in the language about music is the clue that music knows (notice the agency) what we are and what we are not. If we try to fix the language of musical agency, we have fixed music. (One tries to fix so many things in life.) But music is protean. It will not stay fixed for long. The contradictions that we find in music—a surprising chord is an agent, and an act, and a response, and a telling of the agent and act and response—can point the way to finding a different model of subjectivity. Instead of changing how we think about musical agency, then, we might change how we think about ourselves. Music helps us understand those famous reversals in modern thought: knowledge is not power, power is knowledge (Foucault); men do not think in myths, myths think in men (Lévi-Strauss); we do not use language, language uses us (Lacan). Subjectivity is not a metaphor for musical agency, musical agency is a metaphor for subjectivity: protean, chaotic, and pervasively indeterminate with regard to the agents that populate conscious and unconscious thought.

5 Postmodern Quotation, the Signifying Chain, and the Erasure of History

> For every image of the past that is not recognized by the present as one of its own concerns threatens to disappear irretrievably.
>
> —Walter Benjamin, "Theses on the Philosophy of History"

What Are the Symptoms of Postmodernism?

We can understand the increasing and open use of borrowing in contemporary music, starting in the 1960s and continuing to the present, as a symptom of postmodern culture. Here, I take the term *symptom* in its form prior to Lacan's working out of the *sinthome*: some failure in the Symbolic; some truth about which speech must be delivered. Later in the chapter, I focus particularly on the *signifying chain* that the subject knits together in an attempt to deliver the very speech that leads to an understanding of the symptom. Extending a claim by Fredric Jameson, I argue that one of the symptoms of the postmodern condition is a refusal or inability to make that signifying chain. In other words, postmodernism is a form of schizophrenia, although I do not mean that term in the clinical sense but in the more cultural sense of a breakdown in how we view history. Because postmodernism fails to make a signifying chain, it has managed to erase history in favor of the commodification of culture, or, more properly, the culture of commodification.

It may appear nostalgic or even outdated to mention the term *postmodernism,* especially since the most heated debates over it occurred in the mid-1980s and early 1990s (see Lyotard 1984; Hutcheon 1988; Jameson 1991; McGowan 1991). Postmodern knowledge has become an accepted part of the scholarly landscape in music, especially in what we now would have to call nostalgically the *new musicology.* And within the last decade, there have been a number of articles and book-length studies of postmodern music that foreground the issues of postmodernism and culture (see Auner and Lochhead 2002; Gloag 2012). Perspectives on postmodernism and music range from a denial of the usefulness of its new forms of knowledge (especially in music theory), to acceptance of it as the model for examining the world, to a been-there-done-that desire for us to approach some new -ism.

But the proliferation of postmodern culture has only increased in the past decade. Quentin Tarantino's *Inglourious Basterds* (2009) and *Django Unchained* (2012)—"the *D* is silent"—are counterfactual histories, or, more precisely, simulacra that transform the past into a series of cartoon-like characters and events that disconnect us from the history they pretend to invoke. The fulfillment in You-Tube and reality TV of Andy Warhol's prediction that everyone will be world-famous for fifteen minutes breaks down modernism's pretension to attach fame to the extraordinary achievement or the actions of the elite. The explosion of certain technologies, illustrating Marshall McLuhan's aphorism that "the medium is the message" (the iPhone, the iPad, Facebook, Twitter), plays into postmodernism's refusal to acknowledge a truth content to the signifier. After all, it is not important *what* one posts on Facebook; it is only important *that* one posts on Facebook: witness the preoccupation with posting pictures of one's dinner, or cat, or Venti Frappuccino (with extra whip). And even modernist forms of the media (the news on TV), desperately trying to hang on in the postmodern world, have adopted a fragmented style consistent with postmodernism. One watches the announcer in the center screen, while a banner at the bottom scrolls through other Breaking News!, and a banner atop reveals the latest numbers from the NASDAQ, all while a smaller screen in the upper-right-hand corner introduces the next guest to be interviewed. It is clear that postmodernism has not gone away.

Despite these tokens, one has to agree with Lawrence Kramer that "the term *postmodernism* is something of a catchall and susceptible to mere modishness" (1995: 5). Acknowledging that postmodernism covers more concepts than we can combine into some synthesizing theory, Kramer accepts Lyotard's conception of postmodernism as a form of knowledge that eschews grand, unifying narratives in favor of an unrelenting plurality that breaks down modernism's preoccupation with unity and organicism in the first place (for some time the term *hegemony* was obligatory for wagging one's finger at modernism). And the examples listed above perform the cultural work that Lyotard (and Kramer) associate with postmodernism: they break down hierarchies and grand narratives. As useful as this conception of postmodernism may be, though, we may never form a coherent system to make sense of the postmodern condition. Our ability to understand postmodernism may be a victim of its own distaste for coherent (read *hierarchical*) forms of explanation.

Although Lyotard has been important in defining the postmodern condition, I turn my attention more to Jameson's conception of postmodernism as a "cultural dominant . . . [that] allows for the presence and coexistence of a range of very different, yet subordinate, features," whose logic is a consequence of late capitalism (1991: 4). Jameson refuses to systematize the postmodern, perhaps because that would play against the aims of postmodernity in the first place. Yet the opening chapter of his *Postmodernism, or The Cultural Logic of Late Capitalism* discusses a number of interlocking issues, many of which involve quotation or the broader category of intertextuality that is the topic of this chapter. Among these are the erasure of the boundary between high and low culture, the use of quotation as the substance of an artwork, an emphasis on surface over depth, a refusal to psychologize art, a transformation of alienation into fragmentation, a reliance on a form of irony that turns parody into pastiche, an inability to represent experience without borrowing from the past, and a radicalization of textuality that effaces history. This last issue is what troubles Jameson so much, since the failure to historicize plays within the false consciousness that allows capitalism to run amok in the first place. More precisely, late capitalism, which Ernest Mandel defined as *"a period in which all branches of the economy are fully industrialized for the first time,"* spreads the field of commodification to previously unimagined areas (1999: 191; emphasis in original). When a previous generation (modernists, for sure) wanted advice on which mechanic to use, they asked their neighbors; they would not have dreamt of using a computer to ask someone they did not know (named Angie) to collect the advice of people *she* did not know (and pay for that advice, no less). What used to be free advice has become commodified (Angie might say that "you get what you pay for"). And if virtually everything is a commodity, then capitalism must find new ways to hide the means of production and the contradictions at play. Those contradictions, first enumerated by Marx, include once familiar but now repressed aphorisms: technology never shortened the working day (employers simply make fewer laborers do the work of the many); unemployment is desirable because it lowers the cost of labor; people are alienated from the things they produce (do you know who made that iPad you use every day?); capitalism does not fulfill desires, it creates them (when the late Steve Jobs released the first iPad, he admitted that he didn't know what consumers would do with it). Thus the consequences of postmodernism include endeavors to hide the author, his or her style, the unconscious, and, most importantly, the history and ideology within which we all labor, form our identity, and recognize, as Lacan writes, that the subject's "unconscious is his history" (2006a: 217).

A brief example is in order. John Zorn's *Road Runner* for solo accordion (1985) features a series of quotations from a large variety of pieces and genres. The score refers visually to its eponymous cartoon character (the Road Runner) and his nemesis (Wile E. Coyote) with cutouts from comic books, including dialogue balloons with words like *Twang* and *Womp!* The score also features controlled aleatorism in the form of directions to the performer, like "quote Beethoven" and "quote tango," which are interspersed with indications such as "go crazy for two seconds." The references to cartoons in the score and the rapid-fire cuts from one quotation to another have always been a part of Zorn's compositional technique. He has singled out the music of Carl Stalling and Scott Bradley, composers of cartoon music for Warner Bros. in the 1940s, as being influential in his musical outlook (Duckworth 1995: 444). When describing his creative process, Zorn admits, "I write music with the TV on or with music playing, and I work things out"

(Duckworth 1995: 449). As such, *Road Runner* is one of a large collection of his works that relies on collage, quotation, allusion, and a mix of high and mass culture, avoiding the anxiety of contamination that Andreas Huyssen reads in the attitudes of modernism toward popular culture (1986: vii).

Since a performer can realize *Road Runner* in an infinite number of ways within the parameters that Zorn sets, I refer to a particular performance by Branko Dzinovic (see Zorn). Dzinovic begins the piece with a low note, followed by a percussive knock on the accordion, some chromatic noodling in the high register, a quick back-and-forth motion of the bellows (without pitch), and more chromatic noodling before the series of quotations and allusions begins. Each of the introductory sounds, and the quotations themselves, lasts only a few seconds. Among the quotations and allusions are portions of the Hungarian Rhapsody no. 2 by Liszt, the theme song from the French film *Un homme et une femme* (A man and a woman) by Francis Lai, *The Flight of the Bumblebee* by Rimsky-Korsakov, a tango, the theme from the television show *Dragnet,* the German children's song "Mein Hut, der hat drei Ecken," a portion of *Il barbiere di Siviglia* by Rossini, the "Russian Dance" from *Petrushka* by Stravinsky, the opening of the Symphony no. 5 by Beethoven, and so on. The quotations sometimes move from one to another in a seamless manner, but most often they are cut short by a knock on the accordion, a glissando, a dissonant chord, or wild dashing across the keyboard. Although the quotes are from famous pieces of music, the listener has precious little time to identify each one before a breaking device ushers in another quote. Because the quotes are so brief, it is possible that some listeners are able to do little more than realize that they're hearing familiar musical objects without being able to identify them precisely.

As part of an effort to reposition Zorn's music as avant-garde rather than postmodernist, John Bracket claims that in the collage pieces, like *Road Runner,* the composer "is not interested in a 'name that tune' game of listening (or, for that matter, analysis)" (2008: 119). Instead, we are meant to recognize that the quotation has lost its allusive impact to become material for manipulation. The listener committed to postmodern knowledge could reply that it doesn't matter where Zorn's interest lies in stitching together quotes culled from across cultures, time periods, and styles; once the work is released, it becomes a text open to whatever interpretation a listener will make of it. Even trying to adhere to Zorn's intent, though, I find it difficult to avoid the "name that tune" game. The fact that the quotes are often so brief only adds to the fun. What is apparent, whether we play the game or not, is that *Road Runner* refuses to integrate its various quotes into a logical musical discourse, and that it erases the boundary between high and low culture. If we read the inclusion of movie music, television music, and popular songs as a form of irony that undercuts the stuffy elitism of high culture, we soon reach the conclusion that the form of irony employed is a postmodern one, which "acknowledges that all we have are competing contexts and that any implied 'other' position would itself be a context" (Colebrook 2006: 164). In other words, this music does not overturn the high/low opposition to valorize the popular; rather, it equalizes the poles of that opposition so that the detritus of music history becomes the material of the work, regardless of its original place in the aesthetics of high/low art.

The substance of *Road Runner* is a series of quotations, although one could argue that the cutting devices (the knocking of the fist on the accordion, the cluster chords, etc.) are also part of the music's substance. Regarding a similar work by Zorn, *Spillane* (1986), Susan McClary argues that the title's reference to films noirs that take place in 1940s Los Angeles invokes a "narrative schema easily followed by anyone acquainted with urban pulp fiction and the Hollywood movies that translated that genre to the screen" (2000: 146). Similarly, one could hear *Road Runner* as the sound track of a missing cartoon, where the cutting devices are indexical signs of the violence that typically comes to Wile E. Coyote after his attempts to capture the Road Runner backfire. Such an interpretation makes *Road Runner* a quotation of a quotation: a work that quotes the narrative technique of an art form whose sound tracks themselves are tissues of quotations. The postmodern irony, then, extends even to the popular cartoon, as *Road Runner* parodies a genre that parodies the various *peripeteias* of narrative.

The tissue of quotations, an apt metaphor in more ways than one, makes *Road Runner* a flat musical work. There is no depth to the music in the structuralist sense. One is not tempted to place the quotations in a hierarchy or to find a master quote that organizes all the others. The music is all surface, refusing to acknowledge modernity's model of subjectivity, which rests on the notion of interiority. For the Freudian subject, each cultural reference in a dream points to a latent content, which itself leads deeper and deeper through layers of interpretation to the primal scene in the patient's history. But the postmodern subject has no psychology; there is no latent content behind the manifest content of a cultural reference. There is only the quotation itself as it jostles with the surrounding quotations and allusions. If the modern subject suffered from alienation, both in the Marxist and Freudian senses, the postmodern subject suffers from fragmentation, a condition that Lacan uncovered as the necessary price we all pay to become subjects in the first place. In Zorn's music, unmoored bits of culture float by to stand in for our only substance, making *Road Runner* a radical textuality, an intertextuality, that erases the composer and thwarts the historicity of its fragmented elements.

This brief discussion is not meant as a negative or positive appraisal of *Road Runner,* although such strategies are common in discussions of postmodern culture. When McClary describes Zorn's music, for example, she does so within a larger argument that postmodern composition ought to be upheld as a model whose practices are "as vital as those of any other moment in cultural history" (2000: 141). But McClary must face the problem that Zorn's music sometimes includes erotic and violent depictions of Asian women. Coming to the composer's rescue, McClary explains that the composer lived in Japan and was obsessed with the S&M scene there. In addition, she argues that she would rather be in a culture where new music spurs controversy than one where premieres are greeted by silence (150–51). Thus, postmodernism saves us from the problems of modernism, except when it doesn't. As such, the strategy of placing postmodernism in opposition to modernism in forming the far points of ideology turns out to be unhelpful. Once this strategy is set, the game is up, and the possible arguments stand before us like moves in a chess game. One is either pro-postmodern because it represents some corrective swerve from the problems of modernism, or one is anti-postmodern because it has turned our attention from the vital utopianism of modernism. And these positions find their contraries in pro-modernism or anti-modernism. One either denies that postmodernism is a cultural dominant in the first place (modernism still rules the day), or one acknowledges the problems of modernism while believing that the answers to those problems cannot be found in postmodernism (Jameson 1991: 55–66): "The point is that we are *within* the culture of postmodernism to the point where its facile repudiation is as impossible as any equally facile celebration of it is complacent and corrupt" (62). Zorn's music enacts what it does because it is within the culture of postmodernism. As such, it is pointless to bemoan a loss of the values of modernism or to praise some new set of values deemed as a corrective swerve from the problems of modernism. The task at hand is to understand some of the conditions that made a piece like *Road Runner* a possibility in the first place and to see what effect postmodern culture has on our ability to grasp the historical position in which we find ourselves.

How Did We Move from the Work to the Text? (or Intertextuality Revisited)

One feature of postmodernism is its denial of the work concept in favor of a radical textuality, an intertextuality, that values the reader as much as the author. For Jameson, the beginning of the postmodern era coincides with "the 'end of the work of art' and the arrival of the text" (1991: xvii). Briefly, borrowing from Roland Barthes (1981), we can define a *work* as a document tied to its cultural/historical point of origin, its author, and his/her intentions, while a *text* is anything open to interpretation, often without regard to the author's intent, which is another text that is often opaque in the first place. Like all oppositions, this one is apt to collapse: whenever we take a text for interpretation, we end up solidifying it into an object that is work-like; and whenever we attempt to hold limitless interpretation at bay in pursuit of maintaining the work status, we find it impossible to close off the effects of textuality. The rise of textuality has a history that is well known in literary theory (see Clayton and Rothstein 1991), and elsewhere I have discussed its implications for music (Klein 2005: 11–17). As we shall see, though, musicology and theory often ignore or misunderstand textuality in order to uphold a modernist view of subjectivity and interpretation.

Briefly, the conception of the artwork in the nineteenth century involved the unified consciousness of an author who produced a stable work with a singular meaning that the reader could uncover given the proper background in philology, which relied on historical knowledge to map what we now call *signifiers* onto *signifieds*. By the last half of the twentieth century, this conception was turned on its head. The artwork now involves the labor of an author with a decentered consciousness, whose product is a text open to a number of meanings that depend on the labor of a reader who must make do with a signifying system that maps one signifier onto multiple signifieds in a vast, flat web of signification. In the earlier conception, the author had a unified consciousness capable of understanding his interiority (always *his* in the nineteenth century) as separate from the external world. The work was imagined to be closed and stable, like the subjectivity of the author, with a singular meaning tied to the author's consciousness. It is only from a later standpoint that we can see how fraught the relationship between the nineteenth-century author and his work really were. The mode of interpretation under the nineteenth-century ideology included a stable system, in which the reader simply accepted the signs of the work unidirectionally. In the later conception, the author has a decentered consciousness, permeable to the surrounding outside world (the Symbolic). The work has become a text, open and unstable because the author cannot control a semiotic system that maps one signifier onto multiple signifieds. And the mode of interpretation is equally slippery, because the reader must labor to make sense of the text. In Jean-Jacques Nattiez's terms (borrowing from Jean Molino), understanding a text does not run in a single direction from the author/composer through the work to the reader/listener, who receives an uncontestable meaning (1990). Rather, the author/composer creates a text that the reader/listener must interpret with the sign system that she has at hand. If there is a stability to the work, then, where can it be found? Is it in the mind of the composer, whose consciousness was never unified in the first place? Is it in the work itself (the score, or the sounding music), whose signs are as dispersed as the unconscious of the author? Is it in the listener, whose own consciousness is alienated, and whose network of signs may well make of the work something undreamt in the composer's philosophy? The answer in postmodernism is that there is no work; there is only a text, a commodity open to the various interpretive strategies of each reader/listener.

The problem of the open text has made its way into postmodern narratives in the form of a marked uncertainty within the story itself. In Ian McEwan's novel *Atonement* (2001), for example, we are presented with various versions of the same story, leaving the reader to ponder the fiction *as* fiction and to wonder if there ever was a single uncontestable reality to be told in the first place. In Yann Martel's *Life of Pi* (2001), the title character, Piscine Molitor, renders two versions of his travails after a shipwreck. When asked which version is the true one, he simply tells the fictional writer who will tell his tale to choose the one he likes better. One could counter that such uncertainties were a mark of modernism, as well. William Faulkner's *As I Lay Dying*, for example, presents a story through multiple narrators and viewpoints. But if the problem of modernism is a loss of faith in the power of narration itself, or, as Lawrence Kramer puts it, a transformation of narrative into "a version of Lacan's *objet petit a*, the locus of a desire that at best must accept its endless deferral in lieu of fulfillment" (2013: 165), then the problem of postmodernism is a loss of faith in the very reality that a narrative hopes to create. The problem is not one of representation, in which narrative simply cannot do the job, but of reality itself, in which the open text ironically calls for the author to uncover the secret and wave a simulacrum of the *objet petit a* in front of the reader as a sign that the endless deferral of fulfillment lies within an ahistorical reality that refuses to be told. A character in Haruki Murakami's *1Q84* (2011) expresses the conventional wisdom that "there's always only one reality," despite which the novel proceeds to uncover several realities whose first hint comes in the Q of the title itself.

The historical transformation of the work to the text supported ideologies that upheld what Foucault called a *power relation,* "which has its principle not so much in a person as in a certain distribution of bodies, surfaces, lights, gazes; in an arrangement whose internal mechanisms produce the relation in which individuals are caught up" (1977: 202). More simply, people have a place in a social structure, which, in Lacanian terms, is guaranteed by the Symbolic. Bodies (notice that Foucault does not use the more humanizing term, *people*) have their place in this structure, even when they fight against it. In the nineteenth century, for example, the work concept, with its notion that the composer had a unique, closed, and visionary consciousness tied univocally to what we now call *the music itself,* supported a power relation similar to that of the bourgeois structure of society. The composer, like the factory owner, is a controlling consciousness with relation to the performers and listeners: the laborers who are alienated from the very effort they expend to bring the music to life. The composer is primary in the power relation among composers, performers, and listeners: a parallel to the primary place that the bourgeois class has with relation to labor. Once the text concept replaces the work concept, we see a change in the power relation between the composer, the performer, and the listeners. The postmodern author/composer no longer holds the primary position in the production and understanding of the text. There is general agreement, at least among literary scholars, that we must acknowledge the labor that readers/listeners perform in order to make the text meaningful. The larger question is how to understand this new acknowledgment of the reader's labor in terms of the social power relations at play in postmodern society.

To answer this question, we can turn to the changing conception of influence, borrowing, and allusion in postmodern texts. Under the modernist model, influence and quotation/allusion involved dyads of transmission. That is, one author/composer borrowed from another while transforming the precursor's work both to hide the line of influence and to uphold a model of subjectivity in which the composer had access to a unique form of interiority. Charles Rosen nicely articulates the ideology of this model when he writes that in some forms of borrowing there is a "transformation of a model which is so complete that it is almost undetectable and certainly unprovable without a signed affidavit from the composer admitting the borrowing" (1980: 100). Although critics of the mid-nineteenth century recognized that composers often made allusions to the works of other composers, they bemoaned the seeking out of such allusions as a practice that distracted the listener from understanding the unity of the musical work (Reynolds 2003: 2–5). This model of influence, entailing the hiding of one's precursors, was in circulation as late as Harold Bloom's theory of the *anxiety of influence,* in which strong poets gain their strength through an Oedipal struggle with the works of earlier poets (1973). Separately, Joseph Straus (1990) and Kevin Korsyn (1991) made significant extensions of Bloom's work in terms of music. Although Bloom's conception of influence is nuanced, especially with its Freudian aspect, it still upholds an ideology of the author as possessing a special subjectivity that is closed off from the outside world and that controls a work.

A significant change to our understanding of borrowing/influence came with M. M. Bakhtin, whose theory of the novel questioned the idea that the author's voice was univocal (or what he would have called *monologic*): "The novel can be defined as a diversity of social speech types (sometimes even diversity of languages) and a diversity of individual voices, artistically organized" (1981: 262). Instead of organizing borrowings and allusions of the author into a singular voice, Bakhtin embraced the various voices of the novel, although he still insisted on its overall stylistic unity. As an author writes, the speech of another enters his or her discourse, resulting in a double transformation: the authorial voice is changed by the voice of the other, and the voice of the other is changed by the authorial voice. The result is what Bakhtin called *double-voiced* discourse. Although this model sounds suspiciously like Bloom's anxiety of influence, Bakhtin's model views an author's work as the product of a number of different discourses and voices. The one-to-one relationship implicit in Bloom's theory becomes a many-to-one relationship.

Bakhtin's conception of the novel had an impact on Julia Kristeva, whose well-known definition of the text makes clear that it is shot through with quotations, allusions, and influences:

> The text is therefore a productivity, and this means: first, that its relationship to the language in which it is situated is redistributive (deconstructive-constructive), and hence can be better approached through logical categories rather than linguistic ones; and second, that it is a permutation of texts, an intertextuality: in the space of a given text, several utterances, taken from other texts, intersect and neutralize one another. (1980: 36)

Despite a reference to productivity with its implications of agency, the work concept is absent from Kristeva's definition. For Kristeva there is only the text, which is any cultural item open to interpretation: a book, an essay, a painting, music, a map, the furniture in a room, the clothing we wear, the gestures we make, the thoughts we think, and so on. The author is also absent from Kristeva's formulation. We are all authors in the sense that we are all interpreters of texts. Finally, the implicit idea is that we, too, are texts. What we take to be the unconscious is the product of culture, which, like all sign systems, cannot find a fixed place. Or, as we have seen in the words of Lacan, *"the unconscious is the Other's discourse"* (2006h: 10).

As if in response to a new paradigm that recognized the rise of the text at the expense of the work, the late twentieth century more openly displayed quotation without a singular voice that could act as a unifying style. The desire to hide quoted material no longer exists as a cultural dominant in postmodernism. Or, as Linda Hutcheon argues, if "a literary work can actually no longer be considered original . . . [then] this theoretical redefining of aesthetic value has coincided with a change in the kind of art being produced" (1988: 126). Hutcheon's argument includes a quote by George Rochberg, who claims that he had to abandon the notion of originality in writing his String Quartet no. 3, a piece to which we shall return. Jameson is more comprehensive in theorizing the end of the author as primary in producing the text and in discussing the implications for the subject and the problem of originality. For Jameson, postmodernism marks "the end of the autonomous bourgeois monad or ego or individual," but it also "means the end of much more—the end, for example, of style, in the sense of the unique and the personal, the end of the distinctive individual brush stroke (as symbolized by the emergent primacy of mechanical reproduction)" (1991: 15). The open borrowing of material in the postmodern artwork entails the end of the type of personal style that results from hiding and transforming quoted material. The quotes are laid bare, and any personal style comes from a form of arrangement, collage, or interpenetration of genres.

This loss of style is recognized among a few musicologists who work with postmodern music. In an analysis of the many quotations and cultural allusions in Mauricio Kagel's *Die Stücke der Windrose für Salonorchester,* for example, Björn Heile notes that "what is crucial in this context is that the authorial discourse does not assert itself as a personal voice, since there is no single musical element in the example which can unmistakably be described as 'Kagel's music'" (2004: 67). Heile realizes that because Kagel alludes to so many musical discourses, "authorship mostly manifests itself by the selection, combination and inflection of pre-existing musical idioms, not by the assumption of a 'personal voice'" (68). The term *composition* takes on its original meaning: to arrange, organize, put together. And the author function loses the aura of a special and secretive process that can underscore the genius of the creator.

Despite the recognition that open quotation makes it difficult to pin down a composer's style, Heile still tries to rescue Kagel's music from the marks of postmodernism by borrowing Bakhtin's idea of double-voiced discourse. But Bakhtin theorizes this concept under the ideology of a unified work and a voice of the author that happens to include and respond to the voices of other authors and discourses. Bakhtin was recognizing a new form of subjectivity without taking the steps that Lacan would take to argue that the subject was never whole or separate from the Symbolic in the first place. In order for double-voiced discourse to work for postmodern music, one must be able to identify a style in the music of a composer to begin with. Otherwise, what is really at play is the more open and impersonal concept of intertextuality. But this is precisely the concept that many want to avoid in discussing postmodern music, because it denies the singular and humanist agency that we have grown accustomed to thinking about when we discuss a composer and his or her music.

This refusal to let go of an older form of subjectivity has one of its clearest expressions in Richard Taruskin's preface to *Defining Russia Musically*. In a discussion of the mythographic attitude that Slavists take toward cultural theorizing, especially otherness, Taruskin, quoting Clare Cavanagh, cautions that Barthes's "death of the author" has a literal meaning for the Slavist. "It also undoes our capacity, I should say, to ignore the heartless complacency and the frivolity that informs this vein of antihumanistic theorizing" (1997: xxix n.43). The key word in this argument is "antihumanist," which no one wants to be. The oft-quoted passage for this idea of "antihumanist theorizing" appears at the end of Foucault's *The Order of Things*:

> One thing in any case is certain: man is neither the oldest nor the most constant problem that has been posed for human knowledge. Taking a relatively short chronological sample within a restricted geographical area—European culture since the sixteenth century—one can be certain that man is a recent invention within it. . . . As the archaeology of our thought easily shows, man is an invention of recent date. And one perhaps nearing its end. (1994: 386–87)

As Kramer is quick to point out, though, Foucault himself writes that these are not affirmations but questions. Kramer rightly adds: "A subject decentered is a subject still" (1995: 10). And this is the point. Foucault is not saying that there is no such thing as personhood in what we now call the postmodern era; he is arguing that an older conception of personhood, subjectivity, is going away. Despite Barthes's provocative phrase *the death of the author,* the question is not whether the author, or more broadly the subject, has disappeared for good. The question is what kind of subject has come to take the place of a form of subjectivity that Foucault called "a recent invention." Humanism sounds virtuous with its emphasis on self-determination, individual thought, and non-faith-based ethics of behavior, but humanism itself rests on an ideology of subjectivity that may not be accurate. To acknowledge that the subject has less power of self-determination is not anti-humanist or the mark of frivolity but the desire to see what kind of subjectivity is really at play in contemporary culture.

How Does the Simulacrum Play into the Loss of Style?

The impulse to use quotations and allusions as the primary material of music has not disappeared with the 1960s. If anything, the idea that all of culture is up for grabs in putting together new commodities has exploded in ways that Jameson probably did not imagine when he theorized postmodernism in the late 1980s, before internet culture made the proliferation of memes and the production of mash-ups a prevalent form of creative activity. For example, one popular video on YouTube features a techno remix of a leitmotif from the sound track of *The Lord of the Rings* (see "Taking the Hobbits"). As the leitmotif plays on a loop, the video portion primarily repeats a scene from *The Two Towers,* where the character Legolas shouts, "They're taking the Hobbits to Isengard!" The result is a parody of the epic seriousness of the movie. The video was posted by Aaron Hardbarger, who includes a note that reads "(not my work)." But in postmodern culture, it often does not matter whose labor is involved, because there is no style that we can associate with one collage of quotations as opposed to another. In the Marxist sense, through the pervasive use of quotation to eliminate the modernist concept of style, postmodern culture has found a way to hide the labor of those who create artistic forms.

The mixing of allusions and quotations is not just a matter of postmodern popular culture and its preoccupation with new forms of creativity cultivated by technology and internet culture. We can find postmodern allusion in contemporary performances of art music, as well. Another YouTube video features a live performance by Gilles Apap playing his own cadenza to the final movement of Mozart's Violin Concerto no. 3 (see Apap). During the cadenza, Apap quickly departs from the sound world of the eighteenth century, stringing together a number of allusions to popular and folk music. We hear Irish and Hungarian styles of playing, as well as hints of Blues and Bluegrass. Early in the cadenza, Apap whistles a tune, accompanying himself with the violin, played as if it were a guitar. At another point, Apap even sings in a Blues style: "I woke up this morning. Going to play Mozart." The cadenza concludes with a return to one of the themes from Mozart's concerto. Still, Apap cannot resist tossing in a quotation from Mendelssohn's Violin Concerto and another from Tchaikovsky's Violin Concerto. The cadenza as a whole lasts longer than the surrounding movement. And when Apap finally finishes the cadenza, Mozart's voice and style sound odd and out of place, a form of defamiliarization that underscores the historical distance of Enlightenment culture from the postmodern one, while refusing to traverse that distance in any way that could make a logical connection between our current condition and that of our heritage. We can see the effects of this defamiliarization in the reactions of the orchestra members as Apap performs the cadenza. As if to show where they stand in the modern/postmodern divide, some members of the orchestra laugh or smile, and others frown in disgust. Although the cadenza illustrates an incredible virtuosity and improvisatory skill, it manages to parody the high seriousness of the typical classical concert, breaking down the high/low opposition in music.

If postmodernism is still with us, we may well ask when it started, at least for music. Taruskin is clear about this question: the story of postmodernism in music "begins (or we can begin effectively to tell it) with the first performance, on May 15, 1972, of the String Quartet no. 3 by George Rochberg (1918–2005)" (2013). Taruskin offers an excellent analysis of this piece, its cultural and aesthetic issues, and its connection to postmodernism. The problems of Rochberg's String Quartet no. 3—particularly its refusal to update the various styles it borrows—have been a recurring theme in the debates over postmodern music since its premiere. Still, a brief review of the piece and those issues is in order.

First movement ("Modernist")

I. Introduction: Fantasia

Allegro fantastico; violente; furioso (♩* ca.176)

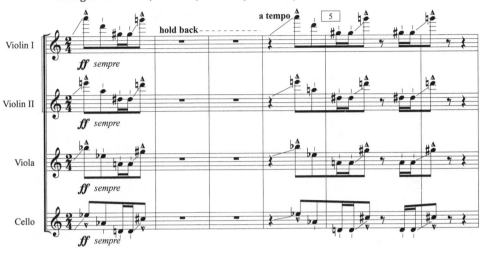

Example 5.1. Rochberg, String Quartet no. 3 (incipits from the five movements)

The quartet is in five movements that create an arch form reminiscent of Bartók's String Quartets nos. 4 and 5. The first movement, the most modernist in the quartet, uses material that returns at the end of the fifth movement (Example 5.1). The second and fourth movements are both marches that sound like spot-on copies (more than simple allusions) of the music of Bartók. At the center of the quartet, the third movement is a theme and variations, imitating Beethoven's late-quartet style with remarkable accuracy. In addition to the obvious replicas of the music of Bartók and Beethoven, the final movement includes the voice of Mahler and a section that closely resembles the fugal passages in the last movement of Beethoven's *Razumovsky* Quartet op. 59, no. 3.

The use of quotation, even in extended passages, was nothing new. Luciano Berio's *Sinfonia* (1969) includes quotations from the music of Beethoven, Berg, Debussy, Mahler, Schoenberg, and many others. And Rochberg's own *Music for the Magic Theater* (1965) uses a collage technique, quoting music of Mozart, Beethoven, Mahler, Webern, Varèse, Stockhausen, and Miles Davis. But these earlier collage pieces, and others like them, surrounded the quotations with ironic musical commentary, or more modernist techniques. In the case of Rochberg's String Quartet no. 3 there is no modernist commentary or transformation; the composers he imitates stand before us as if they have arrived through a time machine.

Second movement ("Bartók")

II. March

Spirited; but grotesque and macabre ($\quad$ = ca. 160-176)

Example 5.1, *continued*

Third movement ("Beethoven")

Rochberg's refusal to transform the composers he imitated was the crux of the matter. In a review of the first recording of the third quartet, Hugh Wood began by remarking on the "alarming expertise" with which Rochberg reproduced the styles of Beethoven and Mahler (1974: 23). But soon enough Wood called the quartet "an awful hotch-potch," and, comparing Rochberg's approach to that of Peter Maxwell Davies, he argued that there is nothing in the third quartet that "raises it above the pastel insipidity of a thousand examples of pastiche" (24). Steven D. Block complained of a similar problem, not only in Rochberg's String Quartet no. 3 but also in his quartets nos. 4–6. Although Block admitted that "there probably aren't many other composers who could match his [Rochberg's] impeccable ability to convince the listener that he is hearing another's music," he concluded that Rochberg's string quartets represented a "necessarily unsuccess-

Fourth movement (Bartók - reprise)

IV. March

Spirited; but grotesque and macabre; precise tempo of II (♩ = 138)

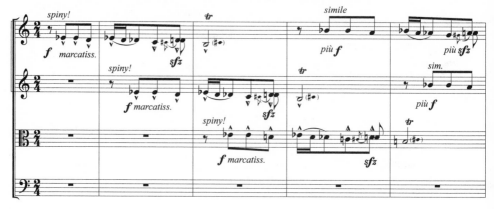

Fifth movement, end ("Modernist" - reprise)

Vivacissimo! Violent! (♩ = ca. 176)

Example 5.1, *continued*

ful attempt to totally recapture a spirit that is not his own and to which he adds nothing" (1982: 408, 409).

Rochberg also had his defenders. Jay Reise argued that behind the changes in style in the first movement of Rochberg's third quartet there was still an underlying unifying principle that required an attention to the interval content of the opening modernist gesture and its connection to the more tonal sections of that movement (1981). One implication of Reise's defense of Rochberg is that the problem of even a collage work can be solved by recourse to the analytical methodologies that music theory developed for modernism. Neither Reise nor the critics of Rochberg's music recognized that the stylistic imitation was the mark of a new paradigm called *postmodernism*. But even after Rochberg's music was recognized as postmodernist, there were attempts to cure the problems of the collage technique by uncovering some unifying principle via music analysis. Catherine Losada, for example, develops a theory of modulation (in a loose sense of that term), showing connections between the various quotations in Berio's *Sinfonia*, Rochberg's *Music for the Magic Theater,* and Bernd Alois Zimmermann's *Musique pour les soupers du Roi Ubu* (2008). Recognizing that these pieces are arguably postmodern, Losada takes a stance that since postmodern works tend to avoid organic unity, if we can find such a unity, a musical work is not postmodern. Further, since postmodernist techniques tend to resist modernist ones, and since modernism itself relies on forms of resistance, postmodernism disappears into an extension of modernism (2008: 297). Heile resorted to parallel arguments to rescue Kagel's music from the marks of postmodernism in that composer's open use of quotation and allusion.

But postmodernism does not need saving, and postmodern music does not need analysis to force it back into a historical category to which it does not belong. Postmodernism is a change in subjectivity, especially in the way that it understands history. Although Wood failed to recognize that Rochberg's music belonged to a new paradigm, he rightly pointed out two characteristics of the composer's remarkable ability to imitate other styles: music had become pastiche, and Rochberg had added nothing to the spirit of the past. As Taruskin recognizes, by abandoning the notion of originality, Rochberg had hit upon a bleak choice: "either renounce expression altogether or borrow a voice" (2013). Further, this borrowed voice is nothing but a *simulacrum,* which in Jean Baudrillard's conception is a copy of something that never existed: "it has no relation to any reality whatsoever" (1994: 6). The simulacrum has no reality because it hides a truth that there is no reality to represent. The point is not that there was no Beethoven, or Mahler, or Bartók, whose music could form the model for a copy. The point is that Rochberg uses a copy of the music of those composers to represent what could no longer be represented. One of the discoveries of postmodernism, then, is that we cannot represent our current experience; we can only borrow from the past to do so (Jameson 1991: 66).

Ironically, Rochberg's eventual turn to the musical simulacrum had its motivation in a growing dissatisfaction with the techniques of high modernism (Gillmor 2009). In a letter of 9 September 1961 to Istvan Anhalt, Rochberg expressed his reaction to a concert in New York, where he heard music of Babbitt, Carter, and Kirchner:

> I came away from the concert feeling one overpowering dissatisfaction: namely, the inability of any of the three composers to make a passionate statement, to produce vibrant music that catches you up & does not let go until it has said all it intends to. In short the burning intensity of a Beethoven or Mahler or the dark somber intensity of a Brahms or the bite of a Schoenberg or Varèse are not there because the engagement with life & reality which produces suffering is not there. (2007: 5)

Unable to find in modernism the means to express anything of the "life & reality which produces suffering," Rochberg turned to the past. And his view of the past and the way a composer ought to approach it was qualitatively different from the usual teleological one. In his essay "No Center" from *The Aesthetics of Survival*, Rochberg argued for a form of creativity based on *ars combinatoria,* because, quoting Rilke, he found that "we . . . were unable to change anyone" (1969: 130). And later, "the art of combination is an attitude, and exploration of deep inner space, mental space" (130). From this point on in Rochberg's writings, we see frequent reference to the *ars combinatoria* that marked his compositions from the 1960s onward.

But it was Rochberg's view of the "deep inner space, mental space" that illustrated the change in historical perspective that we now associate with postmodernism: "I stand in a circle of time, not on a line. 360 degrees of past, present, future. All around me. I can look in any direction I want to. Bella Vista" (132). To make clear that this view of history is not like the old one, Rochberg characterizes the older conception of the past in the next paragraph of his essay: "Time. History. Series of stepwise stages of evolution. Linear view. Cause and effect. The logic of events. Systematization with blinders" (132). Systematization with blinders: this was Rochberg's view of modernism's approach to history, with its linear view, stepwise stages of evolution, and an ever-onward ethos that left the past in the dust. Rochberg's new conception, a 360-degree view of the past, present, and future all available to him, all up for grabs, could well stand as another definition of Julia Kristeva's *intertextuality:* a "permutation of texts" that "neutralize one another." Rochberg did not revive history; he was not picking up a convention, a musical topic, in order to update it and reconfigure its expressive meaning. Roger Scruton illustrates such a creative impulse by considering the musical turn and how it was a "pure ornament in seventeenth-century music," to become an "effect of grace" in Bach, an independent "free and open character" in Mozart, a "major structural motif" in Beethoven, an "expression of a transcendental desire" in Wagner, and so on (1997: 482). Rochberg's conception of borrowing and quotation is not part of this approach to the past. Instead, Rochberg created a simulacrum of the past that detached the cultural issues and expressive troping of Beethoven, or Brahms, or Mahler from the music to leave the listener with a musical past divorced from history. "The past is thereby itself modified: what was once . . . the retrospective dimension indispensable to any vital reorientation of our collective future ... has meanwhile itself become a vast collection of images, a multitudinous photographic simulacrum" (Jameson 1991: 18). Rochberg's history, postmodernism's history, is fragmentary and aleatoric; it stands in for a present that can no longer represent itself to itself.

How Did Stravinsky Bring about the
Loss of Utopian Visions?

Returning to the qualitative differences between borrowing in modernism and postmodernism, we cannot be content to note that postmodernism is more open about borrowing. Taking only one example from modernism, Stravinsky's *Petrushka*, we find that the music moves cinematically from style to style, quote to quote. "So overtly and conspicuously does the score rely on folk and popular tunes of the most familiar sort, and so gaudily are these artifacts of everyday life displayed on the bright surface of the music, that discussion of the ballet's musical texture can easily degenerate into list making" (Taruskin 1996: 695). Taruskin does give us a list of the borrowed material in *Petrushka*, including street vendors' cries, many folk songs, and Émile Spencer's street song *La jambe en Bois*. The ballet mixes quotes from high and low culture, moves through borrowed material without transitions, and does little to hide the quotes. In other words, if we think in terms of open versus closed versions of borrowing, then Stravinsky's *Petrushka* has the marks of postmodernism.

In understanding modern and postmodern forms of borrowing, though, we need to look past the open or closed quotation and toward each era's approach to history. When postmodernism looks to the past, it tends to "obliterate difference and to project an idea of the historical period as massive homogeneity" (Jameson 1991: 3–4). What for modernism was a dialogue with the voices of the past, indispensable for a vision of the future, has become for postmodernism a vast museum of images open to pastiche. Recall that the past as a massive homogeneity, flat and graspable in any direction, was Rochberg's own understanding of musical history. Despite its open use of borrowed material from high and low culture, Stravinsky's *Petrushka* stands as a token of modernism because it attempts to capture the carnival atmosphere of the Russian Shrovetide revelry; that is, the ballet is more than a collection of citations. And *Petrushka* is enmeshed in the historical problems of modernism. Regarding the problem of the human and the automaton, the ballet offers the three puppets, whose emotional range far exceeds the empty displays of the Shrovetide crowd. Regarding the problem of space/time, the ballet features the middle tableaux, where the characters are trapped in their boxes (the enclosure). Regarding the problem of science and religion, the ballet concludes with Petrushka's ironic resurrection, which is negated when his frightening reappearance disintegrates the music into a whimpering alternation of two chords. The borrowed material in *Petrushka* marks the ballet as modernist, because the quotations are situated in the historical period of Stravinsky's Russia, while their apparent resistance to narrative coherence continues the nineteenth century's questioning of Enlightenment values.

But the eclecticism of Stravinsky's later music tended to hide history in a veil of ironically jostling allusions. Adapting a theory of literary borrowing from Thomas Greene's *The Light in Troy*, Martha Hyde uses Stravinsky's music as an example of eclectic imitation, "which treats the musical past as an undifferentiated stockpile to be drawn on at will" (1996: 211). Acknowledging the virtuosity with which Stravinsky plunders history, Hyde nevertheless argues that eclectic imitation plays against the deeper engagement with the past that can show a way to the future. And it is this same conclusion that Jameson reaches when he considers Adorno's famous opposition between Schoenberg and Stravinsky:

> It would therefore begin to seem that Adorno's prophetic diagnosis has been realized, albeit in a negative way: not Schönberg . . . but Stravinsky is the true precursor of postmodern cultural production. For with the collapse of the high-modernist ideology of style . . . the producers of culture have nowhere to turn but to the past: the imitation of dead styles, speech through all the masks and voices stored up in the imaginary museum of a new global culture. (1991: 17–18)

Jameson's imaginary museum of postmodern culture, culled from the past while bereft of history, entails the negation of any utopian possibilities. Without an understanding of the historical positioning of a quote, the tissue of citations cannot lead to a future possibility that continues the history of artistic consciousness.

This symptom of postmodernity often takes the form of an apocalyptic narrative that offers little in the way of a hopeful future. Apocalypse itself has become one of the central themes of postmodern narratives. Often the situation at hand presents itself as some novel difficulty whose history even the characters of the narrative cannot fathom. In the recent movie *Oblivion* (2013), for example, the title itself already gives away the game. A voiceover from the main character, Jack (Tom Cruise), tells us that the Earth has been ravaged by years of war with an alien race called Scavs (the scavenging of history is a theme of the movie). Jack is part of a cleanup crew, seeking what he believes to be the last of the Scavs, while humanity extracts resources from the Earth in preparation for relocation to a moon of Jupiter. [Spoiler alert:] When an old spacecraft crashes on Earth with cryopods from the distant past, Jack learns that the transport ship preparing to relocate humanity is actually an alien ship. Jack is actually one of thousands of clones created by the Scavs to destroy Earth and aid in taking its resources. Jack's memory, his connection to history, has been erased (the oblivion of the movie's title). Although he manages to destroy the alien ship, it is at the cost of his own life. Yet one of his clones manages to find a small green area on Earth, where he is reunited with his wife. Jack is a simulacrum, detached from history and unable to envision a hopeful future that goes beyond a diminished form of pastoralism.

In Cormac McCarthy's novel *The Road*, a post-apocalyptic world is so ravaged that in one scene the unnamed main character and his son express gratitude after finding some mushrooms. We never learn what cataclysm resulted in the scorched earth and the near total erasure of humanity. The characters have no names, no history, and no future. The main character has only one quest, which is to reach the sea, where he trusts in finding some sign that life will find a way to continue. The story is devoid of hope. The father dies, leaving his son with a family whose humanity seems to be intact. But no vision of a better future or a plan of fruitful action is allowed to enter the narrative.

Similar themes weave themselves into the movie *The Book of Eli,* where the title character walks through a post-apocalyptic landscape in the hope of finding a place and a people who will embrace the last remaining bible, which he has in his possession. All we know of this catastrophic future is that it is positioned thirty years after a world war, in whose wake all the bibles were destroyed (except for the one that Eli discovers). Few of the younger generation can read, let alone knit together a society. The break from history is so complete that one entrepreneurial leader, appropriately named Carnegie, tells Eli that the older generation represents the future, because they can recall the values of the past. Carnegie covets Eli's bible, because he knows he can use the word of God to rule his small town more ideologically. Despite Eli's superhuman abilities in combat, which appear to come from his deep faith, Carnegie manages to inflict a mortal wound on Eli and take the bible. Before his death, Eli manages to make his way to San Francisco, where a group of scholars is collecting the few remaining books and works of art. Although Eli no longer owns a copy of the bible, he has read it so many times that he can dictate its every word to the scholars. Meanwhile, Carnegie discovers that the bible he took from Eli is in Braille, which his blind girlfriend, Claudia, claims she cannot remember how to read. Eli dies shortly after the printing of a new bible, and Carnegie clearly will die of gangrene as the result of a gunshot wound at the hands of Eli earlier in the narrative.

Interpreting *The Book of Eli* without a postmodern perspective, we could arrive at a fairly typical working out of the blindness-and-insight theme that runs through narratives from as early as the Oedipus myth. Carnegie's girlfriend is blind, but she can see that Carnegie is capable of great cruelty. Carnegie can see the power of the bible, but he is blind to the values he twists in order to obtain the book. Eli is blind but he can see the values of the past and use them to overcome obstacles. Even the name of Eli's companion, Solara, points to light and sight. And there is an ideological completion that involves tracking how the various forms of insight and blindness overturn themselves. The blind Claudia can see that Carnegie will die of gangrene before he realizes it himself. The characters and the audience are blind to Eli's disability until the end of the movie. In death, Eli enters the realm of a more profound darkness, or, depending on one's point of view, a more profound light. Solara is blind to the possibility of a better world but takes on Eli's quest to fight injustice as she sees the power of the word.

A postmodern reading of the movie is less tidy but more illustrative of the problems of history and the loss of utopian visions. Eli walks through the detritus of history, picking up spare parts (gloves, an iPod, hand wipes, etc.) from what remains of the past. We learn that few people in this post-apocalyptic world can read, let alone remember what the former world was like. In one scene, Solara asks Eli about the world before the apocalypse because, like her contemporaries, she has no connection to the past. The closest thing to a utopian vision that the movie offers comes when Eli explains to Carnegie that he's always hoped to find a place where the bible he owns would be cherished and used to guide a new society. But this expression is little more than nostalgia for a pre-industrial world, which is underscored by the kind of knowledge that Eli represents: he literally has memorized the bible and acts as a present-era Homer, a man who *is* a book. Ironically, the movie concludes with a scene where Eli's vision of the future appears to come true, since he dictates the bible from his unshakeable memory to a scribe who later produces a copy of the book on the first new printing press (another gesture toward the pre-industrial past). But the book doesn't form the basis of a new society, as Eli had hoped. Instead, the scribe simply places the bible on a library shelf, where one assumes it will remain unread, since the scribe expresses more pleasure in owning a bible than in using it to form a new society. The erasure of history in the movie renders a utopian vision as nothing more than a nostalgic yearning for a return to a distant and idealized past. From a Marxist standpoint, that yearning is not only for a pre-industrial world but also a pre-capitalist one. The movie thus stages an opposition between pre-capitalism in the form of Eli and his book, and capitalism in the form of Carnegie and his desire to control the labor of the remaining population.

The loss of utopian visions and their replacement by nostalgia was evident in Rochberg's String Quartet no. 3, where the only alternative to the fragmented present comes in the middle movement in the form of a simulacrum of Beethoven's late quartets. Because Rochberg cannot represent the present except through copies of Bartók, Beethoven, and Mahler, and because he makes no attempt to forge a link to the past in a dialectical way, his music cannot envision a utopian future; it can only offer some past vision as a substitute. The situation is a complete reversal of the narrative paradigms of nineteenth-century music, where a dialectic with the past both questions the Enlightenment and opens up a utopian space to imagine a future that might fulfill the promise of the past, or what Reinhart Koselleck would call a *futures past* (2004). Seth Monahan (2007) offers a clear example in his admirable study of Mahler's Sixth Symphony. Following Adorno, Monahan argues that Mahler engages the tradition of sonata form as a signifier for the total coherence of a social structure that cannot cope with the individual. In discussing one of the themes in the second tonal area of the final movement, Monahan claims that "S1 attempts to fast-forward to a hypothetical Utopian future, beyond the troubled expanses of a sonata still underway" (66). The fact that Mahler's Sixth fails to reach the utopian future it envisions is less important than that the music is in dialogue with a past tradition that stands for some failure to be overcome once a utopian vision is realized.

This approach to both the past and the future in the present goes back at least as far as Chopin, whose larger narrative forms generally open up space for a utopian vision. As I have argued elsewhere (2004), in Chopin's Fourth Ballade, for example, a number of utopian spaces open up in response to a dysphoric waltz, whose series of variations dominates the first section of the piece. Chopin's larger forms are in dialogue with the sonata tradition and with genres new to his time: the waltz, the mazurka (updated with nineteenth-century harmony), the nocturne, and so on. His music engages the past and the present. The first of the

Fourth Ballade's utopian visions comes in the form of a static suspension of time in G♭ major, which interrupts the completion of one of the waltz's variations: the music figuratively opens up space to deny the tragic implications of the waltz. The second utopian vision appears in the form of a pastoral (a siciliano), which we might read as a nostalgic look toward an idealized countryside. Although this idealized theme returns in the form of an apotheosis that might fulfill the promise of its earlier appearance in the ballade, the music realizes the impossibility of nostalgia as an effective form of utopianism; a sudden turn in the musical narrative crushes the pastoral and replaces it with a dramatic struggle in the home key, F minor. Chopin thus offers us a truth claim about his time, in which neither the promise of urban development (in the form of the waltz) nor the nostalgic turn to the past (in the form of the pastoral) can answer the problems of modernity. In terms of the urban/rural opposition, neither side is valued as a path for future action: this apocalypse is more tragic than a postmodern one because its narrator knows his connection to the past and has already foreseen that no solution to the failed Enlightenment is coming soon.

Even when there is no apocalyptic setting for a postmodern work, it often can do little to envision a different future, because it represents the present with the voices of the past. One example is Jennifer Higdon's Concerto for Orchestra (2002), whose title makes an obvious connection to Bartók. Higdon does almost nothing to invoke the pastness of Bartók's music or its connection to historical issues still at play in the present. The first movement, with its rushing octatonic scales and percussive intrusions, is so close in sound to the last movement of Bartók's Concerto for Orchestra that only the listener unfamiliar with Bartók could miss it (Example 5.2). Higdon follows Bartók's work closely, from the five-movement arch form, to a movement featuring the percussion, to a slow central movement. But Higdon's music is not a quotation of Bartók's Concerto: it is another simulacrum. Higdon takes the materials of the earlier concerto without earning them as Bartók had with his close study of Eastern European folk song. The octatonic scales in the opening movement, for example, move apace without a note out of place. There is nothing to signal to the listener a hermeneutic moment to make a real historical connection to some past problem still in play. And where one could argue that the optimistic lift at the end of Bartók's concerto opens a utopian space in light of its historical moment at the end of World War II, any reading of Higdon's music falls short of the same kind of modernist response to history. Higdon offers the listener a token of American optimism from beginning to end, polished like the shiny screen of an Apple product: a commodity that demands nothing from us but that we buy it. For Jameson, the implications of the postmodern artwork are that its erasure of history marks it as aesthetically suspect; postmodernism is a path that does little more than extend commodification into the arts. Scruton expresses a similar distaste for postmodernism, although his outlook shares none of the Marxist underpinnings of Jameson. For Scruton, postmodern music is a form of sentimentality, which "becomes the norm when a culture declines" (1997: 495). Whether or not we wish to wag our finger at postmodernism, the point is not that we should stop listening to Higdon (or Roch-

Example 5.2. Higdon, Concerto for Orchestra, I (opening, strings only)

berg, or Zorn, or Stravinsky, or the cadenzas of Apap). The point is that we should recognize what postmodernism does to history: it erases it.

The Erasure of History, and the Schizophrenic Present

At the beginning of this chapter, I characterized quotation in contemporary music as a *symptom* of postmodernism. To conclude, I will explain this characterization in Lacanian terms and outline how postmodernism's erasure of history marks the present as a series of disconnected moments akin to schizophrenia. As we have seen in earlier chapters, Lacan has several conceptions of the symptom, among which is anything that does not work in the Symbolic. In the case of postmodernism it is our ability to form a signifying chain—a statement both from and about the Symbolic—that comes into question. Lacan associates the Symbolic most strongly with language itself, which is so important to the formation of the subject that even our biological existence is impossible without speech. "For it is important to consider that speech constitutes the subject's being not merely by a symbolic assumption, but that prior to his birth speech determines—through the laws of marriage, by which the human order is distinguished from nature—not only the subject's status but even the birth of his biological being" (2006i: 294). When the subject speaks, he does so with the language of the Symbolic, including its failures and contradictions. "Character analysis presents itself as based on the discovery that the subject's personality is structured like a symptom that his personality feels to be foreign; in other words, like a symptom, his personality harbors a meaning, that of a repressed conflict" (283). A part of the subject's personality resists the language of the Symbolic, and in order to uncover the nature of this resistance, the analyst must help the subject place the symbols of dreams, slips of the tongue, memory disturbances, and so on "in the verbalization of chains of speech in which the subject constitutes his history" (277). For Lacan, these chains of speech, the connection of one signifier to another, are so necessary for the subject that psychosis takes "the form of a broken chain" (2006c: 449). The psychotic patient fails to connect signs into a signi-fying chain that would make sense of his speech. Instead, each signifier stands on its own, causing an unbearable rupture in time and signification, and an accom-panying loss of narrative.

The postmodern condition with its fragmentation, constant quotation, and breaking down of hierarchies is a schizophrenic condition, where every signi-fier is culled from history without a proper context to connect it to a signifying chain. Postmodernism does not update the past to make sense of the present and envision a utopian future; postmodernism quotes bits of various pasts to create a chaotic bricolage. This situation brings us back to Zorn's *Road Runner* and its collection of quotations. Although nothing stops the listener from trying to find a logical connection between one quote and another, the postmodern position plays against that strategy. *Road Runner* is a symptom of postmodernism, a pe-riod witnessing the erasure of the past. Each moment belongs to itself, marking a series of present tenses that only make spatial contacts to every other moment and signifier in time: a vast intertextuality. The postmodern world is flat.

In the case of Rochberg's Third Quartet, or Higdon's Concerto for Orchestra, postmodernism simply takes an entire signifying chain from the past and places it in the present without updating it, creating a simulacrum that speaks the secret of our inability to represent the present moment. This form of quotation would be what Hyde calls *reverential imitation,* except there is no effort to make the past sound new. The postmodern composer simply discovers, consciously or un-consciously, his or her own failure to create a signifying chain, forcing the com-poser to take an entire text from the past as an avatar for a present that cannot find a way to represent itself. One might view this situation as a return of the re-pressed, except there is nothing uncanny about these simulacra. They simply ap-pear without the psychic energy that repetition compulsion lends to repressed material.

But it is pointless to bemoan this situation, because there is no going back. Postmodernism is both progress and catastrophe; it breaks the barriers of hege-monic structures while it upholds a capitalist ideology in which all culture has become a commodity capable of hiding the ideology of capitalism itself. In the Lacanian system (modernist, for sure) there is always a gap between the subject's everyday life and the total knowledge enshrined in the Symbolic, which (as we have seen) the subject addresses without receiving an answer. The answer never comes because the Symbolic is an empty signifier, a dead letter, to which the sub-ject has given his or her agency. Within historical moments prior to postmod-ernism, the subject had to find a way to negotiate everyday life with the Symbolic, which formed the conditions of action and thought at the moment of subjec-tive formation. But the subject can never know the Symbolic fully and precisely because it is the empty signifier that stands in for the total historical and cul-tural conditions in which the subject is born. The subject approaches the series of symptoms in the Symbolic in the hope of uncovering the secret history of his or her existence, one layer at a time. Although there can never be an unmasking scene where all is revealed, there can be a *series* of unmasking scenes, where symptoms give up the secrets of a culture's ideology one by one.

In the postmodern moment, though, the subject risks finding no position from which to perform this series of unmasking scenes that can bring him or her closer to an understanding of the history and culture that make us. The erasure of history refuses a signifying chain that can connect the subject to the very conditions of subjectivity in the first place. This is not to say that an interpreting subject cannot make the effort to trace the real problems and historical contexts of the various borrowings and allusions in a postmodern work. Rather, it is to say that the irony of postmodern quotation hopes to play on the side of capitalism and keep the subject from finding the position from which to discover the history of those quotes and the horizon of their meaning in the present. History is by definition a narrative form, and postmodernism's fragmentation of the signifying chain counters the possibility of that narrative.

In an oft quoted passage, Jameson tells us that "history is what hurts," because it sets the limits to desire and to freedom in a way that the subject may not even realize (1981: 102). Like the Symbolic, history is the law that the subject accepts without knowing, chooses without choosing, and follows without recognizing its footsteps. The Symbolic and history alienate us whether or not we would rather ignore their effects. From this perspective, postmodernism is what helps us to forget our own alienation as we pretend to live in a limitless vista where the total commodification of culture promises a freedom that it cannot deliver. The postmodern subject is not the one who does *not* know, nor even the one who does not *want* to know, but the one who has been convinced that he does not *need* to know.

6 Lutosławski, Molar and Molecular

> Every society, and every individual, are thus plied by both segmentarities simultaneously: one molar, and the other *molecular*.
>
> —Deleuze and Guattari, *A Thousand Plateaus*

The Postmodern Subject (Revisited)

Lacan's model of the subject is not a pleasant one. The subject is alienated and fractured: the site of a symptomatic structure delivered by the Symbolic. Any fantasy of wholeness is nostalgia for a moment that never was. Any vision of a future wholeness is mere wishful thinking. From the nineteenth century through Freud and Lacan, the old ideology of the self falls away in a series of discoveries. The problems of the wound, or the automaton, or the uncanny become the return of the repressed in Freudian thought, only to become the very substance of the subject (an empty substance) in Lacanian thought. The monadic ego of the nineteenth century becomes the undiscovered country for Freud and the undiscoverable country for Lacan. The bourgeois control of the self and the surrounding culture is inverted in Lacan's model: we are the products of the Symbolic, and our every thought is implicated in the symptoms and historical processes of which we may not even be aware. No. Lacan is not for the faint of heart.

Things only get worse once we approach the postmodern subject from the Lacanian point of view. Lacan's only hope for us is to take up the problems of the Symbolic and try to understand them. As we have seen, Lacan's late vision of the symptom, the *sinthome*, involves making sense in an unending series of unmasking scenes that bring us closer and closer to an understanding of the history of our consciousness. What we gain from Lacan's unblinkered view of the self is nothing more than a refusal to be content with what we know. But if postmodernism plays against this making sense of our hidden history, then the Lacanian cure is no cure at all.

But there is a different approach to the postmodern subject that is less bleak and more exuberant in its play with the fragments of culture and of the self. In this chapter, I sketch out this model of the postmodern subject, which comes from Gilles Deleuze and Félix Guattari, particularly their book *A Thousand Plateaus*. The choice may seem an odd one. Guattari, a psychoanalyst who attended Lacan's seminars, was practically the anointed successor to his teacher and mentor until he collaborated with Deleuze on *Anti-Oedipus*, which was highly critical of both Freud and Lacan. Deleuze had no love of Lacan to begin with, although it would be difficult for him to deny that one of the most influential French thinkers of the twentieth century had an impact on his intellectual development. It is possible to read many of the ideas in *Anti-Oedipus* and *A Thousand Plateaus*, for example, as swerves from Lacanian thought that betray the effect of that thought on their theory of the postmodern subject. Such a swerve happens early in *Anti-Oedipus*, where Deleuze and Guattari take up the problem of the signifying chain that was so important to Lacan (and which was a theme of the previous chapter).

> We owe to Jacques Lacan the discovery of this fertile domain of a code of the unconscious, incorporating the entire chain—or several chains—of meaning: a discovery thus totally transforming analysis.... But how very strange this domain seems, simply because of its multiplicity—a multiplicity so complex that we can scarcely speak of *one* chain or even *one* code of desire. The chains are called "signifying chains" (*chaînes signifiantes*) because they are made up of signs, but these signs are not themselves signifying.... These indifferent signs follow no plan, they function at all levels and enter into any and every sort of connection. (1983: 38)

The crucial idea in this passage is that Lacan's signifying chain is a multiplicity. But Deleuze and Guattari take the multiplicity of the subject (and the signifying chain that constitutes him/her) as a positive property. Rather than deny multiplicity or attempt to forge it into a unifying whole, Deleuze and Guattari view it as the escape route from the totalizing impulses of culture. In addition, as we will see, they place importance on the body and its potential to thwart the Symbolic in their formulations of the body as *territorial* (culturally organized), *deterritorial* (escaping cultural control), and *reterritorial* (organized in a new way), a formulation that is akin to Kristeva's notion of the *chora*, though they acknowledge no debt to this concept.

For Deleuze and Guattari, two forms of multiplicity take turns in creating and tearing apart the cultural edifices within which the subject negotiates a form of being in mind and body: the *molar* and the *molecular*. A fuller explanation is forthcoming, but for now we can think of the molar as an impulse to structure the social, while the molecular is an impulse to tear apart structures and make room for new forms of the social and its impact on the mind and body of the subject. Together, the molar and the molecular are creative forces. The molar organizes structures and hierarchies, while the molecular breaks structures apart and makes room for new ones. The molar and molecular are implicated as well in Deleuze and Guattari's notions of milieus, territories, and cosmic expressions, which also receive further explanation later in this chapter. We will discover that instead of focusing on the subject as the one who knows (who makes sense), Deleuze and Guattari focus on the subject as the one (a multiplicity) who expresses, and the one who is plugged into various cultural machines (as we saw in Deleuze's conception of Proust) in order to feel expressions.

Our musical point of entry will be the music of Witold Lutosławski. Again, the choice may seem an odd one, since the Polish composer was no postmodernist but a die-hard modernist. When Deleuze and Guattari speak of music, as they often do, they generally turn to modernist music, as if to show that their model of subjectivity is another discovery of something that was always already before us. Lutosławski may have been a modernist, but his music can be read within the postmodern view of the subject that Deleuze and Guattari developed. The question at the end will be whether this different view of the postmodern subject can make any claim to escape the hard-eyed model that Lacan offers us.

Order and Chaos

A good place to start is with the first movement of Lutosławski's *Jeux vénitiens* (1961), which exhibits an unabashed formal simplicity. The piece works through an elementary alternation between *ad libitum* sections, which rely on the composer's aleatoric technique, and *battuta* sections, which are notated and performed more conventionally. An *ad libitum* (*ad lib*) includes notations for pitch and rhythm, but lacks a common meter for the instrumentalists; each performer plays as if the music were a cadenza, without coordinating their music with the ensemble. The conductor simply stops beating time, and the musicians go off on their own. The resulting textures come from a constrained freedom. A *battuta* section is fully notated in the conventional manner. The conductor regains control of the orchestra through the baton. These alternating sections set up a number of oppositions in *Jeux vénitiens*. The *ad lib* sections are for winds/brass/percussion, while the *battuta* sections are for strings. The *ad libs* are noisy affairs; the *battutas* are more serene. The *ad libs* are active; the *battutas* are static. Joining the two sections are violent stabs in the percussion, like some wily cinematic narrator splicing together bits of shattered time. The whole is a semiotic nightmare, with all the world suspended in a crisis of opposition.

How should we read these oppositions? When I ask my students this question, they invariably reply that the *ad lib* sections signify chaos, and the *battuta* sections signify order. A good first answer. For Arnold Whittall, the concept of limited aleatoric techniques, which Lutosławski first developed in this piece, was "an innovative musical way of working with the spaces between 'chaos' and 'order'" (2001: 255). Limited aleatorism was Lutosławski's way *into* modernism, which Whittall reads as a persistent and intense interaction of opposing elements that resist synthesis. Thus Whittall's analysis moves us from the content to the form. Important as chaos may be to the content of Lutosławski's *Jeux vénitiens,* more important is the form of opposed elements, the engine of unmediated contrast and conflict.

Unpacking Whittall's argument around the content/form opposition, I borrow from Fredric Jameson the notion that content and form really involve four ideological corners, as in a semiotic square. There is the content of the content, the form of the content, the content of the form, and the form of the form (Jameson 2007: xiii–xix). The *content of the content* has no form. At any historical moment there is a swirl of ideas, problems, and symptoms that we can envision without an organizing principle. For *Jeux vénitiens* the content of the content is chaos and order themselves, including their historical dimensions in the Cold War of the 1960s; but it is also everything in Poland's culture during that time: the aftermath of the Polish October (1956), the early liberalism of the Gamułka government, and its later return to repression, among other historical turns. Thinking of the content of the content is difficult without some form to organize the various ideas in a narrative, an assemblage, an artwork, a posting on Facebook, and so on. Thus the *form of the content* is what gives these ideas their shape and organization. In the case of *Jeux vénitiens,* the succession of *ad libs* and *battutas* gives a form to the content (the alternation of sections that might signify order and chaos). The *content of the form* involves the ideology of form as separated from the content. The problem of order and chaos in the 1960s might find its form in a particular narrative structure, in a particular newspaper report, in a particular musical arrangement, and so on. In *Jeux vénitiens,* the content of the form is the very opposition of chaos and order and their refusal to work together or lead one to the other with any transition other than the disruptive strikes from the percussion. As Whittall indicates, the content of the form in this case is the ideology of an opposition that will not find a comforting synthesis: it is the sign of Lutosławski's modernism. All that is missing is the *form of the form,* which is a utopian and absolutist view of music (or other art form) that seeks to deny historical content by focusing on abstract relationships: a trichord that generates a hexachord, or an *Urlinie* spanning a tonal work. *Jeux vénitiens,* for example, is composed of two twelve-tone chords in the *ad lib* sections, and eight-note clusters of semitones in the *battuta* sections. Analysts might content themselves with a study of these pitch elements without making any appeal to what we wrongly call the *extra-musical* content of *Jeux vénitiens.* When Adorno tells us that there is a sediment of subjectivity in even the most modernist works, he is uncovering the ideology behind the form of the form. He is telling us that to study only the form of the form is to overlook the content, which, for him, is a subjectivity dealing with the problem of culture and history (see Williams 1998). Touring the four corners of analysis that Jameson outlines, we might be content with an ideological traversal of the square that moves from the ideas of order and chaos, through the form that those ideas take in the music, through the modernist problem of oppositions themselves, to the utopian dream of an artwork that manages to evade the very content that it first embraced.

But this interpretation that winds around the semiotic square of content and form is too tidy to satisfy a closer reading of *Jeux vénitiens,* because behind the fragile polarity of the oppositional sections, we discover an instability that threatens to challenge the security of chaos *as* chaos and order *as* order. If we listen closely, we discover that the oppositions in the first movement of *Jeux vénitiens* are unstable ones (Klein 2005: 117–21). The first clue lies in a disordered array of quick repeated notes and frozen tremolos that stain the otherwise serene surface of the *battuta* sections. These escaping tics are signs of what Žižek calls "forgetting to forget." What we need to do to get along in our daily lives is to remember to forget the "radical discontinuity" between organic life and the Symbolic order that imposes a structure on it. But sometimes you forget to forget. You confront "a small, compulsive gesture or tic, a slip of the tongue . . . which condenses all you had to forget so that you can swim in your everyday certainty" (Žižek 2008: 18). The *battuta* sections begin as serene, ordered projections of a desirable alternative to the chaotic *ad lib* sections. But soon the tremors mar the surface; their delicate anxiety underscores the impossibility of keeping chaos out. The music forgets to forget the conventionality of chaos and order, and a piece of the Real slips through.

There doesn't appear to be much more to say about the matter. The chaos and order both inside and outside the sections of *Jeux vénitiens* are the form of the content of modernism. *Jeux vénitiens* replays a problem within the project of modernity: the problem of finding a solution where none can be found. The music discovers the idea that oppositions cannot be synthesized because the promise of dialectical thinking is only a "retrograde movement of the true" that starts from the present and moves backward through time to find the putative forms of rational theses and antitheses that have led us here (Deleuze 1991: 18). The same problem occurs again and again in Lutosławski's late music. Interpreting Lutosławski involves unlocking this uncomfortable and unstable opposition between the *ad lib* (chaos) and the *battuta* (order), which promises no synthesis because the opposition itself is a product of a Symbolic order that is itself a symptomatic structure.

Chaos, Milieus, Territories

But what if our first impulse is wrong? What if chaos is not what we think? What if the *ad lib* sections in Lutosławski's music are not signs for chaos? I will rethink the problem of the *ad lib* in terms of subjectivity, starting with chaos. I will show the relationship between chaos and milieus, territories, and music with the help of Deleuze and Guattari's *A Thousand Plateaus*. There is no easy way to summarize Deleuze and Guattari (hereafter "D and G" in citations). The chapters, which the authors call *plateaus,* are an "orchestration of crashing bricks extracted from a variety of disciplinary edifices" (Massumi 1987: xiv). Deleuze and Guattari's many concepts (rhizomes, territories, chaos, assemblages, machines, and so on) collide and intersect in every section of the book, so that "each plateau [chapter] can be read starting anywhere and can be related to any other plateau" (D and G 1987: 22). Having read *A Thousand Plateaus* both ways—first, starting from the beginning and proceeding on the straight and narrow to the end; second, reading at random points each time I picked up the book—I can tell you that it makes little difference how you approach their work. The book is a postmodern entanglement of ideas. And when the authors try to untangle the various ideas in a final chapter that defines their peculiar terms, they really don't do the reader any favors: the definitions are themselves plateaus with the same crashing bricks of thought. With Deleuze and Guattari, you just need to jump in.

Chaos is not just a beginning; it is an end as well, and everything in between. Chaos is not total disorder; it has "its own directional components, which are its own ecstasies" (D and G 1987: 313). Chaos is always all around us, though we may try to understand particular lines in chaos. Those lines are what Deleuze and Guattari call *plateaus*. When Wittgenstein tells us "the world is all that is the case," he has already confined the world to a number of manageable propositions that necessarily exclude chaos (Wittgenstein 1999: 5). Wittgenstein's opening gambit is a line of logic that plumbs through a piece of chaos to understand just that bit of it that propositional logic can structure in the first place. Plumbing a line through chaos is all we can ever do; we can only follow lines through the chaos to understand one portion (plateau) of it. If our desire is to structure chaos in order to make it go away, we have started a losing game. Instead, we must think of chaos as a source of intensities and forces. Chaos is the totality of plateaus without being a totality or hegemony or any structure that aspires to transcendence. We can make sense of some parts (lines) of chaos. We can put together certain areas of chaos. But we can never understand all of chaos.

Different forms of knowledge are like plateaus that slice through chaos to grapple with a piece of it. Science measures chaos. Bureaucracies administer chaos. Philosophy invents concepts for understanding chaos. Art frames chaos. For art, the first order of business within chaos, "the milieu of all milieus," is to make a point of order, a fragile boundary that can protect us from and communicate with the surrounding forces (D and G 1987: 313). Within chaos, one needs to make a safe milieu. In this way, forms of organic life, subjectivities, and the arts share a common strategy. A bird sings a song to mark a safe milieu. A child sings a song to protect herself from the surrounding darkness (311). An artist draws a circle to section off the chaos of the canvas. In music, it is the refrain that makes that first point of order in chaos. A refrain is a milieu in music; it is what tells us that we have found a place we know, a place that can ward off the chaos of sound as an intensity that would otherwise unhinge us. A refrain need not be a recurring melody; it can be a motive, a chord, a system of harmony, a style, a formal schematic, a simple note that functions to mark a point in the flow of sound. The applause before and after a performance is a frame that sections music off from the chaos of sound. Without the refrain, we do not hear music as music because it is an ecstasy in chaos that entangles itself in other ecstasies; until the music has a frame to mark it as music, it is part of the totality of sound that is a plateau within chaos.

Lutosławski's music often begins by making a point of order, forming a frame. In his *Chain 1* (1983), for example, the opening *ad lib* begins on A4, expands outward in register, and collapses onto B3, like a piece of dark matter that ignites before imploding into a single point of density. From B3 as a first point of order, a solo clarinet makes its own quick ascent before returning to the same pitch. The music has made a first milieu around B. But that note is not a tonic nor a center around which other pitches should be measured; it is simply a place to start in the middle of the chaos, or, more properly, the point that has been marked as the place to start. The music's first impulse has been both indexical and creative: I begin here where I have cleared a space. At the end of *Chain 1* the same milieu becomes the source of an intense expression. Beginning at rehearsal 41 the music builds to a climactic moment through an interlocking series of *ad lib* sections that culminate in a registrally expansive twelve-tone chord: the music has reached the moment of its greatest stature and intensity. From here the music moves to the upper register before collapsing on a fiercely repeated B♭4, opening up in register as at the beginning of the piece, and collapsing again on a semitone cluster that spans from A♭4 down to B3. *Chain 1* returns to a transformed version of its first milieu, which acts as the refrain that captures a bit of chaos. The music's refrain is the frame that makes art out of the plateau of chaos that we call *sound*.

Les Espaces du Sommeil (1975). We begin in the middle of things. The strings, vibraphone, celesta, and piano play a texture in the upper register that descends through vertiginous glissandi until it reaches the lower register. The timpani repeats a six-note pattern, C3–B2–D♭3–C3–B2–F3, as if circling to create a ritual point of order. This is the music's first refrain, its frame to cordon off the rest of sound-as-chaos. After the timpani stops, the tenor can enter the fragile opening in the chaotic world. And his first utterance, *dans la nuit,* is as quiet and tenuous as a child warding off the darkness with her simple song. The timpani begins another cycle of its six-note pattern, C3–B2–D♭3 . . . and the tenor completes the pattern with C3–B2–F3 as he sings the opening words. Music has opened a space for the tenor to enter, and once he takes his place in the musical milieu, he opens up that space with an octave leap from C3 to C4. In response, the flutes, clarinets, and trumpets offer their first shimmering texture in the form of an *ad lib.* The music is on its way at last. "One ventures from home on the thread of a tune" (D and G 1987: 311).

Openings like those of *Chain 1* or *Les Espaces du Sommeil* are Lutosławski's way into a piece. But Lutosławski often makes the musical frame more explicit, beginning a piece with an episodic movement that uses a short idea as a refrain (in the conventional sense). Lutosławski claimed that in cases where the episodes form an entire opening movement, their function is merely preparatory for the main movement to come. His episodic first movements "engage the listener's attention and keep him in a state of expectation so that he's ready to absorb a greater quantity of music" in the longer second movement (Kaczyński 1984: 21). But these opening movements are more interesting than Lutosławski lets on, and their form of preparation is more than the whetting of a musical appetite. A Freudian reading of the episodic structure would hear the recurring refrains as a first attempt at mastery, the *Fort-Da* of the music's going and coming. Where did the music go? Here it is! The refrain is not the music, but the refrain is what lets us know that what we've heard *is* music. Whether he knew it or not, Lutosławski was engaged in a plateau of subjectivity that framed a piece of chaos to make it into art.

Concerto for Piano and Orchestra (1987). The first time Lutosławski used the refrain technique for an opening movement, it was in the Quartet (1964), where simple octave C's formed the refrain. And such simplicity is all you need to make a safe musical milieu out of chaos. But in Lutosławski's Piano Concerto the refrain has become expressive. The Piano Concerto begins with an active *ad lib* in the winds, filling the upper register like the chattering of birds. The tremulous texture continues for some time before the strings interrupt and collapse the registral space down to a dyad, G4/Ab4. The piano now has a first fragile milieu. Picking up G# (Ab4) as its lowest note, the piano makes its first tentative utterance. But before we follow the rest of the piano's tale, we might notice that the refrain of the strings with its collapsing texture is more involved than previous refrains in Lutosławski's music. The descent and collapse of register is like the sudden dive of a flock of birds, or the cinematic camera zooming into a scene from the sky above. And these techniques are expressive because they are excessive. If the birds wished to escape a danger or to zero in on a territory, a simple descent would do the trick. Instead, the birds make an acrobatic move: a sudden dive to the left, followed by a sweeping gesture up and over to the right. If the director wished to show us the scene where the opening action will take place, a simple focus of the camera would do the trick. It is not a matter of making a milieu in order to become expressive: the making of the milieu is already expressive. Chaos is excessive; it moves with intensities, vibrations, and densities that we cannot fathom in their raw state. Music frames a bit of chaos to speed up or slow down an intensity or vibration. Like architecture, which makes frames to cordon off bits of chaos, music allows "qualities to be loosened onto the world, no longer anchored in their 'natural' place but put into the play of sensations that departs from mere survival to celebrate its means and excesses" (Grosz 2008: 13).

Once the fragile milieu has become more than a point of order, we have what Deleuze and Guattari call a *territory*. "The refrain is rhythm and melody that have been territorialized because they have become expressive—and have become expressive because they are territorializing" (D and G 1987: 317). A territory is not only a matter of space or the gathering of milieus but also a matter of intensity and expression. The desire to express makes a territory; the firmer boundaries of a territory allow a subjectivity to venture out and make an expression. There is a strange entanglement at work: the subject wants to be expressive, and so it makes a territory; but the making of the territory was already expressive to begin with, though it also allows the subject the safety of more intense expressions. In the first movement of Lutosławski's Piano Concerto, the piano solos between the refrains take up this territorial ambition, spreading through more registral space while becoming expressive in terms of dynamic intensity. Each time the piano responds to the orchestral refrain, it picks up the registral space set by the orchestra and expands its milieu upward. The piano's first statement is quiet and fragile, only opening up spatial territory through tentative moves by half steps. By the third entrance, though, the piano hazards an arpeggio. And at the fourth entrance, the piano loses itself in its first cadenza. The piano gathers registral territory as an act of expression and as a stage for releasing intensity. The dynamic range and articulations increase, the solo line takes on a more singing tone. Although the piano's aspirations have been directional in register, its *becoming* has also been dimensional through those new dynamics, articulations, and melodic expansions.

For Deleuze and Guattari, music channels intensities. Although their descriptions of music reveal a hermeneutic impulse, as have my portrayals of Lutosławski's music, Deleuze and Guattari are more interested in how music, the body, and chaos interact: "The arts produce and generate intensity, that which directly impacts the nervous system and intensifies sensation" (Grosz 2008: 3). Recall from chapter 3 that Deleuze described a Proustian machine producing effects on the reader. The idea of a machine is close to Deleuze and Guattari's approach to the arts: any meanings the arts produce would always already be a part of the Symbolic order intent on reproducing itself within the subject; but when the arts produce an effect in us through intensities, they offer an escape route from the routine, from convention, from the artwork that is read *in advance*. When music harnesses intensities, it does so to affect the body, to shake it loose from the conventions of the Symbolic order.

Symphony no. 3 (1983). Sometimes different milieus come together to create the expressive intensity of a territory. In Lutosławski's Symphony no. 3 the refrain is simple: four repeated E's in octaves. "Make some space for the music," they say. After the opening refrain, the first milieu is expressed by the flutes and piccolo. Soon the oboes make their own milieu below the flutes: theirs is a more staid affair. Now come the horns below the flutes and oboes: their wider intervals, indexical to aspiration, express an almost human subjectivity, but (in Deleuze and Guattari's terms) a subjectivity that harnesses chaos. The three milieus overlap and combine. "The notion of the milieu is not unitary; not only does the living thing continually pass from one milieu to another, but the milieus pass into one another; they are essentially communicating" (D and G 1987: 313). The bee takes flight from its hive and makes its way to the flower, while the bird in a tree above the flower takes flight down to a flowerbed in search of a worm. The buzzing bee, the chirping bird, and the flight of both around the flower are ways in which the milieus of flower, bee, bird, and tree interact. In these ways, milieus communicate, come apart, recombine. Returning to the Symphony no. 3, once the flutes, oboes, and horns come together in the first territory after the opening refrain, the clarinets and bassoons, the harps and piano try to combine their forces as well. The milieus of the various instruments are communicating; their territories are overlapping like those of the bee, the bird, and the flower. But everything slows down. Soon the music just goes away. Silence. Failure. Sometimes the bee makes for the flower, only to discover that its nectar is gone, while the bird swoops down and fails to find food for its young. Milieus can come together, but they can fall apart, too. That's life.

To review: *Chaos* is all the cosmos with its intensities and ecstasies. A *milieu* is a first point of order within chaos, the first chance at subjectivity. Art makes a milieu with a *frame*. Music's frame is a *refrain*. The refrain as a milieu may come together with other milieus to produce a *territory*, which is a form of expression that harnesses the intensities of chaos. Music channels intensities, textures, dynamics, articulations, registers, noises. Music organizes the sounding chaos, but it can also tear the sounds apart, let them die in silence. Music casts vibrations and sounding intensities onto the body. We feel the musical intensity hurled at us. Music is like the Proustian machine. When we are plugged into music, it affects us with its intensities, textures, registers, and so on.

An example. When the hammer blow first comes down in the final movement of Mahler's Sixth Symphony, we can rightly interpret it, like Seth Monahan, as a sign of the monumental failure of the utopian second theme to establish its alternative ontology to the noxious march of the first theme (2007). The moment is like a thunderclap of tragic fate that still captures our imagination a century after the symphony's first moment. Searching YouTube at the time I write this, I can find over a dozen videos that feature nothing but the percussionist raising the hammer to bring it crashing down; and some of these videos set up the *Hammerschlag* with little more than ten seconds of context. The visual is primary here, because the moment can never be loud enough on a computer, or an iPad, or even a computer jacked into a speaker system. Listen to Mahler's Sixth Symphony in a live performance, and you realize that the shock of the hammer comes from the way it shakes the hall and penetrates the chest. Your chest becomes the sign of a composer who once worried about his irregular heartbeat. There, where you feel the intensity of my music: that's where fate has struck me. But the moment is more than fate. It is the reterritorialization of sound into your chest, and legs, and arms. You have felt the music not just as a meaning but also as an intensity that combines your usually segmented self (a hand for grasping, an ear for hearing, a head for thinking) into something new. Music as an intensity has made your whole body into an ear.

Thus, Mahler's music has taken a bit of chaos called *sound* and turned its intensity to the body. This is the focus of Deleuze and Guattari's understanding of music and subjectivity. A subject is not only a mind but also a body. Like the mind that becomes socialized in the Symbolic order, the body is socialized (Deleuze and Guattari would say *territorialized*). But music can release intensities on the body that take apart its conventional responses to the world. When I say that the whole body becomes an ear, I am claiming that music's intensity can penetrate the body and, if only for a moment, restructure it, so that something beyond the conventions of culture can reach it and reorganize it. We not only interpret Mahler's hammer blows as the signs of fate, we feel their intensity as something that changes (Deleuze and Guattari would say *deterritorializes*) our body.

Becoming Intense, Cosmic Expression

Once a number of territorial forces begin to interact, they become intense. "This intense center is simultaneously inside the territory, and outside several territories that converge on it at the end of an immense pilgrimage (hence the ambiguities of the 'natal'). Inside or out, the territory is linked to this intense center, which is like the unknown homeland, terrestrial source of all forces friendly and hostile, where everything is decided" (D and G 1987: 321). As always, things are not easy with Deleuze and Guattari. But we can unpack their writing by thinking first literally in terms of the earth and its biological and topographical territories. A section of the landscape can become teeming with the territories of different life forms: the territories of birds, of insects, of animals, of plants. These territories interact: a dog marks a tree as his territory and growls at a squirrel that climbs that same tree. The growl of the dog and the scraping of the scrambling squirrel become a music of the earth, an expression that becomes intense as the sounds of other animals, insects, birds, the wind in the trees, the crickets in the grass add their voices through the interacting and overlapping territories that they have marked as safe places. As the territories interact, a part of the earth becomes intense, meaning not only that a site takes on multiple activities, but also that color and sound proliferate. "None of these formulations carries the slightest risk of anthropomorphism, or implies the slightest interpretation. It is instead a kind of geomorphism" (D and G 1987: 318–19). And as the earth becomes intense, it is also the site where everything is decided: life and death in the agon of species who share territories made up of milieus that mark safe places from which those species take a line of flight to extend their territory, find a mate, or catch a meal. When you drive a car and approach a squirrel crossing the road, why does it turn around even when it is so close to the other side of the road with its promise of safety? Because the squirrel is returning to its milieu; the other side of the road promises nothing to the squirrel.

The sounds of the earth, this becoming intense with overlapping territories, can also be read as a metaphor for human activity. You are at a party in a large home. There are small milieus and larger territories: three people laughing here, four around the food table, many around the drinks. Each of the milieus is sonically expressive: a low voice among one of the conversations, a humming of delight around the food, the popping of a cork, the laughter after a joke. The milieus communicate. Someone hears the popping of a cork and heads for the drinks, where they share the joke they just heard; the homeowner walks among the milieus and puts together people she thinks ought to know each other better. From the outside of the home, the chatting, chewing, dropped forks, and snippets of jazz are sonically expressive: a "becoming intense" of the party. The party might become too big, too intense. The room is crowded. The intensity of sound is overwhelming. People move out into the street. The neighbors complain. Soon the party has reterritorialized itself into something less pleasant. In the movie *The X Project,* three teens decide to throw an epic party that will raise their status among their peers. But the party gets out of hand. The noise and activity finally lead to a police assault, exploding cars, an aerial presence by the media. And all the noise, noise, noise, noise, noise (to quote the Grinch) has become too much. The sonic expression has nothing to do but to fall apart. The noise itself was territorial, then deterritorial, and finally reterritorial (once the police gained control); and the site of that sound, the territory of the party, was where everything was decided for the three teens.

As the interacting territories become intense, "they cease to be terrestrial, becoming cosmic" (D and G 1987: 327). This building up of intensities into a cosmic expression is the province of the arts, as well. And music's way to that cosmic expression is the refrain. "If the refrain protects us from chaos and entices us to abide and enjoy in a region provisionally enclosed from chaos, music opens up and transforms us, making of both our bodies and of the earth itself a new site of becomings toward a differently contained and directed chaos, to the opening up and exploration of chaotic elements" (Grosz 2008: 56). This viewpoint necessitates the idea that expression is primary in music. As Lawrence Kramer has argued, the primacy of expression is something that music analysis refuses to grasp, even in the face of a growing realization that analytical statements do not represent what we used to call "the music itself" (as if there is such a thing). "Yet the positivist ideal is continually reinstated by the assumption that statements about form or structure are more fundamental and more reliable than statements about expressive content. . . . But there is no warrant for this priority" (Kramer 2012: 22). Similarly, for Deleuze and Guattari, "to express is not to depend upon; there is an autonomy of expression" (1987: 317). But expression for Deleuze and Guattari is not like hermeneutics, though we may approach their ideas with a hermeneutic point of view. Expression does not tell us a secret. Instead, expression does something to us. Like the Debussy machine that produces eternity in us if we are connected to it, the expression machine is meant to change us, reterritorialize us. Our bodies become ears, and the cosmic expression of the earth is an embrace that remakes us.

Cosmic expression is easy to hear in Lutosławski's music. His late pieces often feature one or more sections where various textures (we'll call them milieus and territories) come together into an ecstatic intensity. We hear such intense expression early in *Mi-Parti* (1976). After two attempts to bring together the orchestral forces, a third attempt reaches an early cosmic expression. Our first impulse might be to hear these climaxes, the release of the territorial forces, in terms of the aesthetic opposition of the beautiful and the sublime, as Charles Bodman Rae has pointed out (2001: 17–25). Among the more beautiful passages are the gamelan section near the end of Lutosławski's Symphony no. 3, or the slowly evolving texture that builds to the climax of his Symphony no. 4. When these passages veer toward the sublime, following the classic definition by Edmund Burke, there is the requisite transformation into something awesome and terrible, where "all its [the soul's] motions are suspended, with some degree of horror" (1889: 40, part II, section1). The second climactic passage of *Mi-Parti* is just such a sublime expression. The music becomes too big, too loud, too chaotic. The expression of intensity takes on what Nietzsche heard in *Tristan und Isolde* as "the vast void of cosmic night," which would result in the "expiring by a spasmodic distention of all the wings of the soul" (1995: 78). To make the proper distinctions, though, the Wagnerian sublime in Nietzsche's thinking is one in which the music engulfs the soul in a Schopenhauerian death that is "necessarily horrible because the Will that imposes its omnipotent powers is evil" (Chua 1999: 232). The Will is evil in Schopenhauer's philosophy because, like the *objet petit a* in Lacanian thought, it drives the subject through a never-ending search to satisfy desires that can never really be satisfied at all. For Schopenhauer, the Will leads the subject to suffering. The Will creates desire and drives human action, whose outcomes are negative.

These connections to the Will and its power to create or destroy with indifference, though, are qualitatively different from the sublime intensity in Deleuze and Guattari's conception of territories and milieus harnessing chaos. The sublime intensity for Deleuze and Guattari comes from a buildup of organisms, sound, and activity. "Music molecularizes sound matter and in so doing becomes capable of harnessing nonsonorous forces such as Duration and Intensity" (D and G 1987: 343). Music takes sound apart ("molecularizes sound matter") to connect it (sound) to time-as-quality ("Duration") and to forces that effect sensations in the body ("Intensity"). Although this molecularized sound matter makes music a material of capture (music captures parts of chaos), "a force of the Cosmos," or a cosmic expression, "sometimes one overdoes it, puts too much in, works with a jumble of lines and sounds" (343). Then the molecularized musical territory becomes too big, so that everything inevitably falls apart. "All one has left is a resonance chamber well on the way to forming a black hole." The result is a cosmic force gone awry, tearing up the material forces instead of bringing them together into a consistency that expresses those forces. The climax of *Chain 1* is such a collapse of sonorous force into a black hole. The music tears itself apart and plunges into the gravitational pull of its own making. This falling apart, when it happens in music like *Chain 1,* is not a return to some metaphysical Will, but the chance to form a new territorial assemblage with its own potential to reach a cosmic expression or another black hole. Following this model, after the climactic sections in Lutosławsk's music, it is almost inevitable that some collapse will occur. Thus, one of the composer's favorite techniques for concluding a piece is to have the broken webs of the concluding climax disappear in wisps of disintegrated sound. Unlike a nineteenth-century apotheosis, the sublime molecular structure is not a final telos, but the end of one process and the beginning of another one. Chaos is the end, and the beginning.

Chain 3

I will put together Deleuze and Guattari's ideas about modern music into a sketch of Lutosławski's *Chain 3* (1986). This piece begins with a point of order, a quiet D4 in the violas, a quick expansion of register in the winds, and a return to the D4. The music has drawn the circle of its first milieu and established a point of order through a matter of expression as excess. If it were only a matter of finding a starting point, a simple D4 in the violas would have done the trick. But the expansion and contraction in the winds is an expressive move that points to the first milieu as the result of an artistic act. Having established a point of order, the flutes unfold another milieu with melodic fragments that terminate on that same D4. Soon the basses enter, making their own milieu beneath the flutes. Each of these milieus and those that follow use Lutosławski's *ad lib* technique, creating a molecular texture of overlapping musical lines. After the basses enter, the violins and xylophone capture the force of the upper register to form a new milieu, while the flutes drop out. This process, the chain of which the title speaks, is the plane of consistency that draws together one milieu after another. The flutes communicate with the basses, which communicate with the violins and xylophone. Later the basses drop out as the clarinets enter, and so forth: a musical whisper down the alley in which one group of instruments forms its milieu and then opens it up to the forces of chaos in order to attract the attention of another milieu. Once a new milieu is formed, an old milieu falls away. These acts of communication continue through the first large section of *Chain 3*. Each of the milieus articulates its differences from the previous one through timbre, texture, rhythm, and so on.

Starting at rehearsal 11, the milieus at last come together to form the first territorial section of the piece. The flutes and harp are joined by the violins, leading to a brief pause before the winds, brass, celesta, harps, and piano create a beautiful cosmic expression, magical and sonorous as the morning chorus of birds. As this first territorial expression falls apart, the music turns to a more molar consciousness; that is, while the first large section of the music focused on the creation of a texture, the next section moves to a more traditional style in which a melodic line comes to the fore. The music proceeds in the *battuta* style with a more metrical (Deleuze and Guattari would say *dogmatic*) expression. At rehearsal 17, the violins become intent to take their conventional role in orchestral music and carry a tune. But this kind of molar consciousness is never easy in Lutosławski's music. The violins have moments when they threaten to fall apart in quivering divisions of the melodic line, the first of which appears already in the second measure of the melody. Sometimes these threats to a unified musical consciousness become more prolonged. At rehearsal 22, for example, the violins twitch and writhe in a sustained flurry of sixteenth notes for three measures, after which they lose their train of thought until rehearsal 25, where the flute picks up the melodic material.

The violins refuse to relinquish control for very long. Already at rehearsal 27, they wrest the melody away from the flute. The effort proves too much, though, and the music falls into a more molecular assemblage of forces. By rehearsal 31 the music begins to bring together layers of material until rehearsal 36, where the intensity of the sonorous territories reaches another cosmic expression. This time the expression goes on for some time, threatening to break apart into the black hole of a territory that has gathered too much force, too many lines. The music tears itself to pieces in rehearsals 38 and 39, leaving behind a lonely viola to whimper away. The music won't give up, though. After the viola solo, the strings try to pull the territory back together, reassembling the forces until a beautiful cosmic expression sustains itself at rehearsal 44. Hold on. Don't let go. Let this be the eternal moment that a Romantic dreams of. But Lutosławski is no romantic. He lives where the only recompense for a chaotic world is that the forces of chaos might come together for a while to express intensities and durations. This final cosmic expression quickly falls apart, and the piece ends with the disintegration of the territorial assemblage. The strings make a violent dive to their death. And the cellos end *Chain 3* with a slow descending glissando into the darkness.

The proceeding interpretation uses the metaphors of Deleuze and Guattari as ways of describing the music. *A Thousand Plateaus* becomes a hermeneutic tool. As suggestive as these descriptions are, though, they miss the point if we do not listen to the music as a creation of intensities that the body feels. The mind may make sense of this music, but if we are plugged into the music machine as Deleuze and Guattari conceive it, the body feels intensities and durations that re-organize us, deterritorialize us, so that we feel the world anew.

Lutosławski, Molar and Molecular

Deleuze and Guattari have many good laughs at Freud's expense. They take special delight in his case of the Wolf Man, involving the most famous dream in psychiatric history. As a child, the Wolf Man is terrified by a dream in which he sees six or seven white wolves sitting in a walnut tree in front of his bedroom window (Freud 1989: 404). In terror of being eaten, Freud's patient describes how he suddenly woke up. The dream was so powerful that the Wolf Man even drew a picture of the wolves perched in the tree. Freud had no doubt that his patient's wolf "was undoubtedly his father" (1989: 413). But why the six or seven wolves, when one wolf would do the trick? Freud puzzles and puzzles. He invokes fairy tales, word play, and free association, as is his method in interpreting dreams. But Deleuze and Guattari have a simpler explanation: "Who is ignorant of the fact that wolves travel in packs? Only Freud. Every child knows it. Not Freud" (1987: 28).

Molar and molecular. It was important for Freud to reduce the Wolf Man's six or seven wolves to a singularity, a molar unity, because the threat of the wolves clearly stands in for the threat of the Father. Freud knew from the beginning that he could find a way to make six or seven wolves return to that unity. "Who is Freud trying to fool? The wolves never had a chance to get away and save their pack" (D and G 1987: 28). Freud's effort to explain away the pack of wolves was blind to the possibility that the subject is a multiplicity from the start. Whatever ontology we might imagine for the subject, it is a mistake to see it within the opposition of multiple or one, to treat it "as a numerical fragment of a lost Unity or Totality or as the organic element of a Unity or Totality yet to come" (D and G 1987: 32). The choices are not between the one (healthy) and the multiple (psychotic) but between qualities of the multiple: molar multiplicities and molecular ones.

The molar is not the unified, nor is it the individual within a society; instead, the molar and the molecular are both qualities of multiplicity within the individual and the society. The molar is hierarchical, rooted, rule-like, and signifying; the molecular is dispersed, unfixed, and variable. The molar follows the logic of the organized mass, enlarging and consolidating, capitalizing on past gains. We witnessed the 2,008 drummers playing in perfect synchronization during the 2008 Summer Olympics in Beijing. The sheer number of participants expressed a sublime multiplicity, but their perfection in form and simultaneity, and their organization into straight lines and angled spaces, revealed a molar intelligence, reining in any possibility of chaotic unfolding or freewheeling articulation beyond that of the consolidated whole. By contrast, the molecular follows the logic of the pack, individuals moving to the center and then the periphery, ever ready to make a line of flight away from danger. When the Americans fought the British in the Revolutionary War (the American War of Independence), they did not fight in straight lines and perfect arrays. They fought a molecular war against a molar force. They hid in the trees, ran to the center when necessary, and took a line of flight away from the fighting when necessary. The Americans were a molecular multiplicity.

In *Star Trek: The Next Generation,* the Borg are molar: an organized mass that captures whole civilizations to enlarge its territory. But this does not mean the *Enterprise* is molecular: it is hierarchical, too, with a rigid rule-like structure. Never believe an opposition. The point is not to read the *Enterprise* as all that is good in opposition to all that is bad. The point is to recognize that the Borg's molar nightmare of strict hierarchy, sameness, and paranoia is already part of the *Enterprise,* too. The Borg and the *Enterprise* are both molar and molecular. If forced to choose, one might place the Borg closer to the molar, and the Enterprise closer to the molecular (individuals who make decisions, though tempered by a hierarchy). But it is more accurate to think of all things as a multiplicity of multiplicities with molar tendencies and molecular ones.

These examples are only a place to start, because it is not a matter of creating another opposition that will fall apart once we start to think. The two multiplicities, molar and molecular, work together in what Deleuze and Guattari call *assemblages.* Think of the molar as our impulse to structure chaos, place it in a hierarchy, make all the pieces fit whether they want to or not; and think of the molecular as a dispersive force that breaks up hierarchies, shatters boundaries, makes space for another molar instinct to express itself. And as we cannot find a molar unity that can make sense of all the lines and spaces in the chaos that is the world, so we cannot rely on a totality of molecular impulses, because they would fall apart into a chaos of multiplicities without directional components and intensities.

Returning to *Jeux vénitiens,* our first impulse may be to read the opening section as molecular, because it barely holds together the various musical trajectories. But behind the molecular surface a symmetrical twelve-tone chord places a molar hierarchy on the music. And with each return of the opening section, the music makes molar gains by adding different timbral groups symmetrically in and around the molecular surface. The winds that open this section fall within the boundary pitches of G3 and B♭5. When the brass enters at the return of the opening section, they place themselves precisely in the middle of the winds' register, with boundary pitches of G4 and B♭4. When the pianos enter, their outer pitches, F♯7 and B1, are precisely twenty semitones higher and lower, respectively, than the boundary pitches of the winds. Like the drummers in the Beijing Olympics, the first section of *Jeux vénitiens* expresses a molecular surface contained in a molar unity of space. The opening section is molar and molecular. Its internal consistency sounds like the multiplicity of molecules bouncing into one another, while its external structure is molar and symmetrical.

Similarly, our first impulse may be to read the contrasting section of *Jeux vénitiens* as molar, because the texture seems more unified and singular in its movements. But the gestures of repeated notes that spread through these sections are like molecular impulses that hope to break through the textural unity. That is what molecular subjectivities do: they break down hierarchies. Or, in Foucault's terms, they "free political action from all unitary and totalizing paranoia . . . develop action, thought, and desires by proliferation . . . [and] believe that what is productive is not sedentary but nomadic" (1983: xiii). Rather than read the repeated notes in the second section of *Jeux vénitiens* as signs of anxiety, as I did earlier in this chapter, we can hear them as attempts to molecularize the music. The contrasting section is molar and molecular, though we can make a case that the two sections assemble these multiplicities differently. Through it all, the jabs from the percussion take on a different role in a reading from the molar-and-molecular point of view. The percussive strikes between sections function as refrains and also as molecular impulses that hope to break apart the structured surface to make room for new territorial possibilities.

Rather than go through a number of examples from Lutosławski's music and describe its molar and molecular assemblages, I think it better to discuss what the molar and molecular might mean for understanding this music. It is easy enough to imagine that Lutosławski stages the problems of the modern subject, particularly the difficulties of forming a unified and singular consciousness capable of forging a heroic path in a world that seems bent on crisis and catastrophe. But if we think that such stories of the divided consciousness and the failure of heroic action are particular to the twentieth century, I am afraid we have romanticized the past. As Lawrence Kramer has shown in his study of Schubert, for example, notions of the wounded ego, the failure of subjective positioning, and the divided consciousness were already endemic to the repressive regime of early nineteenth-century Vienna (1998). One does not need to wait for Stalin to imagine a threatened populace. And from a context larger than Vienna, it is not the twentieth but the nineteenth century that first questions Enlightenment values. One can counter that in Lutosławski's music these nineteenth-century problems of subjectivity are magnified. It is not merely that an organized subjectivity fails to accomplish the heroic deed; it is that the subjectivity in Lutosławski's music fails to form itself in the first place. But viewing the problem in this way, to use Bergson's language, is to see differences of quantity instead of quality.

If we are seeking a qualitative difference, I think we find it by reexamining our position on the molecular in Lutosławski's famous *ad lib* sections. Our first impulse may be to view the molecular as the force of chaos that breaks down and prevents the formation of a unified consciousness. But what Deleuze and Guattari are asking us to imagine is that the very notion of a unified subjectivity was always already the product of a historical process that was deeply flawed. Rather than look with sentimentality on the failure of unity as some kind of catastrophe of subjectivity, Deleuze and Guattari reterritorialize the modern subject, viewing it as molar *and* molecular. The subject is not one but several, and the dispersion that we might see as a threat to our subjectivity is in reality what makes us. As Deleuze and Guattari express it in the opening of *A Thousand Plateaus*: "The two of us wrote *Anti-Oedipus* together [referring to their earlier co-written book]. Since each of us was several, there was already quite a crowd" (3).

The modern subject as a multiplicity also has a political commitment in Deleuze and Guattari's work. In the preface to their *Anti-Oedipus*, Michel Foucault writes that he views the book as the "art of living counter to all forms of fascism" (1983: xiii). Summarizing the aims of *Anti-Oedipus*, Foucault presents among its essential injunctions: to "free political action from all unitary and totalizing paranoia," "prefer what is positive and multiple, difference over uniformity, flows over unities, mobile arrangements over systems," and "do not become enamored of power." The molar consciousness for Deleuze and Guattari is the bureaucratic way of controlling the social, and upholding forms of power. Acknowledging our molecular makeup, then, is an answer to those forms of power that try to fashion us in the image of the state. The molecular breaks down hierarchies.

Yet to overturn the molar in favor of the molecular is simply to reverse an opposition and place power in the previously marked term. Cultural oppositions are ripe for deconstruction, because only power upholds them in the first place. To align the molecular with the good and the molar with the bad in Lutosławski's music risks a blindness to the many tensions between those two terms. Returning to *Jeux vénitiens*, we recall that neither the molecular nor the molar finds unqualified alignment with all that is worthy of our emulation. I find similar ambivalences throughout Lutosławski's music. As always, Lutosławski does not give us easy answers. The difficulties we face in understanding Lutosławski's music are similar to those we face in understanding Deleuze and Guattari's model of subjectivity. Where Whittall explained these difficulties in Lutosławski as a result of resistant polarities that refused resolution, though, Deleuze and Guattari would explain them as interacting multiplicities (molar and molecular) that work together to build up (territorialize), tear down (deterritorialize), and build up anew (reterritorialize).

Can the Subject Find a Way Out?

We are left with two views of the postmodern subject. In the first, discussed in chapter 5, postmodernism breaks the signifying chain, disallowing the subject from addressing the very history that makes us who we are. In the second, discussed in this chapter, postmodernism involves a realization that the signifying chain was always a multiplicity whose molar and molecular properties allow the milieus and territories of subjectivity to assemble themselves into cosmic expressions before they break apart to make room for new milieus and territories. In this second view, the subject is always in the midst of change and realignment: the subject is always in the middle of things without being the center of things. In addition, the subject is not only a thinking mind but also a feeling body. Both mind and body are multiplicities that can be territorialized (organized), deterritorialized (disorganized), and reterritorialized (organized anew). This close embrace of multiplicity is not teleological. It is not a matter of history being a comedy whose every moment is tragic. There is no transcendent moment when all is made clear. Instead, there is the acknowledgment that the multiplicities of the molar and molecular are what keep us from fascism and paranoia in all its forms.

The reader will have noticed, though, that these two sides of the subject have involved an inverted relationship regarding modernism and postmodernism. In chapter 5, I examined postmodern music from a modernist (Lacanian) model, which uncovered a crisis via the loss of a signifying chain. And in the present chapter, I have examined modernist music from a postmodernist (Deleuzian) model, which has uncovered a hopeful thought involving molar and molecular multiplicities that promise to break down barriers. The whole reads like an indictment of postmodern music, which falls on the negative side of an unwelcome opposition. But the point is not to make an aesthetic evaluation about postmodern versus modern music. The point is to understand our place in history and to see if it is possible to overcome the crisis of our moment; and our moment, whenever it is, always involves a crisis.

What we need to do, then, is to follow Jameson's advice and try to hold two opposing ideas in our heads: postmodernism (read "late capitalism" for Jameson) "is at one and the same time the best thing that has ever happened to the human race, and the worst" (1991: 47). Postmodernism from the Lacanian view is a catastrophe that keeps us from knowing, and postmodernism from the Deleuzian view is a promise that some new realignment of the subject is always on the horizon. This new realignment involves the possibility of expression or, more precisely, affect as the outcome of a subject whose mind and body are territorialized, deterritorialized, and reterritorialized in new and changing assemblages. An affect, following a tradition that comes from Spinoza, is not a personal feeling but an intensity that changes (has an *affect* on) the body, increasing or diminishing the subject's capacity to act. Thus a Lacanian view of postmodernity involves a subject willing to perform the unending series of unmasking scenes, revealing the historical necessity behind cultural forms. Postmodern cultural forms, in turn, play a part in hiding history, which is why the unmasking scenes are required in the first place. And a Deleuzian view of postmodernity involves a subject willing to use the body to discover the forms of intensity, the affects, that music and the arts produce as they combine, fall apart, and recombine in ever-changing configurations. If there is a way out of the paranoiac view of the subject in Lacanian thought, it is through the promise of the self as a body, as the one who feels the intensities of other bodies, including musical ones.

In the end, it is a matter of acknowledging that we must be both the ones who know (who make sense) and the ones who feel (who are bodies affected). By making sense and feeling an affect we recognize and follow a thread of a tune, wending its way around music and the crises of the modern subject.

Works Cited

Abbate, Carolyn. 1999. "Outside Ravel's Tomb." *Journal of the American Musicological Society* 52/3: 465–530.

———. 2003. "Jankélévitch's Singularity." In Vladimir Jankélévitch, *Music and the Ineffable* (1961), trans. Carolyn Abbate, xiii–xx. Princeton, N.J.: Princeton University Press.

———. 2004. "Music—Drastic or Gnostic?" *Critical Inquiry* 30/3: 505–36.

Adorno, Theodor W. 1991. *Notes to Literature*, vol. 1 (1958). Trans. Shierry Weber Nicholsen. New York: Columbia University Press.

———. 1992a. *Mahler: A Musical Physiognomy* (1960). Trans. Edmund Jephcott. Chicago: University of Chicago Press.

———. 1992b. *Notes to Literature*, vol. 2 (1974). Trans. Shierry Weber Nicholsen. New York: Columbia University Press.

———. 2002. *Essays on Music*. Trans. Susan H. Gillespie. Berkeley: University of California Press.

———. 2004. *Philosophy of Modern Music* (1958). Trans. Anne G. Mitchell and Wesley V. Blomster. New York: Continuum.

Agawu, Kofi. 1987. "Concepts of Closure and Chopin's Opus 28." *Music Theory Spectrum* 9: 1–17.

Apap, Gilles. "Apap, Amazing cadenza_3." Excerpt from performance of Mozart, Violin Concerto no. 3. http://www.youtube.com/watch?v=DmJ7jyIJnn4. Accessed 24 May 2013.

Atwood, William G. 1999. *The Parisian Worlds of Frédéric Chopin*. New Haven, Conn.: Yale University Press.

Auner, Joseph, and Judith Lochhead, eds. 2002. *Postmodern Music/Postmodern Thought*. New York: Routledge.

Bakhtin, M. M. 1981. "Discourse in the Novel" (1934–35). In *The Dialogic Imagination: Four Essays*, trans. Caryl Emerson and Michael Holquist, 259–422. Austin: University of Texas Press.

Barthes, Roland. 1975. *The Pleasure of the Text* (1973). Trans. Richard Miller. New York: Hill and Wang.

———. 1981. "Theory of the Text." In *Untying the Text: A Post-Structuralist Reader*, ed. Robert Young, trans. Ian McLeod, 31–47. London: Routledge.

Baudrillard, Jean. 1994. *Simulacra and Simulation* (1981). Trans. Sheila Faria Glaser. Ann Arbor: University of Michigan Press.

Bellman, Jonathan D. 2010. *Chopin's Polish Ballade Op. 38 as Narrative of National Martyrdom*. Oxford: Oxford University Press.

Benjamin, Walter. 1968. "Theses on the Philosophy of History." In *Illuminations: Essays and Reflections* (1955), ed. Hannah Arendt, trans. Harry Zohn, 253–64. New York: Schocken Books.

Berger, Karol. 1994. "Chopin's Ballade Op. 23 and the Revolution of the Intellectuals." In *Chopin Studies 2,* ed. John Rink and Jim Samson, 72–83. Cambridge: Cambridge University Press.

Bergson, Henri. 1912. *Matter and Memory.* Trans. Margaret Paul and W. Scott Palmer. New York: Macmillan.

Block, Steven D. 1982. "George Rochberg: Progressive or Master Forger?" *Perspectives of New Music* 21/1–2: 407–9.

Bloom, Harold. 1973. *The Anxiety of Influence: A Theory of Poetry.* New York: Oxford University Press.

———. 1995. *The Western Canon: The Book and School of the Ages.* New York: Harcourt Brace.

———. 2000. *How to Read and Why.* New York: Scribner.

Bonds, Mark Evan. 1991. *Wordless Rhetoric: Musical Form and the Metaphor of the Oration.* Cambridge, Mass.: Harvard University Press.

Bracket, John. 2008. *John Zorn: Tradition and Transgression.* Bloomington: Indiana University Press, 2008.

Buhler, James. 1996. "'Breakthrough' as Critique of Form: The Finale of Mahler's First Symphony." *19th-Century Music* 20/2: 125–43.

Burke, Edmund. 1889. *A Philosophical Inquiry into the Origin of Our Ideas of the Sublime and the Beautiful* (1757). London: George Bell and Sons.

Burnham, Scott. 1995. *Beethoven Hero.* Princeton, N.J.: Princeton University Press.

Burstein, Poundie. 1997. "Lyricism, Structure, and Gender in Schubert's G Major String Quartet." *Musical Quarterly* 81/1: 51–63.

Byros, Vasili. 2012. "Meyer's Anvil: Revisiting the Schema Concept." *Music Analysis* 31/3: 273–346.

Cherlin, Michael. 1993. "Schoenberg and *Das Unheimliche:* Spectres of Tonality." *Journal of Musicology* 11/3: 357–73.

Chion, Michel. 1982. *La voix au cinema.* Paris: Cahier du cinéma.

Chua, Daniel K.L. 1999. *Absolute Music and the Construction of Meaning.* Cambridge: Cambridge University Press.

———. 2011. "Listening to the Self: *The Shawshank Redemption* and the Technology of Music." *19th-Century Music* 34/3: 341–55.

Clayton, Jay, and Eric Rothstein, eds. 1991. *Influence and Intertextuality in Literary History.* Madison: University of Wisconsin Press.

Cohn, Richard. 2004. "Uncanny Resemblances: Tonal Signification in the Freudian Age." *Journal of the American Musicological Society* 57/2: 285–324.

Colebrook, Claire. 2006. *Irony.* New York: Routledge.

Cone, Edward T. 1974. *The Composer's Voice.* Berkeley: University of California Press.

———. 1982. "Schubert's Promissory Note: An Exercise in Hermeneutics." *19th-Century Music* 5/3: 233–41.

Daniel, Thomas M. 1997. *Captain of Death: The Story of Tuberculosis.* Rochester: University of Rochester Press.

Deleuze, Gilles. 1991. *Bergsonism* (1966). Trans. Hugh Tomlinson and Barbara Habberjam. New York: Zone Books.

———. 2000. *Proust and Signs* (1964). Trans. Richard Howard. New York: George Braziller.

Deleuze, Gilles, and Félix Guattari. 1983. *Anti-Oedipus: Capitalism and Schizophrenia* (1972). Trans. Robert Hurley, Mark Seem, and Helen R. Lane. Minneapolis: University of Minnesota Press.

———. 1987. *A Thousand Plateaus: Capitalism and Schizophrenia* (1980). Trans. Brian Massumi. Minneapolis: University of Minnesota Press.

Dormandy, Thomas. 2000. *The White Death: A History of Tuberculosis.* New York: New York University Press.

Duckworth, William. 1995. *Talking Music: Conversations with John Cage, Philip Glass, Laurie Anderson, and Five Generations of American Experimental Composers.* New York: Schirmer Books.

Eisler, Benita. 2003. *Chopin's Funeral.* New York: Knopf.

Everett, Yayoi Uno. 2013. "The Tropes of Desire and Jouissance in Kaija Saariaho's *L'amour de loin.*" In *Music and Narrative since 1900,* ed. Michael L. Klein and Nicholas Reyland, 329–45. Bloomington: Indiana University Press.

Fisk, Charles. 2012. "Chopin's 'Duets'—and Mine." *19th-Century Music* 35/3: 182–203.

Forster, E. M. 2002. *Howard's End* (1910). Mineola: Dover.

Foucault, Michel. 1973. *The Birth of the Clinic* (1963). Trans. A. M. Sheridan. New York: Pantheon Books.

———. 1977. *Discipline and Punish: The Birth of the Prison* (1975). Trans. Alan Sheridan. New York: Pantheon.

———. 1983. Preface to *Anti-Oedipus: Capitalism and Schizophrenia* (1972) by Gilles Deleuze and Félix Guattari. Trans. Robert Hurley, Mark Seem, and Helen R. Lane, xiii–xvi. Minneapolis: University of Minnesota Press.

———. 1990. *The History of Sexuality: An Introduction,* vol. 1 (1976). Trans. Robert Hurley. New York: Vintage Books.

———. 1994. *The Order of Things: An Archaeology of the Human Sciences* (1966). Trans. unlisted. New York: Vintage Books.

Freud, Sigmund. 1958. "The 'Uncanny'" (1919). In *On Creativity and the Unconscious,* trans. Alix Strachey, 122–61. New York: Harper.

———. 1961. *Civilization and Its Discontents* (1930). Trans. James Strachey. New York: W. W. Norton.

———. 1965. *The Interpretation of Dreams* (1900). Trans. James Strachey. New York: Avon Books.

———. 1989. "From the History of an Infantile Neurosis ('Wolf Man')" (1918). In *The Freud Reader,* ed. Peter Gay, 400–426. New York: W. W. Norton.

Frisch, Walter. 1984. *Brahms and the Principle of Developing Variation.* Berkeley: University of California Press.

Frye, Northrop. 1990. *Anatomy of Criticism* (1957). Princeton, N.J.: Princeton University Press.

Gallope, Michael. 2012. "Jankélévitch's Fidelity to Inconsistency." *Journal of the American Musicological Society* 65/1: 235–41.

Gay, Peter. 1986. *The Bourgeois Experience, Victoria to Freud: Volume II, The Tender Passion.* Oxford: Oxford University Press.

Gillmor, Alan. 2009. "The Apostasy of George Rochberg." *Intersections: Canadian Journal of Music* 29/1: 32–48.

Gladwell, Malcolm. 2008. *Outliers: The Story of Success.* New York: Little, Brown.

Gloag, Kenneth. 2012. *Postmodernism in Music.* Cambridge: Cambridge University Press.

Goldberg, Halina. 2004. "'Remembering That Tale of Grief': The Prophetic Voice in Chopin's Music." In *The Age of Chopin,* ed. Halina Goldberg, 54–92. Bloomington: Indiana University Press.

Goodkin, Richard E. 1989. "T(r)ptext: Proust, Mallarmé, Racine." *Yale French Studies* 76: 284–314.

Gordon, Edwin E. 2003. *A Music Learning Theory for Newborn and Young Children.* Chicago: GIA.

Gracyk, Theodore A. 1992. "Adorno, Jazz, and the Aesthetics of Popular Music." *Musical Quarterly* 76/4: 526–42.

Green, Leslie. 1998. "Power." In *The Routledge Encyclopedia of Philosophy.* London: Routledge. http://www.rep.routledge.com.libproxy.temple.edu/article/S046SECT3. Accessed 2 June 2014.

Grosz, Elizabeth. 2008. *Chaos, Territory, Art: Deleuze and the Framing of the Earth.* New York: Columbia University Press.

Hatten, Robert S. 2004. *Interpreting Musical Gestures, Topics, and Tropes: Mozart, Beethoven, Schubert.* Bloomington: Indiana University Press.

Hayden, Deborah. 2003. *Pox: Genius, Madness, and the Mysteries of Syphilis.* New York: Basic Books.

Heile, Björn. 2004. "'Transcending Quotation': Cross-Cultural Musical Representation in Mauricio Kagel's *Die Stücke der Windrose für Salonorchester.*" *Music Analysis* 23/1: 57–85.

Hepokoski, James. 1984. "Formulaic Openings in Debussy." *19th-Century Music* 8/1: 44–59.

———. 2012. "Ineffable Immersion: Contextualizing the Call for Silence." *Journal of the American Musicological Society* 65/1: 223–30.

Hepokoski, James, and Warren Darcy. 2006. *Elements of Sonata Theory: Norms, Types, and Deformations in the Late-Eighteenth-Century Sonata.* New York: Oxford University Press.

Hoens, Dominiek, and Ed Pluth. 2002. "The *sinthome:* A New Way of Writing an Old Problem?" In *Essays on the Final Lacan: Re-Inventing the Symptom,* ed. Luke Thurston, 1–18. New York: Other Press.

Holahan, J. M. 1987. "Toward a Theory of Music Syntax: Some Observations of Musical Babble in Young Children." In *Music and Child Development,* ed. J. Craig Peery, Irene W. Peery, and Thomas W. Draper, 96–106. New York: Springer-Verlag.

Howat, Roy. 1983. *Debussy in Proportion: A Musical Analysis.* Cambridge: Cambridge University Press.

Hutcheon, Linda. 1988. *A Poetics of Postmodernism: History, Theory, Fiction.* New York: Routledge.

Huyssen, Andreas. 1986. *After the Great Divide: Modernism, Mass Culture, Postmodernism.* Bloomington: Indiana University Press.

Hyde, Martha. 1996. "Neoclassic and Anachronistic Impulses in Twentieth-Century Music." *Music Theory Spectrum* 18/2: 200–235.

Jameson, Fredric. 1981. *The Political Unconscious: Narrative as a Socially Symbolic Act.* Ithaca, N.Y.: Cornell University Press.

———. 1991. *Postmodernism, or The Cultural Logic of Late Capitalism.* Durham, N.C.: Duke University Press.

———. 2003. "The End of Temporality." *Critical Inquiry* 29/4: 695–718.

———. 2007. *The Modernist Papers.* New York: Verso.

Jankélévitch, Vladimir. 2003. *Music and the Ineffable* (1961). Trans. Carolyn Abbate. Princeton, N.J.: Princeton University Press.

Kaczyński, Tadeusz. 1984. *Conversations with Witold Lutoslawski.* Trans. Yolanta May. London: Chester Music.

Kallberg, Jeffrey. 1988. "The Problem of Repetition and Return in Chopin's Mazurkas." In *Chopin Studies*, ed. Jim Samson, 1–23. Cambridge: Cambridge University Press.

———. 1996. *Chopin at the Boundaries: Sex, History, and Musical Genre*. Cambridge, Mass.: Harvard University Press.

Kaplan, Louise J. 1978. *Oneness and Separateness*. New York: Simon & Schuster.

Keats, John. 2009. *Selected Letters of John Keats: Revised Edition*. Ed. Grant F. Scott. Cambridge, Mass.: Harvard University Press.

Kerman, Joseph. 1982. "Notes on Beethoven's Codas." In *Beethoven Studies* 3, ed. Alan Tyson, 141–59. Cambridge: Cambridge University Press.

———. 2001–02. "Beethoven's Op. 131 and the Uncanny." *19th-Century Music* 25/2–3: 155–64.

Kern, Stephen. 1983. *The Culture of Time and Space, 1880–1918*. Cambridge, Mass.: Harvard University Press.

Klein, Michael. 2004. "Chopin's Fourth Ballade as Musical Narrative." *Music Theory Spectrum* 26/1: 23–56.

———. 2005. *Intertextuality in Western Art Music*. Bloomington: Indiana University Press.

Kolberg, Oskar. 1962. *Lud: Jego zwyczaje, sposdb ycia, mowa, podania, przyslowia, obrzedy, gusla, zabawy, piedni, muzyka i taice* [People. Their customs, habits, language, legends, proverbs, ceremonies, witchcraft, festivities, songs, music and dances]. Cracow: Polskie Wydawnictwo Muzyczne.

Korsyn, Kevin. 1991. "Towards a New Poetics of Musical Influence." *Music Analysis* 10/1–2: 3–72.

———. 2001. "Beyond Privileged Contexts: Intertextuality, Influence, and Dialogue." In *Rethinking Music*, ed. Nicholas Cook and Mark Everist, 55–72. Oxford: Oxford University Press.

Koselleck, Reinhart. 2004. *Futures Past: On the Semantics of Historical Time*. Trans. Keith Tribe. New York: Columbia University Press.

Kramer, Lawrence. 1990. *Music as Cultural Practice, 1800–1900*. Berkeley: University of California Press.

———. 1995. *Classical Music and Postmodern Knowledge*. Berkeley: University of California Press.

———. 1997. *After the Lovedeath: Sexual Violence and the Making of Culture*. Berkeley: University of California Press.

———. 1998. *Franz Schubert: Sexuality, Subjectivity, Song*. Cambridge: Cambridge University Press.

———. 2002. *Musical Meaning: Toward a Critical History*. Berkeley: University of California Press.

———. 2011. *Interpreting Music*. Berkeley: University of California Press.

———. 2012. *Expression and Truth: On the Music of Knowledge*. Berkeley: University of California Press.

———. 2013. "Narrative Nostalgia: Modern Art Music off the Rails." In *Music and Narrative since 1900*, ed. Michael L. Klein and Nicholas Reyland, 163–85. Bloomington: Indiana University Press.

Kristeva, Julia. 1980. "The Bounded Text" (1969). In *Desire in Language: A Semiotic Approach to Literature and Art*, trans. Thomas Gora, Alice Jardine, and Leon S. Roudiez, 36–63. New York: Columbia University Press.

———. 1984. *Revolution in Poetic Language*. Trans. Margaret Waller. New York: Columbia University Press.

Lacan, Jacques. 2006a. "The Function and Field of Speech and Language in Psychoanalysis." In *Écrits* (1966), 237–322. Trans. Bruce Fink. New York: W. W. Norton.

———. 2006b. "The Mirror Stage as Formative of the I Function as Revealed in Psychoanalytic Experience." In *Écrits* (1966), 93–100. Trans. Bruce Fink. New York: W. W. Norton.

———. 2006c. "On a Question Prior to Any Possible Treatment of Psychosis." In *Écrits* (1966), 445–88. Trans. Bruce Fink. New York: W. W. Norton.

———. 2006d. "On the Subject Who Is Finally in Question." In *Écrits* (1966), 229–36. Trans. Bruce Fink. New York: W. W. Norton.

———. 2006e. "Presentation on Psychical Causality." In *Écrits* (1966), 151–93. Trans. Bruce Fink. New York: W. W. Norton.

———. 2006f. "Response to Jean Hyppolite's Commentary on Freud's Verneinung.'" In *Écrits* (1966), 381–99. Trans. Bruce Fink. New York: W. W. Norton.

———. 2006g. "Science and Truth." In *Écrits* (1966), 855–77. Trans. Bruce Fink. New York: W. W. Norton.

———. 2006h. "Seminar on 'The Purloined Letter.'" In *Écrits* (1966), 11–61. Trans. Bruce Fink. New York: W. W. Norton.

———. 2006i. "Variations on the Standard Treatment." In *Écrits* (1966), 323–62. Trans. Bruce Fink. New York: W. W. Norton.

Laitz, Steven. 1992. "Pitch-Class Motive in the Songs of Franz Schubert: The Submediant Complex." Ph.D. diss., University of Rochester, Eastman School of Music.

Lander, Rómulo. 2006. *Subjective Experience and the Logic of The Other*. Trans. and ed. Judith Filc. New York: Other Press.

Lewin, David. 1987a. *Generalized Musical Intervals and Transformations*. New Haven, Conn.: Yale University Press.

———. 1987b. "Some Instances of Parallel Voice-Leading in Debussy." *19th-Century Music* 11/1: 59–72.

Leydon, Rebecca. 2001. "Debussy's Late Style and the Devices of the Early Silent Cinema." *Music Theory Spectrum* 23/2: 217–41.

Liszt, Franz. 1963. "The Mazurkas and Their Social Background." In *Frederic Chopin* (1852), trans. Edward N. Waters, 64–81. London: Free Press of Glencoe.

Lockwood, Lewis. 2005. *Beethoven: The Music and the Life*. New York: W. W. Norton.

Losada, Catherine. 2008. "The Process of Modulation in Musical Collage." *Music Analysis* 27/2–3: 295–336.

Lyotard, Jean François. 1984. *The Postmodern Condition: A Report on Knowledge* (1979). Trans. Geoff Bennington and Brian Massumi. Minneapolis: University of Minnesota Press.

Mandel, Ernest. 1999. *Late Capitalism* (1975). New York: Verso.

Mann, Thomas. 1969. "The Making of *The Magic Mountain*." In *The Magic Mountain* (1924), trans. H. T. Lowe-Porter, 717–27. New York: Vintage Books.

Marx, Karl. 1990. *Capital: A Critique of Political Economy*, vol. 1 (1867). Trans. Ben Fowkes. London: Penguin Books.

Massumi, Brain. 1987. "Translator's Foreword: Pleasures of Philosophy." In *A Thousand Plateaus: Capitalism and Schizophrenia* by Gilles Deleuze and Félix Guattari, trans. Brian Massumi, ix–xv. Minneapolis: University of Minnesota Press.

Maus, Fred Everett. 1988. "Music as Drama." *Music Theory Spectrum* 10: 56–73.

McCarthy, Cormac. 1998. *Cities of the Plain*. New York: Vintage Books.

McClary, Susan. 2000. *Conventional Wisdom: The Content of Musical Form*. Berkeley: University of California Press.

McCreless, Patrick. 1991. "The Hermeneutic Sentence and Other Literary Models for Tonal Closure." *Indiana Theory Review* 12: 35–73.

———. 2011. "The Pitch-Class Motive in Tonal Analysis: Some Historical and Critical Observations." *Res Musica* 3: 52–67.

McGowan, John. 1991. *Postmodernism and Its Critics*. Ithaca, N.Y.: Cornell University Press.

Mickiewicz, Adam. 2004. *Pan Tadeusz* (1834). Trans. Marcel Weyland. http://www .antoranz.net/BIBLIOTEKA/PT051225/PanTad-eng/PT-Start.htm. Accessed 16 October 2013.

Moisala, Pirkko. 2009. *Kaija Saariaho*. Urbana: University of Illinois Press.

Monahan, Seth. 2007. "'Inescapable' Coherence and the Failure of the Novel-Symphony in the Finale of Mahler's Sixth." *19th-Century Music* 31/1: 53–95.

———. 2013. "Action and Agency Revisited." *Journal of Music Theory* 57/2: 321–71.

Monelle, Raymond. 2000. *The Sense of Music: Semiotic Essays*. Princeton, N.J.: Princeton University Press.

———. 2006. *The Musical Topic: Hunt, Military and Pastoral*. Bloomington: Indiana University Press.

Moog, Helmut. 1976. *The Musical Experience of the Pre-School Child*. Trans. Claudia Clarke. London: Schott Music.

Nattiez, Jean-Jacques. 1989. *Proust as Musician*. Trans. Derrick Puffett. Cambridge: Cambridge University Press.

———. 1990. *Music and Discourse: Towards a Semiology of Music*. Trans. Carolyn Abbate. Princeton, N.J.: Princeton University Press.

Nietzsche, Friedrich. 1995. *The Birth of Tragedy* (1872). Trans. Clifton P. Fadiman. New York: Dover.

Notley, Margaret. 2007. *Lateness and Brahms: Music and Culture in the Twilight of Viennese Liberalism*. Oxford: Oxford University Press.

O'Shea, John. 1990. *Music and Medicine: Medical Profiles of Great Composers*. London: J. M. Dent & Sons.

Paschałów, Wiaczesław. 1951. *Chopin a polska muzyka ludowa* [Chopin and Polish folk music]. Cracow: Polskie Wydawnictwo Muzyczne.

Pierce, Alexandra. 2010. *Deepening Musical Performance through Movement: The Theory and Practice of Embodied Interpretation*. Bloomington: Indiana University Press.

Poliński, Aleksander. 1914. *Chopin*. Kijow: L. Idzikowski.

Proust, Marcel. 2003a. *In Search of Lost Time: Volume I, Swann's Way* (1913). Trans. C. K. Scott Moncrieff and Terence Kilmartin, rev. D. J. Enright. New York: Random House.

———. 2003b. *In Search of Lost Time: Volume V, The Captive and the Fugitive* (1923; 1925). Trans. C. K. Scott Moncrieff and Terence Kilmartin, rev. D. J. Enright. New York: Random House.

———. 2003c. *In Search of Lost Time: Volume VI, Time Regained* (1927). Trans. C. K. Scott Moncrieff and Terence Kilmartin, rev. D. J. Enright. New York: Random House.

Rae, Charles Bodman. 2001. "Lutosławski's Sound-World: A World of Contrasts." In *Lutosławski Studies*, ed. Zbigniew Skowron, 16–35. Oxford: Oxford University Press.

Ratner, Leonard G. 1980. *Classic Music: Expression, Form, and Style.* New York: Schirmer Books.

Reichardt, Sarah. 2008. *Composing the Modern Subject: Four String Quartets by Dmitri Shostakovich.* Aldershot: Ashgate.

Reise, Jay. 1981. "Rochberg the Progressive." *Perspectives of New Music* 19/1–2: 395–407.

Réti, Rudolph. 1961. *The Thematic Process in Music.* London: Faber and Faber.

Reynolds, Allison M. 2006. "Vocal Interactions during Informal Early Childhood Music Classes." *Bulletin of the Council of Research in Music Education* 168: 35–49.

Reynolds, Christopher Alan. 2003. *Motives for Allusion: Context and Content in Nineteenth-Century Music.* Cambridge, Mass.: Harvard University Press.

Rings, Steven. 2008. "*Mystéres limpides:* Time and Transformation in Debussy's *Des pas sur la neige.*" *19th-Century Music* 32/2: 178–208.

———. 2012. "Talking and Listening with Jankélévitch." *Journal of the American Musicological Society* 65/1: 218–23.

Rivera, Benito V. 1993. Introduction to *Musical Poetics,* by Joachim Burmeister. Trans. Benito V. Rivera, xiii–lxii. New Haven, Conn.: Yale University Press.

Rochberg, George. 1969. "No Center." Reprinted in *The Aesthetics of Survival: A Composer's View of Twentieth Century Music,* 129–34 (2004). Ann Arbor: University of Michigan Press.

———. 2007. *Eagle Minds: Selected Correspondence of Istvan Anhalt & George Rochberg, 1961–2005.* Ed. Alan M. Gillmor. Waterloo, Ont.: Wilfred Laurier University Press.

Rosen, Charles. 1972. *The Classical Style: Haydn, Mozart, Beethoven.* New York: W. W. Norton.

———. 1980. "Influence: Plagiarism and Inspiration." *19th-Century Music* 4/2: 87–100.

Rosolato, Guy. 1974. "La voix: entre corps et langage." *Revue française de psychanalyse* 38/1: 75–94.

Saariaho, Kaija. "Karita Mattila: 'Parfum de l'instant' (Saariaho)." http://youtu.be /OMIpID-XsKc. Accessed 24 May 2013.

Samson, Jim. 1985. *The Music of Chopin.* Oxford: Clarendon Press.

Schwarz, David. 1997. *Listening Subjects: Music, Psychoanalysis, Culture.* Durham, N.C.: Duke University Press.

———. 2006. *Listening Awry: Music and Alterity in German Culture.* Minneapolis: University of Minnesota Press.

Scruton, Roger. 1997. *The Aesthetics of Music.* Oxford: Oxford University Press.

Sebeok, Thomas A. 1994. *Signs: An Introduction to Semiotics.* Toronto: University of Toronto Press.

Silverman, Kaja. 1988. *The Acoustic Mirror: The Female Voice in Psychoanalysis and Cinema.* Bloomington: Indiana University Press.

Smith, Peter. 2001. "Brahms and Subject/Answer Rhetoric." *Music Analysis* 20: 193–236.

Spitzer, William. 1996. "The Significance of Recapitulation in the 'Waldstein' Sonata." *Beethoven Forum* 5: 103–18.

Stokes, John H. 1918. *The Third Great Plague: A Discussion of Syphilis for Everyday People.* Philadelphia: W. B. Saunders.

Straus, Joseph N. 1990. *Remaking the Past: Musical Modernism and the Influence of the Tonal Tradition.* Cambridge, Mass.: Harvard University Press.

———. 2006. "Normalizing the Abnormal: Disability in Music and Music Theory." *Journal of the American Musicological Society* 59/1: 113–84.

Subotnik, Rose Rosengard. 1978. "The Historical Structure: Adorno's 'French' Model for the Criticism of Nineteenth-Century Music." *19th-Century Music* 2/1: 36–60.

Swartz, Anne. 1975. "The Polish Folk Mazurka." *Studia Musicologica Academiae Scientiarum Hungaricae* T. 17, Fasc. 1/4: 249–55.

———. 1994. "Elsner, Chopin, and the Musical Narrative as Symbols of Nation." *Polish Review* 39/4: 445–56.

Szulc, Tad. 1998. *Chopin in Paris: The Life and Times of the Romantic Composer.* New York: Scribner.

"Taking the Hobbits to Isengard." Video by Erwin Beekveld, 2:09, excerpts from *The Lord of the Rings: The Two Towers.* Directed by Peter Jackson. Los Angeles, New Line Cinema. Posted by Aaron Hardbarger. http://www.youtube.com/watch?v=uE-1RPDqJAY. Accessed 24 May 2013.

Tarasti, Eero. 1994. *A Theory of Musical Semiotics.* Bloomington: Indiana University Press.

Taruskin, Richard. 1996. *Stravinsky and the Russian Traditions: A Biography of the Works through* Mavra, vol. 1. Berkeley: University of California Press.

———. 1997. *Defining Russia Musically: Historical and Hermeneutical Essays.* Princeton, N.J.: Princeton University Press.

———. 2013. "Chapter 9: After Everything." In *Music in the Late Twentieth Century.* New York: Oxford University Press. http://www.oxfordwesternmusic.com.libproxy.temple.edu/view/Volume5/actrade-9780195384857-div1-009003.xml. Accessed 9 July 2013.

Thomas, Adrian. 1992. "Beyond the Dance." In *The Cambridge Companion to Chopin,* ed. Jim Samson, 145–59. Cambridge: Cambridge University Press.

Tolstoy, Leo. 2007. *War and Peace* (1869). Trans. Richard Pevear and Larissa Volokhonsky. New York: Alfred A. Knopf.

Valente, Joseph. 2003. "Lacan's Marxism, Marxism's Lacan (from Žižek to Althusser)." In *The Cambridge Companion to Lacan,* ed. Jean-Michel Rabaté, 153–73. Cambridge: Cambridge University Press.

Vazem, Yekaterina, and Nina Dimitrievitch (trans.). 1988. "Memoirs of a Ballerina of the St Petersburg Bolshoi Theatre: Part 4." *Dance Research: The Journal of the Society for Dance Research* 6/2: 30–47.

Virgil. n.d. *The Eclogues or Bucolics.* Trans. John Dryden. Cambridge: Charles River Editors.

Wagner, Cosima. 1978. *Cosima Wagner's Diaries,* vol. 1. Trans. G. Skelton. London: Collins.

Wheeldon, Marianne. 2005. "Debussy and *La Sonate cyclique.*" *Journal of Musicology* 22/4: 644–79.

Whittall, Arnold. 2001. "Between Polarity and Synthesis: The Modernist Paradigm in Lutosławski's Concertos for Cello and Piano." In *Lutosławski Studies,* ed. Zbigniew Skowron, 244–68. Oxford: Oxford University Press.

Williams, Alastair. 1998. "Torn Halves: Structure and Subjectivity in Analysis." *Music Analysis* 17/3: 281–93.

Wittgenstein, Ludwig. 1997. *Philosophical Investigations* (1953). Trans. G.E.M. Anscombe. Oxford: Blackwell Publishers.

———. 1999. *Tractatus Logico-Philosophicus* (1921). Trans. D. F. Pears and B. F. McGuinness. New York: Routledge.

Wood, Hugh. 1974. "Thoughts on a Modern Quartet." *Tempo* 111: 23–26.

Zakrzewska, Dorota. 1999. "Alienation and Powerlessness: Adam Mickiewicz's Ballady and Chopin's Ballades." *Polish Music Journal* 2/1–2. http://www.usc.edu/dept/polish_music/PMJ/archives.html. Accessed 1 June 2012.

Žižek, Slavoj. 1989. *The Sublime Object of Ideology.* New York: Verso.

———. 2008. *Enjoy Your Symptom! Jacques Lacan in Hollywood and Out* (1992). New York: Routledge.

Zorn, John. "John Zorn: Road Runner (Branko Dzinovic, Accordion)." http://youtu.be/CsGYmGQUuGw. Accessed 24 May 2013.

Index

parallel voice-leading, 53

"Parfum de l'instant" (Saariaho), 61–65, *62, 63*; Other in, 63–64; pitch-class motive in, 62–63; Real in, 65–66

parody, 69, 129–131, 138

particularity, 93–95, 120; loss of in Symbolic, 4, 37, 38, 53, 92

Paschałow, Wiaczesław, 98

past: as act of freedom, 69, 72; agency and, 67–68; postmodern modification of, 144–145

pastiche, 129, 141, 143, 145

pastoral, 88–89, 146, 149

paternal word, 49, 59

pathological life, 116

personality, structured like symptom, 7, 151

personhood, 2, 103, 137

pervasive indeterminacy, 124, 125

Petipa, Marius, 108

Petrushka (Stravinsky), 145–146

phenomenology, 52

Piano Sonata in F major, op. 10, no. 2 (Beethoven), 7

Pierce, Alexandra, 23

pitch-class motive, 10, 21, 22, 25; in "Parfum de l'instant," 62–63

placard, 108

plateaus, 73, 159, 160

plenitude, 44, 47, 56, 57, 59

Poe, Edgar Allen, 19–20

point of order, 159–162

Poland, 157; Great Emigration, 105, 106, 107; Russian conquest of, 104–107, 108

Poliński, Aleksander, 98

political consciousness, 171

popular culture, 129–130

postmodern subject, 5, 131, 153, 154–156, 171–172

postmodernism, 4–5; apocalyptic narrative, 146–148; capitalism and, 129, 152–153, 172; concerns of, 128–129; cultural dominant concept and, 128, 132, 136; erasure of history, 127, 146–149, 151–153, 157, 163; intertextuality, 129, 131, 132–137; irony, 129–131, 153; modernism and, 131–132, 143; refusal to update past, 138, 144, 152; start of in music, 138–139; symptoms of, 127–132, 151

power relation, 22–25, 134

present, 31, 32; as schizophrenic, 151–153

primordial *I*, 41, 43, 44

Prometheus, figure of, 26–27

promissory note, 7–10, 17

Proust, Marcel, 4, 52, 67; three machines, 68, 72–73, 81, 88, 90; time and memory, conception of, 68–71. *See also In Search of Lost Time*

psychiatrization of perverse pleasure, 22

psychoanalyst's role, 17–18, 20–21

psychosis, 60, 151–152

"The Purloined Letter" (Poe), 19

Quatre instants (Saariaho), 60, 61, 65. *See also* "Parfum de l'instant" (Saariaho)

question/answer convention, 53–54

quotation/allusion/borrowing, 134–136, 143; *ars combinatoria*, 144; of Beethoven, 139, 141, *141*; loss of style, 137–138; modernist vs. postmodernist, 145–146; as symptom of postmodernism, 127–132, 145–146, 151, 152

Rae, Charles Bodman, 165

Ratatouille (film), 69–71

Real, 3, 4, 5, 13; in Clarinet Sonata in F minor, op. 120, no. 1, 31, 37; as ghost in the machine, 73; as outside language, 15; in "Parfum de l'instant," 65–66; symptom as message from, 15, 17–18, 66–67, 103, 118; as symptomatic structure, 66; as traumatic, 15, 16, 18, 31, 115

Real, Jankélévitch's, 52

reality, 2, 15–16, 48, 55, 133–134, 143–144

"Reflets dans l'eau" (Debussy), 67, 68, 73, 74–81; apotheosis, 74, 77, *78, 79*, 80, *91, 92*; cadenza, 74–75, 94; crisis, *74*, 77, *77*, 91; dominants "in focus," 77, *78*; epochal time, *91*, 91–92; eternity, 75, 77, *79*; lost time motive, 75–77, *76, 78*; pentatonicism in, 74, *75*, 77; time regained in, 80–81; Tristan chord, 74, 75, 80; Wagnerian signs in, 74, 75, *79*, 80, 91

refrain, 159–162, 164, 170

regret, *70*, 71–72, *79*, 80–81; in "Des pas sur la neige," *84*, 85; in "Hommage à Rameau," *83*; as machine in Debussy's works, 81–88; pastoral, 88–89; time/space opposition, 89–90; *żal*, 105, 106

Reichardt Ellis, Sarah, 3

Reise, Jay, 143

repetition: compulsive, 15, 27, 152; in mazurka, 106, 117–118; uncanny and, 117–118

repressed, return of, 11–12, 19, 117–120, 151–152, 154

"Résonances" (Saariaho), 66

reterritorialization, 64, 155, 170, 171, 172; cosmic expression, 163, 164–165; mazurka and, 98, 99–100, 110

return: desire to, 48–49; Imaginary and, 4, 31, 74; to mother, fantasy of, 4, 47–48; of repressed, 11–12, 19, 117–120, 151–152, 154; of Symptom, 11, 36–37

reverential imitation, 70, 152

Rings, Steven, 51, 83

59–60, 65, 125; "letter reaches addressee," 5, 21, 37, 39, 43 , 120, 125; listening, influence on, 52–53; loss of particularity in, 4, 37, 38, 53, 92–93; matrix of, 16, 41; morality and, 23, 25; resists Imaginary, 55; series of unmasking scenes, 152–153; as set of semiotic structures, 16; story and, 19–20; as symptomatic structure, 37, 49, 66, 119, 154, 158. *See also* Other

symptom, 3; in coda, 27, *30*, 30–31, 37; context as, 102; defined, 17–19; disease as, 112–116; G-flat in Sonata in F minor, op. 120, no. 1, 27, *28*; interpretation of, 17–18, 20–21; invention of, 7–12; language and, 17, 151; meaning for music, 19–22; as message from Real, 15, 17–18, 66–67, 103, 118; morality vs. medical, 22–23; multiplicity of, 102–104; musical, 7, 12, 99, 101; personality structured like, 7, 151; of postmodernism, 127–132; promissory note as, 7; quotation and, 127–132, 145–146, 151, 152; return of, 11, 26–27; as sign, 17–18, 21, 24–25, 29, 35–36, 102–103; subject becomes, 118–119. *See also* sinthome

syntax, 94

syphilis, 20, 22–25, 112

Tarantino, Quentin, 128

Taruskin, Richard, 137, 138, 143, 145

Tchaikovsky, Pyotr Ilyich, *109*, 109–110

television, 128

temporality, end of, 68, 89–90

territory, 98–99; of different life forms, 163–164; molar and molecular, 155; registral, 160–161

textuality, 129, 131, 132, 135

"This Is My Letter to the World" (Dickinson), 5

A Thousand Plateaus (Deleuze and Guattari), 5, 154–155, 158, 170–171

time, 52, 67; attempt to erase subjectivity from, 74; cinema as threat to, 89–90; end of temporality, 68, 89–90; epochal, 90–91, *91*; as multiplicity, 73, 91, 93, 94; pastoral, 88–89; phenomenology of, 4; Proust's conception of, 68–71; as quality of being, 69, 71, 72, 166; regained, 71–72, 80–81, *84*, 88–89, 90–92, *91*; tenants of, 90–92. *See also* lost time

time/space opposition, 4, 68, 72, 89–90, 145

Tolstoy, Lev, 110–111, 123, 125

transcendence, 24, 52, 61

transferences, 24

transmission, dyads of, 134

trimodular block, 27

Tristan und Isolde (Wagner), 61, 165

truth, 15, 16, 55

tuberculosis, 112–116

turning points, 22

uncanny: disease and, 116–117; musical, 11–12, 26–27; repetition and, 117–118

unconscious, 17, 38; gaze and, 41–42; as history, 22, 108, 129; as Other's discourse, 1, 14–15, 52, 135; structured like language, 20

unified consciousness, 132–133, 170

Ur-form of motive, 36

utopian vision, *8*, 11; postmodern erasure of, 146–149, 152, 157, 163

variations, 26–27, 35, 57

Vazem, Yekaterina, 108

vice, 12, 20, 22

Viennese culture, 35–36, 37, 38–39

"Le vierge, le vivace et le bel aujourd'hui" (Mallarmé), 83–85

Violin Concerto no. 3 (Mozart), 138

Violin Sonata (Debussy), 53–54, *54*

Virgil, 88–89

voice leading, 7, *8*, *9*, 10, 11, 53

Wagner, Richard, 27, 61; *Tristan und Isolde*, 61, 165; Valhalla leitmotif, 108–109

Wagnerian signs: in "Hommage à Rameau," 81, *83*; in "Reflets dans l'eau," 74, 75, *79*, 80, 91

War and Peace (Tolstoy), 110–111

Warhol, Andy, 128

Wheeldon, Marianne, 87

Whittall, Arnold, 156, 157, 171

Will, 165, 166

Wittgenstein, Ludwig, 16, 18, 98, 159

Wolf, Hugo, 50

Wolf Man, 168

Wood, Hugh, 141, 143

work concept, 132–136

work-person, 124

wound, in formation of masculine subjectivity, 31–32, 37

The X Project (film), 164

YouTube, 128, 137–138, 163

żal, 105

Zaleski, Bohdan, 106

Zimmermann, Bernd Alois, 143

Žižek, Slavoj, 16, 49, 120; forced choice to enter Symbolic, 37, 65; "forgetting to forget," 157–158; on ideology, 55; Imaginary (mis)recognition, 43; on symptom, 18; on unconscious, 38; *Works: Enjoy Your Symptom!*, 2, 19; *The Sublime Object of Ideology*, 7

Zorn, John, 5, 129–132, 152

MICHAEL L. KLEIN is Chair of the Department of Music Studies and Professor of Music Studies at Temple University. He has published on a variety of topics in *Music Theory Spectrum, Nineteenth-Century Music*, the *Journal of Music Theory*, the *Journal of the American Liszt Society*, and *Indiana Theory Review*. He is the author of *Intertextuality in Western Art Music* (Indiana University Press, 2004). In 2005, he received a publication award from the Society for Music Theory for his article "Chopin's 4th Ballade as Musical Narrative" in *Music Theory Spectrum*. With co-editor Nicholas Reyland, he has recently released a collection of essays entitled *Music and Narrative since 1900* (Indiana University Press, 2012).